LASKER'S GREATEST
CHESS GAMES

[Taken during tournament at Zurich, 1934. Courtesy of H. M. Phillips
and the AMERICAN CHESS BULLETIN]

LASKER'S GREATEST CHESS GAMES

1889-1914

(formerly titled: Dr. Lasker's Chess Career)

with annotations by
FRED REINFELD AND REUBEN FINE

and a biographical introduction by
FRED REINFELD

DOVER PUBLICATIONS, INC., NEW YORK

Published in Canada by General Publishing Company, Ltd., 30 Lesmill Road, Don Mills, Toronto, Ontario.

Published in the United Kingdom by Constable and Company, Ltd., 10 Orange Street, London W. C. 2.

This Dover edition, first published in 1965, is an unabridged and unaltered republication of the work first published by The Black Knight Press in 1935, under the former title, *Dr. Lasker's Chess Career, Part I: 1889-1914*. Although the work was originally planned as a two-volume study, Volume II was never completed, and Volume I is complete in itself.

Library of Congress Catalog Card Number: 65-25711.

Manufactured in the United States of America

Dover Publications, Inc.
180 Varick Street
New York, N. Y. 10014

PREFACE

I LEARNED the moves as a high school youngster, about three months before the great New York Tournament of 1924, so that Dr. Lasker's victory in that extraordinarily difficult contest gave him a vague super-man status in my eyes; but what I lacked in understanding, I made up in enthusiasm! Later on, as I moved out of the tyro class and devoted almost all my time to a minute study of Dr. Alekhine's superb annota-tions in the Book of the New York Tournament (to the fearful detriment of my schoolwork), my appreciation of Lasker's play became more dis-cerning. It was from this book that I caught the ambition of becoming, not President, nor a policeman, nor even a Certified Public Accountant, but merely a writer of chess books, and above all, a book about Lasker!

Even at that time I could not understand why there was no book on Lasker—not only because he is one of the greatest masters in chess history, but because he is one of those relatively few great men who interest us for what they *are,* as well as because of what they *do.* Even in his lifetime Lasker has already become a legend and the intuitive perception of his greatness is so acute among us chess players that the most trivial news item about him arouses indefinable emotional overtones in us.

Mr. H. M. Phillips, because of his friendship of many years' dura-tion with Lasker, is qualified as few are to give us an intimate picture of the man rather than the master. I asked Mr. Phillips to prepare a biographical memoir for the present volume, but he modestly replied that whatever he had to say would contain so much praise as to become monotonous!

The "appreciations" in the present volume have all been translated from the special Lasker issue of the *Wiener Schachzeitung* (January 1929), with the exception of the first one, which was translated from Hans Kmoch's brilliant *Die Kunst der Verteidigung.* The discerning reader will note that these appreciations are by no means unanimous in the views they set forth!

The annotations in this book, the fruit of three years of research and analytical labors, are for the most part original; acknowledgments have been made only where direct quotations were used, or where the utilized material seemed valuable enough (as in the case of difficult analysis) to deserve credit. I want to thank Mr. H. M. Phillips and Mr. L. L. Montgomery for their friendly assistance, and Mr. Irving Chernev (who, incidentally, contributed the substance of the notes to Game No. 54) and Mr. Matthew Green, for their conscientious reading of the proofs.

For the benefit of those readers who may be unfamiliar with some of the signs used in the Games Section, the following explanation is appended:

> White has the better game: $\pm$
> Black has the better game: $\mp$
> Approximately even game: $=$

FRED REINFELD.

August 1935.

~

ACKNOWLEDGMENT

Subscriptions to this volume were received prior to publication from the following:

Dr. G. W. Blanchard
L. Borker
A. A. Burrows
I. Chernev
R. B. Cooke
E. Dimock
Dr. G. C. Dohme
I. M. Tessohn

G. T. Halbert
C. C. McBrian
A. W. Paull
H. M. Phillips
F. Seddon
H. S. Sternberg
S. L. Tatum
Dr. James J. Waygood

CONTENTS

Preface · · · · · · · · · · · vii

Acknowledgment · · · · · · · · · ix

Index of Players · · · · · · · · · 3

Index of Openings · · · · · · · · 4

Lasker's Tournament and Match Record · 5

Appreciations · · · · · · · · · · 7

Biographical Introduction · · · · · · 11

Games · · · · · · · · · · · · 19

1

ENDGAMES

K+P   33
N vs N   27
B vs B   16
R vs R   68, 69
Q vs Q   9

R+B vs R+B   14, 23, 37, 44, 46
R+B vs R+N   30, 38, 49, 51

B vs N   1, 6, 22, 43, 48
R vs N   63
2R vs R+N   66, 73*
2R vs 2R   55
R+B+N vs R+B+N   8

Q+B vs Q+N   70

INDEX OF PLAYERS

(The numerical references are to games)

Albin 13
Alekhine 71, 73
Allies 33, 50, 67
Bauer 2
Bernstein 66
Bird 9, 10
Blackburne 5, 6, 7, 8, 35, 68
Burn 41
Capablanca 74
Delmar 44
Forgács 54
Fox 46
Golmayo 11
Janowski 61, 62, 64, 65, 70
Lee 34, 39
Lipke 1
Maróczy 42
Marshall 49, 75
Mieses 3, 4, 59
Napier 45
Pillsbury 21, 37, 43
Porges 24
Rubinstein 69
Salwe 55
Schlechter 63
Showalter 12, 38
Snosko-Borowski 57
Steinitz 14, 15, 16, 17, 18,
                              20, 22, 25, 28, 29,
                              30, 31, 32, 40
Tarrasch 27, 51, 52, 53, 72
Tartakower 56
Tchigorin 19, 23, 36, 47
Teichmann 48, 60
Vidmar 58
Winawer 26

INDEX OF OPENINGS

(The numerical references are to games)

Albin Counter Gambit ⸴ ⸴ ⸴ ⸴ ⸴ ⸴ 13, 71
Bird Opening ⸴ ⸴ ⸴ ⸴ ⸴ ⸴ ⸴ ⸴ 2
Caro-Kann Defense ⸴ ⸴ ⸴ ⸴ ⸴ ⸴ 34
Center Game ⸴ ⸴ ⸴ ⸴ ⸴ ⸴ ⸴ ⸴ 7
Dutch Defense ⸴ ⸴ ⸴ ⸴ ⸴ ⸴ ⸴ 4, 43
English Opening ⸴ ⸴ ⸴ ⸴ ⸴ ⸴ ⸴ 56
Evans Gambit ⸴ ⸴ ⸴ ⸴ ⸴ ⸴ ⸴ ⸴ 19
Four Knights' Game ⸴ ⸴ ⸴ ⸴ ⸴ ⸴ 33, 62
French Defense ⸴ ⸴ ⸴ ⸴ ⸴ ⸴ ⸴ 25, 36, 38, 53,
57
From Gambit ⸴ ⸴ ⸴ ⸴ ⸴ ⸴ ⸴ ⸴ 10
Giuoco Piano ⸴ ⸴ ⸴ ⸴ ⸴ ⸴ ⸴ ⸴ 29, 31, 50
Petroff Defense ⸴ ⸴ ⸴ ⸴ ⸴ ⸴ ⸴ 48, 75
Queen's Gambit ⸴ ⸴ ⸴ ⸴ ⸴ ⸴ ⸴ 42
Queen's Gambit Declined ⸴ ⸴ ⸴ ⸴ 8, 15, 16, 20,
21, 41, 44, 63,
65, 70, 72
Queen's Pawn Opening ⸴ ⸴ ⸴ ⸴ 12, 23, 35, 37,
64
Ruy Lopez ⸴ ⸴ ⸴ ⸴ ⸴ ⸴ ⸴ ⸴ ⸴ 6, 9, 14, 17,
18, 22, 24, 26,
27, 28, 30, 32,
39, 46, 47, 49,
51, 52, 54, 55,
58, 60, 61, 66,
67, 69, 73, 74
Scotch Game ⸴ ⸴ ⸴ ⸴ ⸴ ⸴ ⸴ ⸴ 59, 68
Sicilian Defense ⸴ ⸴ ⸴ ⸴ ⸴ ⸴ ⸴ 11, 45
Vienna Game ⸴ ⸴ ⸴ ⸴ ⸴ ⸴ ⸴ ⸴ 1, 3, 5, 40

DR. EMANUEL LASKER—SUMMARY OF RESULTS:
1889-1914
TOURNAMENTS

Year		Prize	Played	Won	Lost	Drawn
1889	Amsterdam	2	8	5	1	2
1890	Graz	2	6	3	—	3
1892	London	1	11	8	1	2
1892	London	1	8	5	—	3
1893	New York	1	13	13	—	—
1895	Hastings	3	21	14	4	3
1895-6	St. Petersburg	1	18	8	3	7
1896	Nuremberg	1	18	12	3	3
1899	London	1	28	20	1	7
1900	Paris	1	18	14	1	3
1904	Cambridge Springs	2-3	15	9	2	4
1909	St. Petersburg	1-2	18	13	2	3
1914	St. Petersburg	1	18	10	1	7
	Totals		200	134	19	47

MATCHES

Year		Played	Won	Lost	Drawn
1889	v. Bardeleben	4	2	1	1
1890	v. Bird	12	7	2	3
1890	v. Miniati	5	3	—	2
1890	v. Mieses	8	5	—	3
1890	v. Englisch	5	2	—	3
1891	v. Lee	2	1	—	1
1892	v. Blackburne	10	6	—	4
1892	v. Bird	5	5	—	—
1893	v. Golmayo	3	2	—	1
1893	v. Vasquez	3	3	—	—
1893	v. Showalter	10	6	2	2
1893	v. Ettlinger	5	5	—	—
1894	v. Steinitz	19	10	5	4
1896-7	v. Steinitz	17	10	2	5
1907	v. Marshall	15	8	—	7
1908	v. Tarrasch	16	8	3	5
1909	v. Janowski	4	2	2	—
1909	v. Janowski	10	7	1	2
1910	v. Schlechter	10	1	1	8
1910	v. Janowski	11	8	—	3
	Totals	174	101	19	54

5

APPRECIATIONS

by HANS KMOCH

THE factors which place Dr. Lasker far above his predecessors are his much greater elasticity of outlook and his infallible, ever calm and objective judgment. He is called the Philosopher, and in point of fact there could be no apter characterization of Lasker the chess player as well as Lasker the man. Why the Philosopher?—is it because he has received the degree of Ph. D. or because he has written books on philosophy? These are factors, to be sure. But the true reason is revealed to us in the self-analysis which is offered by a perusal of his writings. In them we perceive a man and a thinker who has comprehended very precisely the limits of human thought, a man who has never—unlike many other artists and chess masters—wasted a moment on anything which ranges beyond these limits; a man who from the very start knew just how to apply his genius in the most effective way.

Man's powers are very great; they are enormous. They are slight only in comparison with eternity and infinity, but for us mortals they are very great indeed. Only in the rarest instances does a man arise who can approach these limits. Many great minds have been shattered because they could not endure this feeling of being continually hemmed in; many weaklings have set up their castles of dreams beyond these limits, thereby concealing or revealing that they were unable to attain to material possessions or firm convictions within the limits. Lasker has always striven only for the attainable and has devoted his considerable abilities and powers to this one end.

Not that he has carelessly neglected these other matters. Without a doubt he has understood the intangible and unknow-able more fully than any man who has devoted his life to "impractical" meditation. Lasker has analyzed his powers and wishes in mathematical terms; he has systematically apportioned his abilities; he has prescribed several goals and at the same time he has not overlooked the continuous flux of transcendental forces. He has interpreted them mathematically and taken them into consideration as unavoidable necessities. In this way good luck and bad, chance and the like have simultaneously filtered

7

through his fingers. He was never overjoyed nor painfully surprised. Every player knows the shattering influence of some unfortunate mis-chance, or the discouraging results which ensue if his powers suddenly relax (if only for a moment) and occasionally before relatively simple tasks; not necessarily because he was too optimistic: he may merely be one of those people who have been fortunate so long that they have already forgotten there is such a thing as misfortune. Such mishaps as a rule influence their victim subsequently for quite a while; they give him a feeling of uncertainty, confuse his thoughts, and rob him of his self-confidence—for some time at least. And all because he did not realize the existence of an indefinite number of obstacles and even less the possibility of their occurrence.

Lasker is enabled to exploit all his energies to the utmost through the circumstance that at every move, in fact every thought—that is to say not only over the board but mentally as well—he never forgets the enemy's practical threats, and at the same time he holds in reserve a certain amount of fighting spirit to cope with any remote theoretical contingencies. It is as if his personality were split: one half defends on the back lines, the other far advanced in the forefront of the conflict.

by ARON NIMZOWITSCH

WE can appreciate how far ahead of his time Lasker was, if we bear in mind that Tarrasch was the *praeceptor mundi* of the chess world up to about 1911. There is no master, living or dead, whose maneuver-ing ability approaches that of Lasker. The theory of complexes of weak squares of a definite color is relatively new, yet Lasker played many remarkable games with this theme (for example, his game with Tar-takower at St. Petersburg 1909) twenty and even thirty years ago.

by RICHARD RÈTI

LASKER is neither dogmatic nor mystical; he relies on healthy common sense. With this concept he seeks to understand the world and the game of chess.

An example will make clear Lasker's boundless faith in the principle of common sense. Lasker had defeated one of his great rivals in a match, and some time later he lectured on the match at the Vienna Chess Club. In the discussion after the lecture a member of the audience inquired, "Why did you almost always choose variations in the opening which your opponent had previously declared unsatisfactory? Had you studied his analyses and found mistakes in them?" "I did not study anything," Lasker replied, "but the variations in question consisted of developing moves which were so sound and reasonable that they could not be so bad as my opponent thought. I was therefore convinced that he had misjudged these variations, that his understanding of them was faulty. I wanted to take advantage of this state of affairs."

by RUDOLPH SPIELMANN

LASKER'S games are a unique source of pleasure. He is not merely successful: his games are more profound than those of any other player. Positional chess and combinative play, fantasy and technique, all these he fuses into a wonderful harmony. Such a harmony can be achieved over a long period of years only by a powerful personality which is nevertheless capable of self-control at all times. As an experienced tournament player myself, I know how to judge such ability, to estimate and admire it. I have been playing in tournaments for many years, and I know how difficult it is to retain self-control when one has to guide one's boat through the sea of an infinite number of chess possibilities. That is why many prefer to stay close to the shore and play for a draw.

Not so Lasker: he is always unafraid, always ready for the struggle. To me that is a sign of true greatness, for I know how often, in pursuing such dangerous lines of play, I lost my bearings, how often I suffered cruel disappointments; sometimes one attacks too late, sometimes too soon; one overlooks some trifle, or commits a microscopic positional error, and at once the catastrophe nears.

But Lasker! His eyes, his thoughts are everywhere. I speak from experience, for I have frequently tried to analyze with him. The result was really discouraging for me; no sooner had I hit on a good idea or a pretty combination, than Lasker waved it aside; for he had long ago already discarded it in his thoughts! It is true that we often find Lasker in difficult positions, but this is the result of conscious daring rather than of unconscious error. He is the ideal Fighter!

Let us hope that he will retain his greatness for a long time to come, and that he will have opportunities to add to his many triumphs of the past.

by DR. SAVIELLY TARTAKOWER

IT is frankly admitted that the "psychological chess" of which one hears so much nowadays is based to a great extent on Lasker's games. It is characteristic of Lasker's philosophy of life that he was the first to demonstrate that in chess not only a brilliant combination (Morphy), or a methodical system (Steinitz), but (and chiefly!) a knowledge of the opponent's personality, his weak and strong points, is an important element in obtaining victory.

While Morphy believed in miracles, Tarrasch believed in dogmas. But Lasker was always guided by his unswerving belief in the elasticity of the position. Only in this manner—and not by means of the usual fatuous explanations, such as individual style and will to win—can the universality of his chess creations be explained; a universality which enabled him for decades to steer clear of all schools, tendencies and imitations—only in the end to become the father of ultra-modern chess.

BIOGRAPHICAL INTRODUCTION

Dr. Emanuel Lasker was born in Berlinchen, a suburb of Berlin, on the 24th of December, 1868. We are told that he learned the moves at the age of 12 from his brother, Dr. Berthold Lasker, himself a very fine player, by the way. The youthful Emanuel, according to Mason's account, did not take up the game seriously until he was 15, but his progress does not seem to have been meteor-like, since his earliest important success was first prize in a tournament at the *Kaiserhof* in Berlin in 1889. A month later he acquired the title of *Master,* according to the German custom, by winning the *Hauptturnier* at Breslau from a good field. Leopold Hoffer, a discerning judge of chess ability, commented, in connection with the game against Lipke, "The young master will be a formidable opponent in future contests." Truly a prophetic judgment! Lasker's newly acquired honors secured him an entry at Amsterdam, where he made a promising start (his celebrated game with Bauer was played in the first round), leading Hoffer to remark that "Herr Lasker, a rising player from Berlin, shows considerable talent for the game, and will probably be the future master." Later Lasker fell back and finally finished second to Amos Burn. Seen from the perspective of his later achievements, this does not seem a great feat, considering the rather weak field; but it is consistent with his development up to that time, so that Hoffer was fully justified in writing after the tournament that "Young Lasker only confirmed the opinion we expressed about him when we watched him at Breslau. He is only 21 years of age, but possesses already the qualities of a first-class master—erudition, judgment of position, quickness of conception, imagination, great enthusiasm for the game, and above all, he is a man of culture and more than average intellect."

Unfortunately, very few of Lasker's games from the next few years have been preserved. He took part in two tournaments of only minor importance in 1890, at Berlin and Graz, and did not particularly distinguish himself. In the same year, however, he inflicted decisive defeats on Jacques Mieses and on the veteran Bird. Here he displayed for the first time that uncanny mastery of the imponderables of match play that has set him apart from all other masters. True, there have always been explanations: the style of Mieses was not suited to match play, and this was even more true of Bird, already a declining force for several years.

Displaying "good position judgment", the ambitious young master now paid a long visit to England, where he proceeded on his way to fame with a succession of victories which amazed the chess world. His easy defeats of Miniati and Lee in match play and his victory in the B. C. A. Tournament led to the arranging of the Quintangular Tournament in 1892, where Lasker met Bird, Blackburne, Gunsberg and Mason, the best contempory English players. The result was a convincing victory for Lasker, followed by equally decisive defeats of Blackburne and Bird in match play. Despite some sour comments on the soundness of his play, Lasker's place among the foremost players of the day could no longer be denied.

He now reversed the procedure of the illustrious Paul Morphy by coming to the New World. Here he continued his long series of triumphs, including matches with Golmayo, Vasquez and Showalter, and overwhelming scores in set games against the leading players of the Manhattan, Brooklyn and Philadelphia Chess Clubs. At a tournament held in New York, he won every game, despite the participation of Pillsbury, Showalter, Hodges and Albin! The result was that in 1894 —at the age of 26!—he was in a position to challenge Steinitz for the World's Championship.

Steinitz's matches with Tchigorin and Gunsberg had already revealed that his powers were seriously on the wane. The encounter at once took an unfavorable turn for the older master; and although Steinitz rallied pluckily toward the close of the match, the result was a foregone conclusion before ten games had been played. An examination of the games of the match will show that the youthful Lasker well deserved his victory, despite the unintentional aid of his adversary. The contemporary critics were much more zealous in castigating Steinitz than they were in praising Lasker. Their appraisal of the match was preponderantly negative: they felt that Steinitz had lost the match, rather than that Lasker had won it. Bardeleben's tartly phrased comments, possibly colored by personal animus, summed up the opinion of a goodly portion of the chess world: "Lasker lacks Steinitz's profundity, but he makes up for this by his extraordinary self-possession. His play is quite free from oversights, and that is the main cause of his victory over Steinitz. Another interesting characteristic of Lasker's play is that when he has a bad game he defends himself with serenity and circumspection, thus making his opponent's task as difficult as possible; whereas most players lose hope in such positions and make blunders which hasten the end. Lasker's play in the opening is generally correct but never forceful, and occasionally he passes by blunders of his opponent without exploiting them. Generally speaking Lasker belongs to the Modern School: his style is not particularly aggressive, his combinations lack fire, but his position judgment is sound and above all his play is characterized by extreme caution, so that it is very difficult to attack him successfully. He is more skillful at defense than at attack, to which he turns only when there is a definite, obvious advantage to be gained, or when he is at so great a disadvantage that defensive play no longer offers any prospects." (*Deutsche Schachzeitung*)

Toward the close of 1894 Lasker returned to Europe, where he became seriously ill. He recovered slowly, under the expert and devoted care of his brother. During the spring of the following year, he accepted an invitation to play in the forthcoming Hastings tourney, and it was about this time that he gave a series of lectures in England which later made up the substance of his *Common Sense in Chess*. The result of the Hastings Tournament was a disappointment for Lasker, for to miss first prize in a tournament which attracted so much attention was a distinct blow to the Champion's prestige. Besides, a victory was urgently needed to dispel the doubts of those critics who were unconvinced by the match with Steinitz. Lasker did not do himself justice at Hastings, as evidenced by the relatively low aesthetic standard of his games there; yet even his rival Tarrasch grudgingly admitted that at Hastings "Lasker has proved for the first time that he is a strong player." (!)

Later on in the same year Lasker amply justified his position by a striking triumph at St. Petersburg in the famous Quadrangular Tournament. Not only was his victory a decisive one, but his games were on a high artistic plane. His defeat of Steinitz and Tchigorin was crushing, and while he lost his individual series to Pillsbury, he had the satisfaction of defeating the American master in a superb game.

Despite the fact that the Nuremberg Tournament in the summer of 1896 had an even stronger entry than Hastings, Lasker soon took the lead and was never in any danger of being overtaken. Maróczy, Pillsbury, Tarrasch, Steinitz, Janowski, Schlechter, Tchigorin were left far behind! There followed the return match with Steinitz at Moscow, which resulted in an even more overwhelming defeat for Steinitz. One has the feeling, when playing over the games of this match, that Lasker was hardly ever extended, and had matters very much his own way. Yet his easy superiority did not blind Lasker to Steinitz's genius, and one recalls with pleasure the eloquent tribute Lasker has paid to the memory of his great rival in the *Manual of Chess*.

Satisfied with these achievements, Lasker now retired from active play for several years, until the London 1899 Tournament, which resulted in his most impressive victory to date, as he was first by a clear lead of 4½ points! This time Lasker's play aroused universal enthusiasm, and Marco expressed the general mood when he exclaimed exuberantly in the *Wiener Schachzeitung*, "Lasker was there, Lasker I, Lasker the Unique!" The following year at Paris, Lasker again achieved an easy victory, although his final lead (2 points ahead of Pillsbury) was not so great as at London.

From this time on, Lasker's appearances in tournament play became quite rare. He did not compete again until Cambridge Springs 1904, where he tied for second prize with Janowski. Lasker played some fine games in this tournament, interspersed with uneven chess which had a harmful effect on his score. Marshall's notable victory in this tournament led to talk of a match, which finally took place in 1907; but from the very first game it was clear that the American master was far from Lasker's equal in match play. Another decisive defeat was inflicted by Lasker on Tarrasch the following year, for a precisely opposite reason: Marshall, it seems, had too much vitality, and Tarrasch too little, to play well in a match against Lasker.

In this year (1908) Tchigorin died, and it was decided to hold a Memorial Tournament in his honor the following year at St. Petersburg. Despite the absence of Tarrasch, Maróczy and Marshall, and the poor form of Schlechter and Vidmar, the tourney was a most formidable one. Lasker was severely handicapped almost from the start by losing a sensational game in the third round to his chief rival, Rubinstein, who played the best chess of his life in this tournament. The Champion soon regained the lost ground when Rubinstein was defeated by Dus-Chotimirski, who, however, performed the same feat on Lasker a few rounds later! As the contest entered its second half, the pace set by the two leaders became so fierce that 3½ points separated them from the next players at the close. In the final round, Lasker had to win in order to be mathematically certain of a tie. Lasker produced some of his greatest strategical masterpieces in this tournament, while the unique merits of his Book of the Tournament have been praised by no less an authority than Alekhine.

There followed a short match with Janowski, which Lasker drew only with difficulty, and then a longer match, in which the Franco-Polish master was decisively worsted.

We come now to perhaps the most dramatic chapter in Lasker's colorful career: the match with Carl Schlechter in 1910. The struggle was limited to the strangely short number of ten games, draws to count. Contrary to expectations, the first series in Vienna produced extremely interesting and hard-fought games. The first four games were drawn, Lasker frequently being in hot water against the "Drawing Master," who played at the very height of his form on this occasion. The fifth game proved a sensation. After a colorless opening, Lasker obtained a microscopic advantage, and by subtle and patient maneuvering he gradually increased it until Schlechter, in desperation, offered a Pawn to obtain an attack. To the probable surprise of both players, the attack disclosed hidden powers as it progressed, and Schlechter, exploiting his advantage to the utmost, soon brought the game to a victorious close!

The scene now shifted to Berlin, where the games were equally exciting. Despite Lasker's desperate efforts to win, the next four games were drawn. This led to the following queer situation: in order to retain the championship, Lasker *had* to win the final game, whereas Schlechter, to wrest the championship from him, merely had to draw! Lasker, with the White pieces, played at once for the attack; but to the amazement of the spectators, so did Schlechter!! He explained later on that he would have considered it unworthy to win the title by playing for a draw. Schlechter soon took the initiative and pushed the attack vigorously, spurning several chances to draw. At one point, he had a fairly easy win, but overlooked it; Lasker took full advantage of his mistake, and playing with great care, finally won after 70-odd moves, thus retaining the title.

Later in the year Lasker administered a crushing defeat to Janowski in their return match. Meanwhile two younger stars had arisen: Capablanca and Rubinstein. There was much talk of a match, but nothing definite was accomplished, and the three masters met for the first time at the great St. Petersburg Tournament in 1914. The action of the Tournament Committee in inviting two masters long past their prime, and in arranging a second tournament to be played by the first five prize-winners of the preliminary tournament, aroused considerable dissatisfaction at the time. The result of the peculiar arrangement was that Rubinstein, Nimzowitsch and Bernstein fell through badly and did not qualify for the second tournament. Lasker played some beautiful games in the preliminary section, but a loss to Bernstein and a draw with Nimzowitsch brought him into the finals fully a point and a half behind Capablanca, who started like a whirlwind. The outlook was dark for Lasker: in an eight game tournament against Capablanca, Alekhine, Tarrasch and Marshall, he had to concede a point and a half to Capablanca! Nor was this all: Lasker could not afford to spare any precious points or half-points, every game had to be played for a win, risks had to be taken—and against such masters! And Lasker succeeded! Unquestionably Lasker's play in this tournament shows him at the height of his skill, for truly only a Superman could perform such a feat and at the same time play masterpieces almost every day!

The result of the tournament was really decided by the celebrated game with Capablanca two rounds before the close. Of the conclusion to this game Lasker wrote, "The spectators had followed the final moves breathlessly. That Black's position was in ruins was obvious to the veriest tyro. And now Capablanca turned over his King. From the several hundred spectators, there came such applause as I have never experienced in all my life as a chess player. It was like the wholly spontaneous applause which thunders forth in the theatre, of which the individual is almost unconscious." And on this glorious note of triumph we conclude the volume devoted to the first part of Lasker's Chess Career.

LASKER'S GREATEST
CHESS GAMES

GAME No. 1

Breslau 1889 (Hauptturnier)
Vienna Game

White	Black
Dr. E. Lasker	**P. Lipke**

1 P-K4	P-K4
2 Kt-QB3	Kt-KB3
3 P-KKt3	

Louis Paulsen's move, popularized by Mieses about this time; it is excellent against 2 . . . Kt-QB3, but not against Black's last move, which allows 3 . . . P-Q4!

3	B-B4
4 B-Kt2	O-O
5 KKt-K2	P-Q3
6 O-O	Kt-B3
7 P-Q3	B-K3

Preparing for . . . P-Q4, which White prevents by

8 Kt-Q5!	BxKt

Otherwise B-Kt5 would be annoying.

9 PxB	Kt-K2

White now has a superior position because of the greater mobility of his two Bs.

10 B-Kt5!

Avoiding 10 P-B4, which would yield control of Q4 to Black.

10	Kt-Q2

Of course neither Kt can capture the QP because of the resulting pin.

11 P-Q4	PxP

11 . . . B-Kt3; 12 PxP, PxP? (to keep White's Kt out of Q4; safer is 12 . . . KtxP) would be unsatisfactory because of 13 P-Q6, PxP; 14 QxP±.

12 KtxP

The Kt is very well placed at this centralized post.

12	P-KR3
13 B-K3	Kt-K4

More logical is 13 . . . Kt-KB3 and if then 14 P-QB4, Q-Q2 followed by . . . Kt-B4.

14 Q-K2	Q-Q2
15 P-KR3	QR-K

. . . Kt-B4 was better. The principle that exchanges are useful to relieve cramped positions was not generally known at this time.

16 QR-K	P-R3

He cannot play . . . Q-R5 at once with any effect, since the continuation would be 17 P-Kt3! QxRP? 18 R-R, Q-Kt7; 19 KR-Kt (19 Q-Q2 would also serve the purpose), Q-B6; 20 Kt-Kt5, Q-Kt5; 21 R-R4 trapping the Q.

17 P-KB4	Kt (K4) -Kt3
18 Q-B2	

Preventing . . . Kt-B4 (which would be answered by KtxKt followed by BxB, winning a P) and also threatening P-B5-B6.

18	BxKt

Black has little choice in view of the above-mentioned threat. If 18 . . . Q-R5; 19 P-Kt3 and the Q must retreat, for if 19 . . . QxRP? 20 R-R, Q-Kt7; 21 Q-Q2! and again the Q is trapped.

19 BxB	Kt-B4
20 B-QB3	RxR
21 RxR	R-K
22 B-B3	RxRch
23 QxR	

Lasker has managed the opening and middle game play expertly and now has a decided advantage.

23 . . . .   Kt (B4)-K2

Or 23 . . . Q-K2; 24 QxQ, Kt
(B4) xQ; 25 B-QR5, P-Kt3; 26
B-B3±.

24 K-Kt2   Q-R5

Lipke cannot resist this tempta-
tion. His safest policy would have
been to mark time.

25 Q-Q2   QxRP
26 Q-Q4

Position after White's 26th move

26 . . . .   P-KB3

If instead 26 . . . Kt-B4; 27
Q-K4

I 27 . . . Kt (Kt3)-K2; 28 P-
KKt4 (28 B-KKt4 QxQP! 29 Q
xQ, KtxQ; 30 BxKt, Kt-K6ch,
etc.), Kt-R5ch; 29 K-Kt3, KtxB;
30 QxKt (K7), QxQP; 31 Q-K3
winning.

II 27 . . . Kt (B4)-K2; 28 P-
B5, Kt-K4; 29 BxKt, PxB; 30 Q
xP with a winning game.

27 Q-K4   Q-Kt8
28 P-R4

Threatening P-R5.

28 . . . .   K-B

The only move.

29 B-R5   P-KB4

Again forced: if 29 . . . Kt-R;
30 Q-R7, Kt-B2; 31 BxP! winning.

30 Q-Q4!

But not 30 Q-K6, QxPch; 31
K-R3, Q-K5 and White will be
lucky to draw.

30 . . . .   QxPch
31 K-R3   Q-K5
32 QxPch   K-K
33 BxKtch   K-Q2

The only chance. If 33 . . .
KtxB; 34 QxKtch, K-Q2 best; 35
Q-B7ch, K-B (or 35 . . . K-Q; 36
B-B6ch); 36 Q-K6ch and White
will win quickly.

34 BxPch!

A very pretty move which
ensures a won ending, whereas 34
K-R2 would only draw after 34
. . . Q-K7ch; 35 K-Kt, Q-K6ch;
36 K-B, Q-B6ch followed by . . .
QxPch and . . . QxKB.

34 . . . .   QxBch
35 Q-Kt4

After the exchange of Qs,
White's K side Ps will win easily.

35 . . . .   QxQch

Nor would 35 . . . K-K; 36
QxQ, KtxQ; 37 K-Kt4 be any
better for Black.

36 KxQ   KtxP
37 B-Q2

But not 37 K-R5? KtxB; 38
PxKt, P-R4 and Black will at least
draw.

37 . . . .   Kt-B3ch

38	K-B5	K-K2
39	P-KKt4	P-Q4
40	P-Kt5	PxP
41	BPxP	Kt-Q2
42	P-Kt6	K-B
43	P-R5	P-Q5
44	P-R6	K-Kt
45	P-R7ch	K-R

Or 45 . . . K-Kt2; 46 B-R6ch, K-R; 47 K-K6 and wins.

46	K-K6	Kt-Bch
47	K-B7	Resigns

Despite his relative inexperience, Lasker's handling of the Bishops and in fact his whole conduct of this difficult game could not have been improved upon even by Steinitz.

GAME No. 2

Amsterdam 1889

Bird Opening

White	Black
Dr. E. Lasker	**J. H. Bauer**

1 P-KB4

The only recorded instance of Lasker's adoption of this rarely played opening.

1	. . . .	P-Q4
2	P-K3	Kt-KB3
3	P-QKt3	

Not the most precise continuation: 3 Kt-KB3 would have been better, for now Black could play 3 . . . P-Q5, completely disorganizing his opponent's plans.

3	. . . .	P-K3
4	B-Kt2	B-K2
5	B-Q3	

Clearly revealing his intention of obtaining a K side attack, and doubtless better than B-K2, or P-Kt3 followed by B-Kt2.

5	. . . .	P-QKt3
6	Kt-QB3	B-Kt2
7	Kt-B3	QKt-Q2
8	O-O	O-O
9	Kt-K2	

Reinforcing the projected attack by opening the QB's diagonal and bringing the Kt to the other wing.

9 . . . . P-B4

Here Black should have seized the opportunity of ridding himself of one of the dangerous Bs by 9 . . . Kt-B4; 10 Kt-Kt3, KtxB; 11 PxKt, ⌐-B4 etc. (*Deutsche Schachzeitung*).

10	Kt-Kt3	Q-B2
11	Kt-K5	KtxKt

This is rather risky and demands careful play on Black's part from now on. 11 . . . P-Kt3 would have been safer despite the weakening of the diagonal.

12 BxKt Q-B3

With the transparent threat of . . . P-Q5.

13 Q-K2 P-QR3?

In order to play . . . Kt-Q2 without having to fear B-Kt5. But as will soon become clear, 13 . . Kt-Q2 was imperative.

I 14 B-Kt2, B-B3 etc.

II 14 Q-R5, P-B4 with a good game.

III 14 B-Kt5, Q-B; 15 BxKt, QxB; 16 Kt-R5, P-B3 and White cannot afford to go in for 17 Q-Kt4, P-Kt3; 18 B-Kt2, P-B4; 19 Q-Kt3, K-B2 winning a piece.

13 . . . Kt-K5 was also a playable alternative.

Position after Black's 13th move

14 Kt-R5!

After this there is no saving the game for Black.

I 14 . . . Kt-K; 15 BxP, KtxB; 16 Q-Kt4.

II 14 . . . P-R3; 15 BxKt, BxB; 16 KtxBch, PxKt; 17 Q-Kt4 ch, K-R; 18 Q-R4, K-Kt2; 19 R-B3, KR-Q; 20 R-Kt3ch, K-B; 21 QxP±.

III 14 . . . P-Q5; 15 BxKt, BxB; 16 Q-Kt4, K-R (16 . . . P-K4; 17 B-K4!); 17 R-B3, R-KKt (17 . . . PxP; 18 KtxB, P xKt; 19 Q-R4); 18 BxKRP! KR-Q; 19 Q-R3, B-K2; 20 B-K4! and wins.

14 . . . .   KtxKt

Leading to a brilliant refutation which has since served as a classic example of the power of the united Bs.

15 BxPch!

Black no doubt expected 14 Qx Kt, P-B4 etc.

15 . . . .   KxB
16 QxKtch   K-Kt
17 BxP!!

A really beautiful move which adds lustre to Lasker's combination.

17 . . . .   KxB

. . . P-B3 would lose quickly because of R-B3-Kt3.

18 Q-Kt4ch!

In order to win one of the Bs four moves later.

18 . . . .   K-R2
19 R-B3   P-K4
20 R-R3ch   Q-R3
21 RxQch   KxR
22 Q-Q7

This move crowns the combination begun on his 14th move.

22 . . . .   B-KB3
23 QxB   K-Kt2

Not 23 . . . PxP; 24 QxKtP, K-Kt2; 25 R-KB. But Black's game is hopeless anyway.

24 R-KB   QR-Kt
25 Q-Q7

Rightly disdaining the Q side Ps in favor of the attack.

25 . . . .   KR-Q

He must create a flight square for his K.

26 Q-Kt4ch   K-B
27 PxP   B-Kt2

27 . . . BxP? would of course lose the B.

28 P-K6

This settles matters.

28 . . . .   R-Kt2
29 Q-Kt6   P-B3
30 RxPch!   BxR
31 QxBch   K-K
32 Q-R8ch   K-K2
33 Q-Kt7ch   Resigns

GAME No. 3

Berlin 1889

Vienna Game

White   Black
J. Mieses   **Dr. E. Lasker**

1 P-K4	P-K4
2 Kt-QB3	B-B4
3 P-KKt3	Kt-QB3
4 B-Kt2	P-Q3
5 Kt-R4	

KKt-K2 was better.

5	B-K3
6 KtxB	PxKt
7 P-Q3	Kt-B3
8 Kt-K2	Q-Q3!

After the routine 8 . . .O-O; 9 O-O followed by P-KB4, White would obtain a strong attack.

9 P-KB4   P-KR4

To discourage White from castling K side.

10 P-B5

Blocking the position does not appreciably help White. Mieses should rather have continued with P-KR3 followed by B-K3, Q-Q2 and (eventually) O-O-O.

10	B-Q2
11 B-Kt5	

Again B-K3 was simpler and better.

11. . . .	Kt-R2
12 B-K3	O-O-O
13 Kt-B3	

Planning a risky attack against Black's K which is not justified by White's insufficient development. 13 Q-Q2 could have been played quite safely.

13 . . . .   Kt-B3

14 Kt-Kt5	Q-K2
15 P-B3	P-B5!?

15 . . . P-R3 was more prudent.

16 P-QKt4?

For here 16 Q-R4 and if 16 . . . P-R3; 17 PxP! would have yielded a powerful attack.

16 . . . .   KtxKtP!

An obvious sacrifice, but the sequel has many pretty points.

17 KtxPch

After 17 PxKt, QxPch followed by . . . QxKt Black would win easily.

17 . . . .   K-Kt
18 PxKt

Declining the sacrifice would leave White with a hopelessly disorganized game.

18 . . . .   QxPch
19 K-B

Or 19 Q-Q2, P-B6; 20 Q-B (20 Q-B2, B-R5; 21 QR-Kt, Q-R4 with . . . P-B7 dis ch to follow), P-QKt3 regaining the piece with the superior game.

19 . . . .   Kt-Kt5

The most forceful; but the simple 19 . . . P-QKt3 would have proved equally effective in the long run.

20 B-Kt	B-R5
21 R-Kt	Q-R6
22 Q-K2	RxP
23 P-R3	

Despite his material advantage, White's position is untenable; if for example 23 Q-Kt2, R-Q8ch; 24 RxR, QxQ or 29 K-K2, Q-Q6 mate.

23 . . . .   KR-Q!!

White probably expected 23 ...
Kt-K6ch; 24 BxKt, RxB; 25 QxBP,
KxKt; 26 QxQBP with counter-
play.

     24 PxKt   P-B6!

The point of the foregoing sacrifice: White has no adequate defense against the threat of . . .
P-B7.

     25 Kt-B6ch

Equally hopeless would be 25
B-K3, P-B7; 26 R-B, RxB or 25
Kt-Kt5, BxKt; 26 RxB, R-Q8ch;
27 K-B2, R(Q)-Q7 etc.

     25 . . . .   BxKt
     26 B-K3   P-B7!

But not 26 . . . RxB? 27 QxR,
P-B7; 28 RxPch! and wins.

     27 QxP   RxB

Position after Black's 27th move

     28 K-B2

If 28 QxB, R-Q8ch! 29 K-B2
(if 29 RxR, PxQ), R-Q7ch and
White is lost:

I 30 K-B, R-K8ch!! 31 KxR,
Q-K6ch and mate next move.

II 30 K-Kt, R-K8ch; 31 K-R2,
RxRch; 32 KxR, R-Q8ch followed
by . . . RxR.

     28 . . . .   R-B6

White resigns: if 29 Q-Kt2, Q-
B4ch followed by . . . R-B7 wins
quickly.

A spirited game in which the
youthful Lasker carries out the
attack in the most elegant style.

GAME No. 4

Match 1890

Dutch Defense

White	Black
Dr. E. Lasker	**J. Mieses**
1 P-Q4	P-KB4
2 P-QB4	

Passing up the opportunity of
playing the Staunton Gambit (2
P-K4), for which see Game No.
43.

2 P-KKt3 (Steinitz's idea) is at
present considered stronger than
the text.

     2 . . . .   P-B4
     3 PxP   Q-R4ch

Unnecessarily complicating matters; simply . . . P-K3 was preferable.

     4 Kt-B3   QxBP
     5 P-K4   PxP
     6 KtxP   Q-B2

The unfortunate excursion of
the Q has enabled White to gain
important time.

     7 Kt-R3!

Very good! This Kt is to be
brought to Q5 without loss of time

     7 . . . .   P-KKt3

Or 7 . . . Kt-KB3; 8 KtxKtch, KPxKt; 9 B-Q3±.

8 Kt-B4	B-Kt2
9 Kt-Q5	Q-Q
10 B-Kt5	BxP

Black's position is so hopeless that he has already passed the stage where "Pawn-grabbing" can do him any harm!

11 Kt-Q6ch	K-B
12 Q-B3ch	B-B3
13 Kt (Q5) xB	

If now 13 . . . PxKt (B3); 14 KtxB, QxKt; 15 BxP, KtxB; 16 QxKtch etc. After Black's actual reply, Lasker has at his disposal an even more advantageous line.

13	KtxKt
14 BxKt	PxB
15 Q-Q5!	

Position after White's 15th move

15	Q-K2ch

15 . . . K-Kt2 would likewise be inadequate after 16 Q-B7ch, K-R3; 17 O-O-O! followed by R-Q3 with a winning attack.

16 K-Q2	K-Kt2

Now the only defense against the two threats of KtxB and R-K.

17 R-K	Q-B

Probably hoping for 18 R-K8, QxR; 19 KtxRch, RxR and the win for White is by no means easy.

18 P-KR4!

An ingenious resource for freshening up the attack. The immediate threat is P-R5-6 mate!

18	P-KR4
19 R-R3!	

This was the real purpose behind Lasker's last move: he doubles Rs on the K file without loss of time, after which the attack must be irresistible.

19	Kt-B3
20 R (R3) -K3	

Threatening R-K8, which would win the Q for only a R.

20	Q-Q

This costs a piece, but Black has no way of saving the game.

21 R-K8

Winning a piece outright; but 21 K-B! would have been more conclusive: all the White threats remain, and Black cannot play 21 . . . Q-R4 because of 22 R-K7ch, K-R3; 23 Kt-B7ch, K-Kt2; 24 KtxR dis ch, and mate in three.

There followed: 21 . . . RxR; 22 RxR, Q-R4ch; 23 QxQ, KtxQ; 24 RxB, RxR; 25 KtxR, Kt-B3; 26 Kt-Q6, P-Kt3; 27 B-K2, P-B4; 28 B-B3, Kt-K2; 29 Kt-Kt5, P-R4; 30 Kt-B7, Kt-B; 31 Kt-Q5, K-B2; 32 K-B3, K-K3; 33 K-Q4, P-Q3; 34 Kt-B4ch, K-B3; 35 B-Kt7, Kt-R2; 36 Kt-Q5ch, K-K3; 37 KtxP, resigns.

GAME No. 5

London 1892

Vienna Game

White	Black
J. H. Blackburne	**Dr. E. Lasker**
1 P-K4	P-K4
2 Kt-QB3	Kt-KB3
3 P-B4	P-Q4
4 BPxP	KtxP
5 Q-B3	P-KB4

More usual is the line of play recommended by Steinitz: 5 . . . Kt-QB3; 6 B-Kt5, KtxKt; 7 KtP xKt, Q-R5ch; 8 P-Kt3, Q-K5ch, etc. The text leads to more complicated play.

6 Kt-R3

This is too slow; 6 P-Q3 seems best with the continuation 6 . . . KtxKt; 7 PxKt, P-Q5; 8 Q-Kt3, Kt-B3; 9 B-K2, B-K3 and now 10 P-B4!? (an innovation), B-Kt5 ch; 11 K-Q, Q-Q2; 12 R-Kt, R-QKt; 13 B-B3, O-O; 14 Kt-K2, B-B4; 15 Kt-B4, Kt-K2; 16 P-KR4 and White has a much better game than he usually obtains in this variation (Reinfeld-Thompson, Correspondence 1927).

6 . . . .   P-B3

Rather conservative; on 6 . . . Kt-B3; Tarrasch gives 7 B-Kt5, Q-R5ch; 8 K-B as best for White.

7 Kt-K2?

Blackburne wishes to dislodge Black's Kt by P-Q3 without allowing an exchange. But this is not an unmixed blessing, since White's minor pieces are so badly posted. 7 P-Q3 was essential, instead of the time-wasting text.

7	B-K2
8 P-Q3	Kt-B4
9 P-R3?	

Altogether incomprehensible.

9	O-O
10 B-K3	QKt-Q2
11 BxKt	

If instead 11 P-Q4, Kt-K5 followed by . . . Q-Kt3. 11 Q-B4 would lose the KP after . . . Kt-K3 (12 Q-Kt3? B-R5).

11	KtxB
12 KKt-B4	Q-Kt3!

Very strong! White's best reply would have been 13 P-QKt3, but not 12 O-O-O because of 12 . . . Kt-R5 nor 12 R-QKt because of 12 . . . Kt-Q2.

13 P-QKt4

Creating a new weakness which enables Black to institute an energetic attack.

13	Kt-Q2
14 P-Q4	P-QR4!
15 R-QKt	

15 P-B3 would of course be useless: 15 . . . PxP; 16 BPxP, BxPch etc.

15	PxP
16 PxP	

(See diagram on next page)

16 . . . .   BxPch

This is not so much a sacrifice as a profitable investment!

17 P-B3	BxPch
18 KtxB	QxP

The ultimate result of the game cannot be in doubt; Black gets four Ps for the piece, open lines for the attack and White's K is dangerously exposed.

Position after White's 16th move

19 Kt (B4)-K2

He must provide for . . . R-R6.

19	QxP
20 Q-B4	Q-B3
21 Kt-Q4	Kt-B4!

Threatening to win a piece by . . . Kt-K3!

22 Q-Q2	Kt-K5
23 KtxKt	BPxKt
24 Q-K3	R-R5
25 Kt-B2	

White must give way: a plausible continuation after 25 R-Q would be . . .P-B4; 26 Kt-B2, P-Q5; 27 Q-Q2, P-K6; 28 Q-K2, B-Kt5.

25	R-R7
26 R-B	B-Kt5!
27 B-K2	BxB
28 KxB	Q-Kt7
29 K-Q	Q-Kt4!
30 R-K	

If 30 K-K, Q-Q6; 31 Q-K2, P-Q5 wins easily.

30 . . . .   R-Kt7!

Not 30 . . . Q-Q6ch; 31 QxQ, PxQ at once because of 32 Kt-Kt4. Blackburne misses the point and loses at once.

| 31 Q-K2 | Q-Q6ch |
| 32 QxQ | PxQ |

White resigns, as he must lose a piece. Lasker's play throughout is characterized by superb vigor.

GAME No. 6

London 1892
Ruy Lopez

White	Black
Dr. E. Lasker	**J. H. Blackburne**

1 P-K4	P-K4
2 Kt-KB3	Kt-QB3
3 Kt-B3	Kt-B3
4 B-Kt5	P-Q3

The Steinitz Defense; modern masters prefer either 4 . . . B-Kt5 or . . . Kt-Q5.

5 P-Q3

Likewise indicating his preference for a closed, solid game of the Steinitzian type. Nowadays 5 P-Q4 is considered the refutation of this defense: 5 . . . B-Q2; 6 Bx Kt, BxB; 7 Q-Q3, PxP (or 7 . . . Kt-Q2; 8 P-Q5, Kt-B4; 9 Q-B4, B-Q2; 10 P-QKt4±; Niemzowitsch-Breyer, Gothenburg 1920); 8 KtxP, P-KKt3; 9 B-Kt5, B-Kt2; 10 O-O-O ±; Alekhine-Brinckmann, Kecskemet 1927.

5	B-K2
6 P-KR3	O-O
7 B-K3	

More in the spirit of the opening was Kt-K2 at once, followed by P-KKt4, Kt-Kt3 etc. If 7 Kt-K2, P-Q4? 8 BxKt, PxB; 9 KtxP, Q-Q3; 10 B-B4, Kt-R4; 11 B-R2±.

```
7 . . . .            Kt-K
8 P-KKt4             P-QR3
9 B-R4               B-K3
10 Kt-K2             P-Kt3
11 Kt-Kt3            Kt-Kt2
```

11 . . . P-B4 would leave his white squares too weak.

```
12 P-B3              P-QKt4
```

But here Black misses his opportunity: 12 . . . P-B4 would have equalized. If then 13 KtPxP, PxP.

I 14 B-R6, P-B5; 15 Kt-K2, B-B3; 16 R-KKt, Q-K! 17 Kt-Kt5, B-Q2; 18 B-Kt3ch, K-R with a good game (19 Kt-B, Kt-QR4! 20 B-B2, Q-Kt3!).

II 14 PxP, KtxP; 15 KtxKt, BxKt; 16 B-R6, R-B3; 17 B-Kt3ch (or 17 R-Ktch, R-Kt3), K-R and again White has no advantage.

```
13 B-Kt3             P-Q4
```

Now it is too late for . . . P-B4; for if 13 . . . BxB; 14 QxB, Kt-QR4; 15 Q-Q, P-KB4; 16 KtPxP, PxP; 17 B-R6, P-B5; 18 BxKt, KxB; 19 Kt-B5ch ±.

```
14 B-R6              Q-Q2
```

14 . . . PxP would be equally unsatisfactory because of 15 BxB! PxKt (or 15 . . . PxB; 16 Kt (Kt3) xP); 16 B-Kt3±.

```
15 Q-K2              P-Q5
```

Weakly played; 15 . . . KR-Q, gaining control of the Q file, would still have left him with a playable game.

```
16 BxB               QxB
17 O-O!              KR-Q
```

Or 17 . . . PxP; 18 PxP, P-Kt5; 19 P-Q4! ±.

18 KR-B!

A very fine move which definitely establishes White's superiority since he forces the closing of the Q file.

```
18 . . . .           R-Q2
19 PxP               KtxP
20 KtxKt             PxKt
21 P-B4
```

Lasker has cleverly built up a K side attack.

```
21 . . . .           P-QB4
22 P-K5
```

Threatening to win a piece by BxKt followed by P-B5-6.

```
22 . . . .           R-Q4
23 R-K
```

Renewing the threat.

```
23 . . . .           B-R5
24 Q-B3              BxKt
```

After R-K2, this exchange would have been forced anyway.

```
25 QxB               P-B4?
```

Black's game was already critical, and it is questionable whether he had any adequate defense; but the text is a blunder which allows Lasker to win in elegant style.

```
26 PxP e.p.          QxBP
27 Q-Kt2!
```

An important finesse: after 27 Q-B3, QR-Q; 28 B-Kt5? is refuted by . . . RxB.

(See diagram on next page)

```
27 . . . .           Q-Q3
```

27 . . . Q-B2?; 28 R-K7!

```
28 R-K7!             Kt-K3
29 R-K               QxR
```

The Kt has no squares: if 29 . . . Kt-B2; 30 RxKt, or 29 . . .

Position after White's 27th move

Kt-B; 30 R-K8.

| 30 QxR | R-K |
| 31 P-B5 | |

Wins a piece. There followed: 31 . . . Q-R5; 32 RxKt, Q-Kt6 ch; 33 Q-Kt2, QxQch; 34 KxQ, RxR; 35 PxR, P-B5; 36 PxP, PxP; 37 K-B3, P-B6; 38 PxP, PxP; 39 K-K3, resigns.

GAME No. 7

Match 1892

Center Game

| White | Black |
| **J. H. Blackburne** | **Dr. E. Lasker** |

1 P-K4	P-K4
2 P-Q4	PxP
3 QxP	Kt-QB3
4 Q-K3	P-KKt3

The usual continuation now- adays is 4 . . . Kt-B3; 5 Kt-QB3, B-Kt5; 6 B-Q2, O-O; 7 O-O-O, R-K and Black has a satisfactory game. Lasker's move is less direct but equally good.

| 5 B-Q2 | B-Kt2 |
| 6 Kt-QB3 | Kt-B3 |

| 7 O-O-O | O-O |
| 8 P-B3 | |

After 8 B-QB4, Kt-QR4! 9 B-K2, Black could safely play 9 . . . P-Q4!

| 8 . . . . | P-Q4 |
| 9 Q-B5 | |

White's position is awkward; the text only leads to simplifications favorable to Black.

| 9 . . . . | PxP |
| 10 B-KKt5 | Q-K |

Forced.

11 BxKt	BxB
12 KtxP	B-Kt2
13 B-Kt5	Q-K4!

Forcing the exchange of Qs, after which Black by virtue of his two Bs has the better game.

| 14 QxQ | KtxQ |
| 15 Kt-K2 | P-QR3! |

By a series of deft maneuvers, Lasker now restricts the mobility of White's minor pieces.

| 16 B-Q3 | P-KB4 |
| 17 Kt (K4) -B3 | |

Or 17 Kt-B5, P-Kt3; 18 Kt-QKt3, B-K3 etc.

| 17 . . . . | B-K3 |
| 18 K-Kt | |

Being unable to formulate any plan, he drifts aimlessly.

18	KR-Q
19 Kt-B4	B-B2
20 B-K2	Kt-B3!

The Kt is no longer useful at K4, since Black has already suc- ceeded in driving back his oppon- ent's minor pieces one rank.

| 21 RxRch | RxR |
| 22 R-Q | R-K! |

Exchanging Rs would simplify unduly. The text threatens 23 . . . BxKt, 24 PxB, P-KKt4 winning a piece.

   23 B-B   P-QKt4!
   24 Kt-Q3

Threatening Kt-B5.

24 P-QR4 appears to be strong, but after 24 . . . BxKt! 25 PxB, Kt-K4 Black retains his advantage.

   24 . . . .   B-Q5
   25 Kt-K2   B-Kt3

The change of diagonal has enabled Black to control the important square K6 a second time.

   26 P-QKt3

To bring his K into play. The maneuver creates new targets for attack but the weakness of the black squares would have proved decisive in any case.

   26 . . . .   K-Kt2
   27 P-B3   K-B3
   28 K-B2   Kt-K2

Centralization!

   29 Kt(K2)-B   Kt-Q4
   30 K-Kt2?

A blunder which loses the exchange. 30 K-Q2 would have prolonged the game.

(See diagram next column)

   30 . . . .   P-Kt5!
   31 KtxP

There is no defense. If 31 PxP, B-Q5ch; 32 K-R3, Kt-K6 or 31 P-QB4, B-Q5ch.

   31 . . . .   Kt-K6
   32 R-K   Kt-B5ch
   33 BxKt   RxR

There followed: 34 BxP, R-Kt8; 35 P-Kt3, R-Kt7ch; 36 K-R3,

Position after White's 30th move

RxKRP; 37 Kt-K2, R-Kt7; 38 Kt-B2, P-Kt4; 39 B-Q3, P-R4; 40 K-Kt4, B-B7; 41 P-R4, P-B4ch; 42 K-Kt5, QBxP; 43 P-R5, P-QB5; 44 BxQBP, BxKt; 45 P-R6, B-Q8; 46 Kt-Q4, BxKt; 47 PxB, BxP; 48 P-Q5, B-K7; 49 BxB, RxB; 50 P-R7, R-QR7; White resigns.

GAME No. 8

Match 1892

Queen's Gambit Declined

White	Black
Dr. E. Lasker	**J. H. Blackburne**
1 P-Q4	P-Q4
2 Kt-KB3	Kt-KB3
3 P-B4	P-K3
4 Kt-B3	QKt-Q2
5 B-B4	

The older continuation which was generally played until Pillsbury popularized B-Kt5.

   5 . . . .   P-B3

This gives Black a cramped game; 5 . . . PxP; 6 P-K3, Kt-Q4 is an alternative.

   6 P-K3   Kt-R4
   7 B-Kt5   B-K2

8 BxB	Qx]
9 B-Q3	P-KKt3

Inaugurating a plan which is of dubious value positionally. 9 . . . KKt-B3, to be followed later by . . . PxP and . . . P-K4, held out more prospects of equalizing.

10 Q-K2	O-O
11 O-O	P-KB4

Attacks in this opening on Black's part generally have little hope of success.

12 KR-Q	QKt-B3
13 QR-B	B-Q2

This B is destined to play an ineffectual role throughout the game: an indication that Black has not played the opening properly.

14 Kt-K5	B-K
15 Q-B2	

Black has, with his 11th move, stopped the advance of the White KP. The White Q is therefore now available for the Q side (Lasker).

| 15 . . . . | R-Q |

Here and later on . . . P-B5 can always be countered effectively with P-K4.

16 P-QR3	Kt-Q2
17 Kt-B3!	

Rightly refusing to allow Black to free his game a bit by exchanging.

| 17 . . . . | Kt-Kt2 |
| 18 R-K! | |

White intends a Q side attack; and, therefore, makes first preparations to take advantage of any forward movement that Black might undertake on the K side, beginning with . . . P-B5 (Lasker).

18 . .	Kt-B3
19 P-QKt4	Kt-K5
20 Kt-K5	KtxKt
21 QxKt	Kt-R4
22 P-QR4	

White makes steady progress.

| 22 . . . . | Kt-B3 |
| 23 P-Kt5 | |

P-B5, to be followed by this move, was also quite good. The intention behind the advance of the Q side Ps is to weaken Black's Ps, and the masterly way in which Lasker executes this plan is most instructive.

| 23 . . . . | Kt-Q2 |
| 24 Kt-B3 | PxBP |

White threatened now P-B5, followed by P-R5-6, to establish a dangerous passed P at B5 (Lasker).

| 25 QxP | Kt-Kt3 |
| 26 Q-Kt3 | PxP |

. . . R-B offered somewhat better prospects.

27 PxP

After this recapture the positional struggle is concluded in White's favor: the QRP is decidedly weak.

Position after White's 27th move

27	B-B2
28 Kt-K5	R-B
29 R-R	R-R
30 R-K2	KR-B

. . . Kt-B would save the RP, but leave Black hopelessly tied up; a plausible continuation would be 30 . . .Kt-B; 31 KR-R2, K-Kt2; 32 B-K2, R-Q; 33 B-B3, K-B; 34 Q-B3, K-K; 35 R-B2, Kt-Kt3; 36 Q-B7 or 34 . . . B-K; 35 Q-B5! QxQ; 36 PxQ, BxP; 37 BxP, R-Kt; 38 P-B6 with a winning game in either variation.

31 KR-R2	Q-B2
32 P-Kt3	

RxP could also be played at once.

32	Q-B6
33 QxQ	RxQ
34 RxP	RxR
35 RxR	R-B2

The attack has now succeeded. White has the advantage of a P plus on the Q side. What remains is to convert this into positional superiority—not an easy process, as still there are hardly any assailable points in the Black camp (Lasker).

36 K-B	B-K
37 K-K2	K-B
38 K-Q2	K-K2
39 R-R3	K-Q3
40 P-B3!	

The logical procedure. White must threaten to break through on the K side.

40	R-B
41 P-K4	R-B2

Black has of course nothing

better than wait for White to carry out his plans.

42 R-R

So as to be able to switch the R to the other wing if necessary.

42	R-B
43 P-R4!	R-B2
44 R-QKt	R-B
45 K-K3	K-K2
46 P-R5!	K-B3

46 . . . BPxP; 47 BxP would be decidedly in White's favor.

47 RPxP	RPxP
48 R-KR	K-Kt2

Here, after some maneuvers to complete the third hour (we played 18 moves an hour), the game went on at move 55, the position being unchanged (Lasker).

55 P-Kt4!	PxKtP
56 PxP	R-R
57 P-Kt5!	

With the decisive threat of Kt-Kt4-B6.

57	R-R6
58 K-Q2	R-R7ch
59 K-K3	R-R6
60 K-B4	Kt-Q2
61 B-B4	Kt-B
62 R-QB	

The threat of invasion at B7 leaves Black without resource.

62	R-R4
63 B-Q3	BxP
64 R-B5 and wins.	

Positional chess of the highest order throughout.

GAME No. 9

Match 1892

Ruy Lopez

White	Black
Dr. E. Lasker	**H. E. Bird**

1 P-K4	P-K4
2 Kt-KB3	Kt-QB3
3 B-Kt5	Kt-Q5

One of the many eccentricities for which the British master was noted. It has also been adopted on occasion by Blackburne, Tarrasch and Alekhine. While the move provides the best defense to the Four Knights' Game (the Rubinstein Variation), it is not wholly satisfactory in the Ruy Lopez.

4 B-B4

Less energetic than KtxKt, but sufficient to maintain a slight lead in development.

4	KtxKtch
5 QxKt	Kt-B3
6 P-Q4?!	P-Q3

Canny play. After 6 . . . PxP; 7 P-K5, Q-K2; 8 Q-K2,Kt-Kt Black would have difficulty completing his development.

7 Q-QKt3	Q-K2
8 PxP	PxP
9 O-O	P-B3

If 9 . . . KtxP; 10 BxPch, Qx B; 11 Q-R4ch etc.

10 Q-KB3	P-KR3
11 Kt-B3	P-KKt4

12 P-QR4

In order to fortify the position of the KB; also with a view to fixing the Q side Ps later on with P-R5.

12	B-K3
13 Q-K2	Kt-Q2
14 R-Q	

Intending perhaps to double Rs should Black fianchetto his KB. Bird therefore protects the weak square Q3.

14	Q-B3
15 B-K3	B-QKt5

After an unorthodox start, Black has obtained a fair game which promises interesting possibilities. But the text is aimless, and . . . B-K2 at once would have saved time.

16 Kt-R2!	B-K2
17 P-QKt4	Kt-Kt3
18 B-Kt3	

Better than 18 BxB, QxB and Black threatens . . . Kt-B5.

18	O-O
19 P-R5	Kt-B
20 QR-Kt	Kt-Q3
21 Kt-B3	P-R3

Creating a weakness on the black squares which allows his opponent to gain further terrain; but if he wishes to dispute the Q file, he cannot leave the QRP unprotected.

22 B-Kt6!	Kt-K
23 Kt-R4	Kt-Kt2
24 P-QB3	BxB
25 RxB	Kt-K3
26 P-Kt3	B-Q
27 R-Kt2	Q-Kt3
28 R(Kt2)-Q2	P-R4

This belated counter-action offers Black little hope, as the liquidation which now follows is much in Lasker's favor.

29 BxB!	QRxB

After 29 . . . KtxB; 30 R-Q7 followed by Kt-B5 would paralyze Black's game.

30 RxR	RxR
31 RxRch	KtxR
32 Kt-B5!	

The key to the ending! "So many masters of the modern school would have proposed and accepted a draw at this point," runs a contemporary comment, from which we see that "modernism" is not a matter of absolute time, but of relativity.

32	P-Kt5
33 Q-Q3	Kt-K3

. . . Q-B3 would not help because of Q-Q7!

34 KtxKt

Very cautious play; at any rate more artistic than the simple and obvious 34 KtxKtP, Kt-Kt4; 35 Kt-B5 etc.

34	QxKt
35 Q-Q8ch	K-R2
36 Q-Kt5	P-B3

Black cannot save the P.

37 QxPch	K-Kt2
38 K-Kt2	Q-Q2

The ending is most instructive; despite its apparent simplicity, it demands the most sustained concentration (Mason).

39 P-R3	PxPch
40 QxP	Q-Q6
41 Q-Kt4ch	K-B2
42 Q-B3	Q-B5
43 Q-K3	K-K3
44 P-B3	K-Q3
45 K-B2	Q-R7ch
46 Q-K2	Q-K3
47 Q-Q2ch	K-B2

48 P-Kt4!

Lasker intends to break up the hostile Ps by P-KKt5 followed by the march of his K to KB6.

48	Q-B5
49 Q-K3	Q-R7ch
50 K-Kt3	Q-R8

Position after Black's 50th move

51 P-Kt5!	PxP
52 K-Kt4	Q-Kt7
53 KxP	K-Q2

. . . Q-Kt7ch would be useless in view of 54 K-B5 and if 54 . . . Q-Kt6; 55 K-K6! followed by Q-Q3 etc.

54 K-Kt4

K-B6 would have been quicker.

54	Q-KR7
55 K-B5	Q-Kt6
56 K-B6!	

Bringing about a Zugzwang position: if 56 . . . K-B2; 57 K-K6! followed by Q-Q3, or if 56 . . . Q-R7; 57 Q-Kt5 or Q-Q3ch wins easily.

56	P-B4
57 Q-Kt5!	Q-R7

Or 57 . . . QxPch; 58 Q-B5ch,

QxQch; 59 KxQ, K-Q3; 60 K-B6
and wins.

58 Q-B5ch	K-B3
59 Q-B8ch	K-Kt4
60 QxBPch	K-R5
61 QxP	Resigns

GAME No. 10

Match 1892
From Gambit

| White | Black |
| **H. E. Bird** | **Dr. E. Lasker** |

1 P-KB4	P-K4
2 PxP	P-Q3
3 PxP	BxP
4 Kt-KB3	P-KKt4

This move (introduced by Lasker) is now considered Black's strongest continuation.

5 P-Q4

Better is 5 P-KKt3, P-Kt5; 6 Kt-R4, B-K2; 7 Kt-Kt2, P-KR4; 8 P-Q4, P-R5; 9 B-B4 etc.

5	P-Kt5
6 Kt-K5	BxKt
7 PxB	QxQch
8 KxQ	

White has retained his extra P, but it is weak and cannot be held permanently.

| 8 . . . . | Kt-QB3 |
| 9 B-B4 | |

A good line of play at this point is 9 B-Kt5! KtxP; 10 Kt-B3, B-K3; 11 P-K3, P-KB3; 12 B-R4! K-B2; 13 B-Q3, KtxB; 14 PxKt, Kt-K2; 15 Kt-K4 (Brinckmann-Tartakower, Kecskemet 1927). Or 12 . . . O-O-O ch; 13 K-K, R-B (not 13 . . . Kt-B5; 14 BxKt, Bx

B; 15 P-QKt3, B-K3; 16 R-KB ±); 14 P-QKt3, Kt-K2; 15 Kt-K4 etc.

| 9 . . . . | B-K3 |
| 10 P-K3 | |

The advance of the P two squares would weaken Q4 and deprive the Kt of a valuable post at K4.

10 . . . .   KKt-K2

Castling immediately would be somewhat more precise, as White could not then play his K to K2.

| 11 B-QKt5 | O-O-O ch |
| 12 K-B | |

Needlessly banishing the QR from the scene of operations. K-K2 was simpler and better.

12	B-Q4
13 R-Kt	P-QR3
14 B-K2	B-K3
15 Kt-B3	

Missing an excellent continuation in B-KKt5!—which Lasker promptly prevents.

15	P-R3
16 B-Q3	Kt-Kt3!
17 BxKt	PxB
18 R-Q	QR-K!

Avoiding the simplifying exchange which would allow White to bring his K and QR into play.

19 P-K4

This move is open to the objections set forth in the note to White's 10th move.

| 19 . . . . | P-KKt4 |
| 20 B-Kt3 | KR-B |

In order to obtain control of the KB file before capturing the KP.

21 P-Kt3

Too soon; Kt-Q5 first was correct.

21	P-KR4
22 R-Q2	P-R5
23 B-B2	KtxP
24 B-K3	

Overlooking the splendid plan which Lasker has in mind. He should have played K-Kt2.

Position after White's 24th move

24	P-R6!

Initiating a beautiful combina tion which is fully 13 moves deep.

25 BxP

If 25 PxP, PxP; 26 BxP? Kt-B6; but 25 P-Kt3 was relatively better.

25	P-Kt6!!
26 PxKtP	

Again PxRP would be refuted by Kt-B6.

26	R-B8ch!

In order to remove White's K from the passed P as far as possible.

27 K-Kt2

Forced, for if 27 Kt-Q, P-R7 or if 27 R-Q, PxP; 28 B-K3, B-Kt5.

27	RxR
28 KxR	P-R7
29 R-Q	Kt-Kt5
30 R-R	

Else . . . Kt-B7 wins outright.

30	B-B2

Now we see why Lasker drove the K away: the KP cannot be defended.

31 K-Kt2	P-B3!!

The finest move in the game.

32 K-B	B-Kt3
33 K-Q2	RxP!

The first point of the whole winning combination; Black is bound to regain the exchange with interest.

34 Kt-Q	R-Q5ch
35 K-K2	RxKt!

The second point: if 36 KxR, Kt-B7ch wins.

36 RxR

Here is revealed the object of Lasker's fine 31st move; had he not played . . . P-B3, mate would now be threatened, which would give White enough time to defend himself.

36	B-K5
37 R-Q8ch	K-B2
38 R-Q	BxKtP
39 B-Q8ch	K-B
40 B-Kt6	B-Q4
41 P-B4	P-R8=Q
42 RxQ	BxR

and White resigned on the 63rd move.

GAME No. 11

Match 1893

Sicilian Defense

White	Black
Dr. E. Lasker	**C. Golmayo**
1 P-K4	P-QB4
2 Kt-KB3	P-KKt3
3 P-Q4	PxP
4 KtxP	B-Kt2

The order of Black's opening moves is incorrect; this could have been exploited by 5 P-QB4!—leading into the Dragon Variation, which however was as yet unknown.

5 Kt-QB3	Kt-QB3
6 B-K3	Kt-B3
7 B-K2	O-O
8 P-B4	P-Q3
9 O-O	Kt-KKt5?

Black could have continued with . . . B-Q2. The simplifying text-move looks so plausible that it is instructive to see how conclusively Lasker demolishes it.

10 BxKt	BxKt

Forced; if 10 . . . BxB? 11 Kt xKt wins a piece.

11 QBxB	BxB
12 Q-Q2!	

The refutation: White threatens to cut off the B with P-B5. But once the B retreats, White has R-B3-R3 and Q-R6 at his disposal—and in addition!—Kt-Q5 and P-B6.

12	B-K3

13 P-B5	B-B5

. . . B-Q2 was better.

14 R-B3	KtxB
15 QxKt	B-R3

He could have at least postponed the evil hour with 15 . . . Q-Kt3; 16 QxQ, PxQ; 17 P-QKt3, B-R3; 18 Kt-Q5.

16 Kt-Q5

Strengthening the attack decisively and also preventing . . . Q-Kt3.

16	R-B?

Position after Black's 16th move

17 P-B6!	R-B5

Or 17 . . . P-K3; 18 Kt-K7ch, K-R; 19 Q-K3, R-KKt; 20 R-R3, Q-B; 21 KtxQR and if 21 . . . QxKt; 22 RxPch, KxR; 23 Q-R3 mate.

18 Q-Q2	PxP
19 Q-R6	P-B4
20 R-KR3	Resigns

A game of theoretical value.

GAME No. 12

Match 1893

Queen's Pawn Opening

White	Black
Dr. E. Lasker	**J. W. Showalter**

1 P-Q4	P-Q4
2 Kt-KB3	Kt-KB3
3 P-K3	P-K3
4 B-Q3	P-QKt3
5 QKt-Q2	B-Kt2
6 Kt-K5	B-Q3
7 P-KB4	O-O

It is well known that Black will be subjected to a violent attack in this variation unless he is able to play . . .Kt-K5. The text is at any rate premature, as it supplies White with an immediate and tangible objective.

8 Q-B3!	P-B4
9 P-B3	

The one flaw in White's game is that the Pawn configuration allows no scope for his QB.

9	Q-B2
10 P-KKt4	Kt-K
11 Q-R3	P-Kt3
12 P-Kt5	BxKt

Black wants to play . . . Kt-Kt2, which if played at once would allow Kt-Kt4-B6ch. The text creates a weakness on the black squares which is relatively bearable because of the limited scope of the QB.

13 BPxB	Kt-Kt2
14 KR-Kt	Kt-Q2

Intending to move the KR and play . . . Kt-B if R-Kt4-R4.

15 Kt-B3	KR-B
16 B-Q2	P-QR3

Losing a tempo for the Q side counter advance. He could have played . . . P-B5 followed by . . . P-Kt4 and . . . P-QR4.

17 Q-B	P-Kt4
18 P-KR4	P-B5
19 B-B2	R-B
20 Q-R3!	

If 20 Kt-R2, P-B4; 21 KtPxP e.p., KtxBP!

20	P-QR4
21 Kt-R2!	

Lasker is beginning to operate on the black squares: the Kt is headed for B6.

21	P-Kt5
22 Kt-Kt4	

If 22 PxP, P-B6!

22	P-Kt6
23 B-Q!	

Better than 23 PxP, PxP; 24 BxQKtP, Q-Kt3; 25 R-R3, P-R5!

23	Kt-KB4
24 P-R5	K-Kt2
25 Kt-B6	R-R
26 B-Kt4	

Position after White's 26th move

26	Kt-K2?

A deplorable error. Black should have played . . . QKtPxP, making it rather difficult for White to carry out his plan of getting the QR into play. 26 . . . P-R5 was also a possibility, although in that case White could block the Q side with 27 P-R3. After 26 . . . P-R5; 27 QRPxP Black would have to reply 27 . . . BPxP but not 27 . . . RPxP? 28 RxR, BxR; 29 Px P, BPxP (29 . . . RPxP; 30 QxR ch! KxR; 31 R-Rch, K-Kt2; 32 R-R7ch, K-B; 33 R-R8ch and mate next move); 30 BxKt, KPxB (30 . . . KtPxB; 31 Q-R6ch, K-B2; 32 P-Kt6ch); 31 Q-R6ch, K-B2; 32 P-K6ch! KxP; 33 Q-Kt7, R-Q, 34 KtxKt and the Kt cannot be recaptured.

27 BxP!

Fairly obvious, but it leads to some pretty play.

27	KtxP

Not 27 . . . PxB; 28 QxP, Kt-Kt3; 29 Kt-K8ch!! and wins; for after 29 . . . RxKt; 30 P-R6ch forces mate.

28 PxKt	PxB

But not 28 . . . QxP; 29 P-R6 ch, K-B; 30 Kt-Q7ch.

29 QxP	R-R3

On 29 . . . B-B? 30 Kt-K8ch! still wins; while if 29 . . . KR-KB? 30 KRPxP, RPxP; 31 R-R, R-R; 32 Kt-K8ch! etc.

30 P-R6ch!	K-B
31 Q-Q7!	

Forcing the exchange, for if 31 . . . Q-Kt; 32 KR-B, Kt-B4; 33 RxKt, PxR; 34 Q-Kt7 mate.

31	QxQ
32 KtxQch	K-K
33 Kt-B5	R-R2

On 33 . . . R-Kt3, White has 34 PxP, PxP; 35 RxP if nothing better is available.

34 PxP	PxP
35 KR-B	B-B3

. . . Kt-B4 would enable a longer resistance.

36 KtxP	P-R5
37 Kt-Q4	R-B
38 R-B6	B-Q2
39 P-K6	B-B?

39 . . . B-B3 was better, although 40 P-B4! PxP; 41 B-Kt4, B-R; 42 K-Q2 followed by QR-KB would win easily.

40 Kt-Kt5!	Resigns

The R is lost! If 40 . . . R-R4; 41 P-B4.

The best part of this game is in the variations which did not occur.

GAME No. 13

New York 1893
Albin Counter Gambit

White	Black
Dr. E. Lasker	**A. Albin**
1 P-Q4	P-Q4
2 P-QB4	P-K4

The present game seems to have been the earliest occasion on which this opening appeared in master play.

3 QPxP	P-Q5
4 Kt-KB3	Kt-QB3
5 P-QR3	

Not bad, but White could play QKt-Q2 at once, followed by the fianchetto of the KB with a definitely superior game.

5	B-Kt5
6 P-R3	BxKt
7 KtPxB!	KtxP
8 P-B4	Kt-QB3

Of course not 8 . . . KtxP? 9 Q-R4ch. But 8 . . . Kt-Kt3 was preferable.

9 B-Kt2	Q-Q2
10 P-QKt4	P-QR3

If at once . . . R-Q; 11 P-Kt5, Kt-R4; 12 Q-R4, P-QKt3; 13 B-Q2±.

11 B-Kt2	R-Q
12 Kt-Q2	KKt-K2
13 Kt-Kt3	

Position after White's 13th move

13	Kt-B4

After 13 . . . Kt-Kt3; 14 P-Kt5 would be tempting, say 14 . . . PxP; 15 PxP, Kt-R2; 16 Qx P! QxKtP; 17 QxKt, QxKt; 18 QxP, QxQ; 19 BxQ, KtxP; 20 B-B6ch, K-K2; 21 B-K5, Kt-K3; 22 P-K3 and White should win. But Black answers 14 P-Kt5 with 14 . . . KtxP!, for example 15 PxKt, KtxBch; 16 K-B, QxBP; 17 KtxP? Kt-K6ch and wins; or 14 . . . Px

P; 15 PxP, KtxP; 16 B-KB3, Kt-K4! 17 KtxP, KtxBch; 18 PxKt, B-B4∓.

However, after 13 . . . Kt-Kt3, White plays 14 Q-Q2, B-Q3 (or 14 . . . Q-B4; 15 BxKtch, PxB; 16 KtxP±); 15 KtxP, BxBP; 16 P-K3±.

14 Q-Q3

Safe and sound. 14 P-Kt5, Px P, 15 PxP, Kt-R2; 16 KBxP, Kt xP would have led to nothing definite.

14	B-K2
15 B-K4!	Kt-Q3

The weakness of Black's QP has prevented him from obtaining a natural development. The result is that his position is already lost. If he tries 15 . . . P-KKt3 at this point, then 16 BxKt(B5), PxB; 17 P-Kt5, PxP; 18 PxP, Kt-R2; 19 QxQP, QxQ; 20 BxQ and wins.

16 Kt-B5	Q-B
17 B-KB3!	

Lasker is in no hurry. 17 Ktx RP would have won a P, but after 17 . . . KtxB; 18 QxKt, O-O; 19 P-Kt5, KR-K! Black's splendid development would be adequate compensation.

17	O-O
18 R-KKt	

Again KtxRP would not have been wholly convincing, for Black could reply 18 . . . Kt-K; 19 P-Kt5, B-Q3 with counter-chances.

18	Kt-K
19 Kt-Kt3	Q-Q2

Not 19 . . . QxP?? 20 R-R.

20 O-O-O	Q-Q3
21 K-Kt!	QxBP

22 R-Kt4	Q-R3
23 BxKt	PxB

23 . . . QxB; 24 KtxP would
be no better.

24 RxQP	R-Q3
25 P-B5	R-K3
26 QxP	QxP
27 R(Q4)-Q3	Q-Kt7
28 Kt-Q4	R-B3

A blunder which loses quickly;
but even after 28 . . . R-Kt3; 29
R-KB3! Black's position would
have been hopeless.

29 R-K3	B-Q
30 Kt-B2	RxP
31 RxB	Resigns

An unorthodox conclusion to an
unorthodox game.

GAME No. 14

Match 1894
Ruy Lopez

White	Black
Dr. E. Lasker	**W. Steinitz**
1 P-K4	P-K4
2 Kt-KB3	Kt-QB3
3 B-Kt5	P-Q3
4 Kt-B3	

Not quite so good as 4 P-Q4,
B-Q2; 5 Kt-B3, which Lasker had
played previously in this match.
While 4 P-Q4 threatens to win a
P, the text is relatively innocuous,
so that Black can equalize quickly.

4	P-QR3
5 B-B4	

Or 5 B-R4, B-Q2=.

5	B-K3
6 BxB	PxB
7 P-Q4	PxP

8 KtxP	KtxKt
9 QxKt	Kt-K2
10 B-Kt5	Kt-B3!
11 BxQ	

After 11 Q-K3, B-K2 Black
has nothing to fear.

11	KtxQ
12 O-O-O	Kt-Kt4?

Here Steinitz shows poor judgment, since he will be left with a
doubled, isolated QKtP and a weak
QP. 12 . . . P-QB4; 13 B-Kt5
would also be unfavorable for
Black, but he could simply have
played 12 . . . RxB; 13 RxKt, B-
K2 with an even game.

13 KtxKt	PxKt
14 BxP	RxP

Black could have won the KP
by 14 . . . R-R3, forcing 15 P-
K5 (else . . . K-Q2), P-Q4; 16
P-QR3, K-Q2 although even then
White would still have the better
game. Now Black threatens to
come out a P ahead by . . . R-R3.

15 B-Kt6	B-K2
16 P-QB3	K-B2
17 K-B2	KR-R
18 K-Kt3	R(R7)-R5
19 P-B3	R(R)-R3
20 B-Q4	P-KKt3
21 R-Q3	K-K
22 KR-Q	

(See diagram on next page)

22	P-K4

Obviously a very bad move, but
a difficult one to avoid in view of
Black's P position. There were two
plausible alternatives at his disposal:

I 22 . . . K-Q2; 23 B-B5, R-
B3; 24 BxP, RxB; 25 RxRch, Bx
R; 26 P-K5, R-R3; 27 P-KB4, K-

Position after White's 22nd move

B2; 28 PxBch, RxP; 29 R-Q4! with the better end-game. If Black exchanges Rs he is lost: 29 . . . Rx R; 30 PxR, K-B3; 31 K-Kt4, K-Kt3; 32 P-KKt3, P-R3; 33 P-R3, P-R4; 34 P-R4, K-B3 (or 34 . . . K-R3; 35 K-B5, K-R4; 36 K-Q6, and wins); 35 K-R5, K-Q4; 36 KxP, KxP; 37 K-Kt6, K-B5; 38 KxP, K-Kt6; 39 K-B6 and wins. In the R and P ending resulting from 29 . . . R-R3, on the other hand, White has a considerable advantage: 29 . . . R-R3; 30 R-K4, K-Q2; 31 R-K5, R-R4 (or 31 . . . R-Kt3; 32 K-Kt4); 32 P-Kt3 winning a P.

II 22 . . . R-B3; 23 B-B2, K-Q2 (23 . . . R(R5)-R3? 24 K-Kt4!); 24 B-Kt3, K-B2; 25 R-Q4, RxR; 26 RxR, R-B4; 27 K-Kt4±.

The text not only permanently weakens the QP, but allows White to attack the QKtP as well.

23 B-K3   K-Q2

Enables White to post his B on the diagonal QR3-KB8. But Black must protect the KtP, for White already threatens R-Q5.

24 B-B5!   R-R8

25 R(Q)-Q2	K-K3
26 B-R3	P-Kt4
27 R-Q5	R-Kt3
28 K-Kt4	P-Kt5

In contrast to his weak and colorless play in the early part of the game, Steinitz plays now with great energy. Lasker's play however is also on a high level.

The object of the text is of course to weaken White's K side Ps.

29 K-R5

Lasker suggests the following variation as superior to the text: 29 PxP, R-K8; 30 K-R5, B-Q; 31 RxP, R-R3 dbl ch; 32 K-Kt4, Rx Pch; 33 K-Kt3. The move actually played has the merit of simplicity.

| 29 . . . . | R-R3ch |

Or 29 . . . B-Q; 30 RxP!

30 KxP	P-R4
31 R-Q	RxR
32 RxR	PxP
33 PxP	R-R

After 33 . . . K-B3 Black would be condemned to passive play.

34 K-Kt6	R-KKt
35 KxP	R-Kt7
36 P-R4	R-R7
37 K-B6	BxP
38 RxPch	K-B2
39 K-Q5	B-B3

If 39 . . . R-Q7ch; 40 KxP, B-Kt6ch; 41 P-B4, RxR; 42 BxR, P-R5; 43 B-B5, P-R6; 44 B-Kt and White wins easily with his four passed Ps (Lasker).

40 R-Q7ch	K-Kt3
41 K-K6	P-R5
42 R-Q	P-R6
43 R-Ktch	R-Kt7

Or 43 . . . B-Kt4; 44 B-K7, R-Kt7; 45 RxR, PxR; 46 B-B5 and wins.

44 RxRch	PxR
45 B-B5	B-Q
46 P-Kt4	K-Kt4
47 K-Q7	B-B3
48 P-Kt5	K-B5
49 P-Kt6	Resigns

Lasker's best game in this match.

GAME No. 15

Match 1894
Queen's Gambit Declined

White	Black
W. Steinitz	**Dr. E. Lasker**
1 P-Q4	P-Q4
2 P-QB4	P-K3
3 Kt-QB3	Kt-KB3
4 P-B3	

A premature attempt to create a strong P center which only serves to weaken the position of White's K.

| 4 . . . . | P-B4 |
| 5 PxBP | |

White already has the inferior game. If 5 PxQP, KtxP; 6 Ktx Kt (or 6 P-K4, KtxKt; 7 PxKt, PxP; 8 QxP, Kt-B3∓. Here 8 PxP is not possible because of 8 . . . B-Kt5ch; 9 K-B2, B-B6 winning a P), QxKt; 7 PxP, QxQBP ∓.

5	BxP
6 PxP	KtxP
7 P-K4	

7 KtxKt, PxKt; 8 P-K3, O-O; 9 B-Q3, Q-K2! (incidentally preventing BxPch followed by Q-B2 ch); 10 K-B2, R-K would leave

Black with a strong attacking game.

7	KtxKt
8 QxQch	KxQ
9 PxKt	

The result of White's faulty opening strategy is that he is left with an isolated P on an open file.

| 9 . . . . | Kt-B3 |
| 10 Kt-R3 | |

Developing the Kt this way is preferable to the routine B-Q3 followed by Kt-K2, for now White will be able to bring his Kt to Q3; whereas in the alternative variation, . . . Kt-K4 is apt to prove embarrassing.

10	K-B2
11 Kt-B4	R-Q
12 Kt-Q3	B-Q3
13 P-KB4	

Probably fearing . . . Kt-K4; but the text weakens his K side Ps. A better continuation is 13 B-Q2,Kt-K4; 14 KtxKt, BxKt; 15 O-O-O.

13	P-QKt3
14 Kt-B2	B-B4
15 B-K2	B-Kt2
16 Kt-Q3	

Now White realizes that his 14th move prevented the development of the QB. Steinitz's play in this game is rather poor.

| 16 . . . . | B-KB |
| 17 P-B5 | |

Another weakening of his P position! 17 B-K3 was quite playable.

| 17 . . . . | P-K4 |
| 18 B-Kt5 | |

Presenting Black with another tempo. Again B-K3 was better.

| 18 . . . . | P-B3 |
| 19 B-K3 | QR-B |

Lasker's logical and well-considered development of his pieces is in marked contrast to Steinitz's planless movements.

| 20 O-O-O | K-Kt |

Position after Black's 20th move

21 Kt-B2?

How many mistakes it sometimes requires to lose a game! The text costs a P, whereas after 21 K-Kt2, Black could not play . . . Kt-R4; 22 Kt-B2, RxR; 23 RxR, B-R6ch; 24 KxB (not 24 K-B2, B-Kt5; 25 B-Q2, B-B4), RxPch; 25 K-Kt2, RxB because of 26 B-Q3 winning the exchange.

21	Kt-Q5!
22 BxKt	PxB
23 B-Q3	

Or 23 P-B4, B-R3.

23	PxP
24 P-KKt4	B-R6ch
25 K-B2	

If 25 K-Kt, RxB! followed by . . . P-B7ch.

| 25 . . . . | B-B3 |
| 26 K-Kt3 | B-B4 |

27 Kt-R3

27 KR-B would cost White another P after 27 . . . BxKt; 28 RxB, BxP.

27	B-K6
28 B-B2	B-Q7
29 Kt-B2	R-Q5

Lasker finishes neatly. He now threatens . . . B-R5ch.

30 K-R3	B-K
31 Kt-Q3	RxP
32 Kt-Kt4	R-Q5
33 B-Kt3	P-QR4
34 Kt-B2	P-QKt4!
Resigns	

A well-played game by Lasker, unfortunately marred by Steinitz's feeble defense.

GAME No. 16
Match 1894

Queen's Gambit Declined

White	Black
Dr. E. Lasker	**W. Steinitz**
1 P-Q4	P-Q4
2 P-QB4	P-K3
3 Kt-QB3	Kt-KB3
4 Kt-B3	B-K2
5 P-K3	O-O
6 B-Q3	P-B4
7 PxBP	PxP

The exchange of Qs is bad because of the distance of the Black K from the center.

| 8 BxP | QxQch |

8 . . . BxP would at least save a tempo.

9 KxQ	Kt-B3
10 P-QR3	BxP
11 P-QKt4	B-Kt3

Black does not develop his pieces

harmoniously. The QB should be posted at Kt2, where it is placed much more effectively than at Q2. Lasker's exploitation of his slight— to many players non-existent!— advantage is little short of miraculous.

12 K-K2	B-Q2
13 B-Kt3	QR-B
14 B-Kt2	P-QR4

Obtaining QB4 for his pieces, but it turns out to be of no value. Worse yet, the move weakens the Q side Ps. 14 . . . KR-Q followed by . . . K-B-K2 was unquestionably a better course.

15 P-Kt5	Kt-K2
16 Kt-K5	B-K
17 P-QR4	B-B2

Black's game is badly developed and consequently he cannot formulate a logical plan.

| 18 Kt-B4 | B-Q2 |

At first sight it seems that White can now gain a P by 19 P-Kt6, B-Q; 20 KtxP, KBxP; 21 KtxP. Black, however, can regain the P with a superior position by playing 22 . . . R-Kt; 23 Kt-Q6, BxKP! 24 Kt(Q6)-Kt5 (or 24 PxB, RxB; 25 KR-QKt, Kt(K2)-Q4; 26 Ktx Kt, KtxKt; 27 B-Q4, RxR; 28 R xR, BxP∓), B-B4 followed by . . . B-B3 and . . . Kt-Q4 with a good game. Lasker evidently believes that the position is not yet ripe for forceful measures and therefore plays

19 QR-QB!

(See diagram next column)

Now White threatens 20 B-R3, for if 20 . . . KR-K; 21 P-Kt6,

Position after White's 19th move

B-Q; 22 Kt-Q6 while if 20 . . . B-Q; 21 KR-Q (21BxKt, BxB; 22 KtxP, RxKt! 23 RxR, B-Kt5; 24 R-B7, BxKt; 25 RxP is somewhat risky) with a decidedly superior position.

19 . . . . Kt(K2)-Q4?

Allowing Lasker to obtain a decisive end-game advantage. But Black had a difficult position in any event:

I 19 . . . R-K; 20 P-Kt6, B-Q? 21 Kt-Q6 winning the exchange.

II 19 . . . P-QKt3; 20 KR-Q, KR-Q; 21 Kt-Q6, R-Kt; 22 P-K4, B-K; 23 P-K5, Kt-Kt5; 24 Kt (B3)-K4, BxKt; 25 PxB, Kt-Kt3; 26 P-R3, Kt(Kt5)-K4; 27 P-Kt3 with a winning game.

Relatively best seems . . . R-R, although Black's game would be badly cramped.

| 20 KtxKt | KtxKt |
| 21 Kt-K5! | |

To this move Black has no adequate reply:

I 21 . . . KR-Q; 22 KtxB, Rx Kt; 23 BxKt, RxB; 24 P-Kt6 winning.

II 21 . . . B-K; 22 BxKt, PxB; 23 Kt-Q3! P-B4 (23 . . . B-Q2; 24 Kt-B5 winning a P); 24 B-R3, R-B3 (24 . . . B-R4ch; 25 P-Kt 4! BxPch; 26 P-B3); 25 R-B2 and Black has no defense against KR-QB.

III 21 . . . Kt-B3; 22 KR-Q, BxKt (or 22 . . . KR-Q; 23 Ktx B, KtxKt; 24 RxKt, RxR; 25 P-Kt6, QR-Q; 26 PxB, R-Q7ch; 27 K-K and wins); 23 BxB±.

| 21 . . . . | BxKt |
| 22 BxB | P-B3 |

White threatened 22 P-K4, Kt-B3; 23 P-B3 followed by B-B7.

23 P-K4!   PxB

Forced for if 23 . . . Kt-Kt3; 24 B-B7 winning a P and if 23 . . . Kt-K2; 24 B-Q6, KR-K; 25 BxKt, RxB; 26 RxRch, BxR; 27 R-QB, B-Q2 (27 . . . R-K? 28 RxB! RxR; 29 BxPch); 28 K-K3 with a won ending.

24 PxKt	K-B2
25 KR-Q	K-K2
26 P-Q6ch	K-B3

Black's P position is now very weak.

27 K-K3

Stronger than 27 R-B7, RxR; 28 PxR, B-B; 29 R-Q8, K-K2.

| 27 . . . . | RxR |
| 28 RxR | R-B |

To prevent R-B7.

| 29 RxR | BxR |
| 30 B-B2 | |

Now we see how accurately Lasker has judged the end-game. Black is lost, for if he now plays

30 . . . P-KR3 or 30 . . . P-KKt 3 White wins by posting his B at K4 and bringing the K to the Q side, thus: 30 . . . P-KKt3; 31 B-K4, K-B2; 32 K-Q3, K-K; 33 K-B4, K-Q2 (or 33 . . . P-Kt3; 34 B-B6ch followed by K-Q3-K4 winning the KP); 34 K-B5, P-Kt3ch; 35 KxP, KxP; 36 KxP, K-B4; 37 P-Kt6 winning easily.

| 30 . . . . | K-B2 |
| 31 ˙BxP! | P-QKt3 |

If Black plays to win the B, White's K has time to make a decisive inroad on the Q side: 31 . . . P-KKt3; 32 K-K4, K-Kt2 (32 . . . K-B3; 33 P-KKt4, P-Kt 3; 34 P-Kt5ch, KxP; 35 KxP); 33 KxP, KxB; 34 K-B6, K-Kt; 35 K-K7, K-Kt2; 36 K-Q8! etc.

32 K-K4

B-K4 would also win quickly.

| 32 . . . . | K-B3 |
| 33 P-Kt4 | P-Kt4 |

33 . . . B-Kt2ch would prolong the game a bit.

34 K-B3	K-B2
35 B-K4	K-K
36 P-R4	

In order to obtain a passed P on the K side. 36 . . . PxP; 37 P-Kt5, K-B2; 38 P-Kt6ch, K-Kt2; 39 K-Kt4 would be quite hopeless for Black.

36	K-Q2
37 P-R5	K-K
38 K-K3	Resigns

One of Lasker's best games in the first match.

GAME No. 17

Hastings 1895
Ruy Lopez

White	Black
Dr. E. Lasker	**W. Steinitz**

1 P-K4	P-K4
2 Kt-KB3	Kt-QB3
3 B-Kt5	P-QR3
4 B-R4	P-Q3
5 O-O	Kt-K2

One of the many defenses which Steinitz invented, but which have not found favor with other masters. Nowadays the usual reply is 5 . . . B-Q2; 6 P-B3, P-KKt3 or 5 . . . P-B4.

6 P-B3	B-Q2
7 P-Q4	Kt-Kt3

Black gets an easier game with . . . P-KKt3.

8 R-K	B-K2
9 QKt-Q2	O-O
10 Kt-B	

The maneuver with the QKt was invented by Steinitz himself!

10 . . . .   Q-K

The critics are unanimous in applying to this move such epithets as "bizarre", "typically Steinitzian", "peculiar", and the like. In reality the text begins a profound maneuver. Black wishes to force his opponent to play P-Q5. Once the center is stabilized by this advance, Black can undertake a promising attack on the Q side. Unfortunately, Black's KKt is not very well placed for the execution of this plan. That Steinitz hardly deserved all the criticism heaped on him because of the present encounter,

may be seen from the following game played in the return match (White: *Lasker;* Black: *Steinitz*): 1 P-K4, P-K4; 2 Kt-KB3, Kt-QB 3; 3 B-Kt5, P-Q3; 4 P-Q4, B-Q2; 5 Kt-B3, KKt-K2; 6 B-Kt5, P-B3; 7 B-K3, Kt-B; 8 Kt-K2, B-K2; 9 P-B3, O-O; 10 B-Q3, Kt-Kt3; 11 Kt-Kt3, K-R; 12 O-O, Q-K; 13 R-QB, Kt-Q; 14 R-K, P-QB4; 15 Kt-R4, Kt-R5; 16 R-B2, P-QKt4; 17 P-KB4, Kt-K3; 18 P-B5, Kt-Q; 19 P-Q5 (finally!), Kt-Kt2; 20 Kt-B3, P-B5; 21 B-K2, B-Q; 22 Kt-R4, P-Kt3; 23 B-Kt4, P-Kt4; 24 Kt-B3, Kt(Kt2)-B4; 25 P-R4, PxP; 26 KtxRP, Kt-Q6; 27 R-KB, Kt(R5)xKtP. Black has won a P and should win the game; Lasker escaped with a draw subsequently only because of a tactical oversight on his opponent's part later on.

As we shall see later on, it is not because of his "bizarre" moves that Steinitz loses this game.

11 B-B2

Black threatened . . . KtxP, hoping in this way to provoke P-Q5.

11 . . . .   K-R

Black plays inconsistently. The text is intended to prepare for . . . P-B4, which at present would lose a P, thus: 11 . . . P-B4; 12 PxB P, BxP; 13 BxB, RxB; 14 PxP followed by 15 Q-Kt3ch and 16 QxP. But 11 . . . B-Kt5 was the logical continuation of Black's plan.

12 Kt-Kt3	B-Kt5
13 P-Q5	

Black has finally forced the advance of the QP and should now continue . . . Kt-Q, as in the game previously quoted.

13 . . . . Kt-Kt

Whereas this move is really pointless, as will soon appear.

14 P-KR3 B-B
15 Kt-B5

To prevent . . . P-QB3.

15 . . . . B-Q
16 P-KKt4 Kt-K2
17 Kt-Kt3 Kt-Kt

Position after Black's 17th move

The *Deutsche Schachzeitung* inclines to the opinion that Steinitz allowed his sense of humor to get the better of him in bringing about the present position. This imputation of humorous intent is however merely a sign of the annotator's laziness. It is clear that after . . . P-KKt3, . . . B-B3-Kt2, . . . Kt-K2 and . . . P-KB4, Black will have a promising game.

18 K-Kt2 Kt-Q2

Again Steinitz changes his plan.

19 B-K3 Kt-Kt3

The Kt is of course quite ineffective on this square, but it is to be brought to K2.

20 P-Kt3 B-Q2
21 P-B4

Now White has the initiative on both wings.

21 . . . . Kt-B
22 Q-Q2 Kt(B)-K2
23 P-B5 P-KKt3
24 Q-B3

Threatening the sacrifice at K5, in case Black plays . . . P-B4.

24 . . . . P-B4?

Overlooking the threat. . . . P-B3 followed by . . . Q-B2-Kt2 was indicated.

25 KtxKP! PxKt
26 QxPch Kt-B3
27 B-Q4!

Not 27 P-Kt5, KtxQP!

27 . . . . PxKtP
28 PxP BxP

Or 28 . . . KtxQP; 29 QxQ, RxQ; 30 PxKt, RxR; 31 RxR, K-Kt (31 . . . BxP; 32 R-K8ch, K-Kt2; 33 Kt-K4); 32 BxKt, BxB; 33 Kt-K4 etc.

29 Q-Kt5 Q-Q2
30 BxKtch K-Kt
31 B-Q B-R6ch
32 K-Kt KtxP

This sacrifice of a piece loses quickly. The only way of putting up any fight at all consisted in 32 . . . RxB; 33 QxR, KtxP.

33 BxB Kt-B5
34 B-B6 Q-Q7
35 R-K2!

The simplest method of putting an end to Black's demonstration.

35 . . . . KtxRch
36 BxKt Q-Q2

37 R-Q	Q-B2
38 B-B4	B-K3
39 P-K5	BxB
40 Kt-B5	Resigns

A vigorous conclusion to a well-played game by Lasker. Unfortunately his great opponent did not do himself justice.

GAME No. 18

St. Petersburg 1895-6
Ruy Lopez

White	Black
Dr. E. Lasker	**W. Steinitz**
1 P-K4	P-K4
2 Kt-KB3	Kt-QB3
3 B-Kt5	P-QR3
4 B-R4	P-Q3
5 P-Q4	B-Q2

At present the reply . . . P-QKt4 has a considerable vogue.

6 P-B3	Kt-B3
7 QKt-Q2	B-K2
8 O-O	O-O
9 R-K	R-K
10 Kt-B	B-KB

The contemporary critics, who almost invariably "annotated by result," seize the opportunity at this point of expressing their amazement at Steinitz's stubborn adoption of this defense. Had he not already lost several games with it in the championship match?!

11 Kt-Kt3	P-KKt3
12 P-KR3	B-Kt2
13 B-B2	

This move will be necessary sooner or later if White wishes to continue with B-K3 and Q-Q2.

| 13 . . . . | B-QB |

Steinitz's moves were often criticized unjustly, but this last move is really obscure.

14 P-Q5

Leading to a position of a frequently recurring type: White endeavors to break through on the Queen's wing by attacking Black's Pawn ‑ formation (P ‑ QB4 ‑ B5), while Black counters with an attack on the other flank against his opponent's Pawn-formation (. . . P-KB4 or . . . P-QB3).

| 14 . . . . | Kt-K2 |
| 15 B-K3 | R-B |

It cannot be said that Steinitz carries out the attack in the most economical manner. Here he should have played 15 . . . K-R; 16 Q-Q2, Kt(B3)‑Kt, to be followed by . . . P-KB4.

| 16 Q-Q2 | Kt-K |
| 17 B-R6! | |

The removal of Black's important B turns out to be very useful later on.

17	K-R
18 QR-Q	Kt-Kt
19 BxBch	KtxB
20 P-B4	P-KB4
21 Q-B3	PxP?

One rarely finds a positional blunder of this magnitude on the part of a player like Steinitz.

The right move was 21 . . .P-B5; 22 Kt-B, P-KKt4; 23 Kt(B3)-R2, P-KR4; 24 P-B3, Kt-R3 with a most difficult and complex struggle in prospect. The text gives Black the open KB file, but this is altogether outweighed by White's command of K4.

22 BxP	Kt-B3
23 Q-K3	KtxB
24 KtxKt	

Subsequently Lasker utilizes the beautiful position of this Kt in masterly style.

24	R-B5

The R is not well-posted here; 24 . . . B-B4 would have been somewhat better.

25 P-B5	**B-B4?**

Expecting perhaps 26 Kt(B3)-Q2, BxKt; 27 KtxB, Kt-B4; 28 Q-QB3, Kt-Q5; 29 R-Q2, but even then White's game is superior.

26 Kt(B3)-Kt5!	

Strangely enough this move forces the win of the exchange no matter how Black replies — the chief threats being QxR! or P-KKt 3, depending on how Black replies.

Position after White's 26th move

26	Q-Q2
27 QxR!	

This elegant continuation is more conclusive than 27 P-KKt3, RxKt; 28 KtxR, BxP etc.

27	PxQ
28 Kt-B6!	

The point! White must regain the Q with the exchange to the good and in command of the seventh rank, for if now 28 . . . R-Q; 29 KtxQ, RxKt; 30 P-B6 and Black can go home.

28	Kt-K3
29 KtxQ	KtxKt
30 R-K7	K-Kt
31 Kt-B6ch	K-B
32 RxBP	Resigns

GAME No. 19

St. Petersburg 1895-6
Evans Gambit

White	Black
M. Tchigorin	**Dr. E. Lasker**
1 P-K4	P-K4
2 Kt-KB3	Kt-QB3
3 B-B4	B-B4
4 P-QKt4	BxP
5 P-B3	B-B4
6 O-O	P-Q3
7 P-Q4	B-Kt3!

Laskers' defense, which gives Black a solid center, secures him from attack and at the same time guarantees him a normal develop-ment.

8 P-QR4

White, to be sure, could regain his P by 8 PxP, PxP; 9 QxQch, KtxQ; 10 KtxP, B-K3; but his Q side Ps would be weak and his game undeveloped. Here we see the main strength of Lasker's Defense: when White adopts the Evans Gambit he wants to play an "immortal" game; instead he is confronted with the unpleasant alternative of (1) turning into a dry ending in which he has to

work hard to stave off defeat, or
(2) giving up the P for a slight
semblance of an attack that can
be parried with ease.

    8 . . . .   Kt-B3

A simple move, but a very effective one.

    9 B-QKt5

Preventing Black from castling
because of 10 BxKt, PxB; 11 P-R5.

9	P-QR3
10 BxKtch	PxB
11 P-R5	B-R2
12 PxP	KtxP
13 Q-K2	

Here he might at any rate have
recovered his P with Q-R4; but he
feels that he must attack; hence
he plays the objectively weaker
move.

13	P-Q4
14 Kt-Q4	

This move looks like an oversight, but it is probably a last desperate attempt to save the game:
evidently he does not foresee
Lasker's 17th move.

14	KtxQBP!
15 KtxKt	BxKt
16 Q-Q3	P-QB4!

It is very questionable whether
Black could win after 16 . . .Bx
Kt in view of his weak Q side Ps
and the Bs of opposite color. But
it is significant to note that White
is already reduced to temporary
expedients and petty threats.

    17 Q-Kt3

Now Black cannot castle, because of 18 B-R6, BxP; 19 QxB,
PxB; 20 KtxP etc., while 17 . . .

P-Kt3, would be bad because of
B-Kt5-B6.

17	B-K3!
18 B-Kt5	

After 18 QxP Black would
obtain a crushing attack on the
KKt file by 18 . . . K-Q2 followed
by . . .KR-Kt etc.

18	Q-Q2
19 QR-B	P-KB3!
20 PxP	PxP
21 B-B4	KR-Kt
22 Q-B3	O-O-O
23 KR-K	P-B5!

White threatened Q-K2.

24 Q-K2	B-KB4
25 Q-R2?	

White is too intent on his attacking plans.

Position after White's 25th move

25	RxPch!

The *reductio ad absurdum* of
White's whole plan of the game.

    26 K-R

Or 26 KxR, B-R6ch; 27 K-R,
Q-Kt5 etc.

26	RxP

White resigns, for if 27 Kt-K2,
B-K5ch, or if 27 B-Q2, Q-Q3 etc.

GAME No. 20

St. Petersburg 1895-6
Queen's Gambit Declined

White	Black
W. Steinitz	**Dr. E. Lasker**
1 P-Q4	P-Q4
2 P-QB4	P-K3
3 Kt-QB3	Kt-KB3
4 B-B4	B-K2
5 P-K3	O-O
6 R-B	P-B4
7 PxBP	BxP
8 PxP	PxP

But not 8 . . . KtxP? 9 KtxKt etc.

9 Kt-B3
9 KtxP would lead to no advantage for White: 9 KtxP, Ktx Kt; 10 RxB, B-K3! (not 10 . . . KtxB; 11 QxQ, KtxPch; 12 BxKt, RxQ; 13 RxB! RxR; 14 BxP±); 11 B-B4, KtxB; 12 QxQ (12 Px Kt, Kt-Q2), KtxPch; 13 K-B, Ktx Pch∓; or 11 BxKt, RxB; 12 B-B4, Q-K2; 13 RxKt, Q-Kt5ch; 14 Q-Q2, QxB∓.

9 . . . .   Kt-B3
10 B-Q3
If 10 KtxP, KtxKt; 11 RxB, Kt xB; 12 QxQ (if 12 PxKt, Q-K2 ch), KtxPch; 13 BxKt, RxQ=.

10 . . . .   P-Q5
11 PxP   KtxP
On 11 . . . R-Kch; 12 Kt-K2! Black must not play 12 . . . Bx P? 13 RxKt! PxR; 14 KtxB, Qx Kt; 15 BxPch.

12 O-O
Safer is 12 KtxKt, BxKt; 13 O-O.

12 . . . .   B-KKt5

13 Kt-QKt5?
There is no reason for this "attacking" move: 13 B-K2 leaves White with a playable game, thus: 13 B-K2, KtxBch; 14 QxKt, R-K; 15 Q-Kt5! Q-Kt3 (or 15 . . . BxKt; 16 QxB=); 16 Kt-K5 and Black's advantage is certainly very slight.

13	BxKt
14 PxB	Kt-K3!
15 B-K5	Kt-R4
16 K-R	Q-Kt4
17 B-Kt3	QR-Q!

As so often happens in Lasker's games, he carries out a positional maneuver by a tactical threat.

18 Q-B2   Q-R3

Position after Black's 18th move

The point of Lasker's trap is that the natural move 19 KR-Q is now impossible, as is shown by the subjoined analysis, which it is hoped will not terrify or bore the reader by its great length, since it contains variations of absorbing interest and great beauty. After 19 KR-Q Black would play 19 . . . R-B! to which there are fourteen plausible replies:

I 20 Q-R4 (or Q-Kt3), BxP!

21 RxR, KtxBch; 22 K-Kt2, RxR winning.

II 20 Q-Kt, P-R3; 21 Kt-B3 (if 21 Kt-R3, Kt-Q5; 22 B-K4, Kt-K7), KtxBch; 22 PxKt, B-K6; 23 R-B2, Kt-Q5; 24 R-Kt2, Ktx P; 25 B-K4, Kt-Q7; 26 Q-Q3, KtxB and wins.

III 20 Q-Q2, KtxBch; 21 PxKt, B-K6 and wins.

IV. 20 Q-K2, BxP! 21 QxB, R xR and wins.

V 20 Kt-B3, Kt-Q5 etc.

VI 20 B-K4, BxP!! 21 QxR, BxB.

(a) 22 PxB, KtxPch; 23 K-Kt 2, Q-R5; 24 Q-B2, Kt-B5ch; 25 K-Kt, Kt(Kt6)-K7ch; 26 K-B, Q-R7; 27 K-K, Q-Kt8ch; 28 K-Q2, R-Qch; 29 B-Q3 (or 29 Q-Q3, KtxQ; 30 RxQ, Kt(Q6)xR dis ch followed by . . . KtxR), Q-B7; 30 R-B, Q-Kt7; 31 K-K3, Kt-Q4 ch; 32 K-K4, Q-Kt3ch and mate next move.

(b) 22 Q-B4, B-Kt; 23 R-B2, (if 23 Kt-Q6, Q-B5), P-R3; 24 Kt-B3, Kt-Kt6ch; 25 K-Kt2 (or 25 K-Kt? B-R2ch; 26 K-Kt2, Kt-B5ch; 27 KxKt, Q-Kt4 mate), P-QKt4; 26 Q-Kt3 (if 26 Q-B6, Kt-B5ch; 27 KxKt, Kt-Q4 dis ch; or 27 K-B2, QxPch; 28 K-K, Kt-Kt7ch), KtxB; 27 KtxKt (if 27 PxKt; QxPch; 28 K-B, Q-R8ch; 29 K-K2, Q-Kt7ch; 30 K-Q3, Q-B6ch); QxPch; 28 K-B, Q-R8ch; 29 K-K2, Kt-B5ch; 30 K-Q2, R-Qch winning.

(c) 22 QxP, BxP; 23 KxB, Kt-B5 dis ch; 24 K-Kt3, Q-Kt4 ch; 25 K-B2, Q-Kt7ch and mate next move.

(d) 22 Q-B2, B-B5; 23 QR-Kt, Kt-Kt6ch; 24 K-Kt2, KtxB; 25 Q xKt, QxPch; 26 K-B, Kt-Kt4 with a winning attack.

VII 20 B-K2, KtxBch; 21 Px Kt, B-Kt8! and wins.

VIII 20 B-B, BxP; 21 QxR, KtxBch; 22 K-Kt2, KtxB; 23 Rx Kt (if 23 KxB, Q-K6ch; 24 KxKt, QxPch; 25 K-K, Kt-B5; 26 R-Q2, Q-K6ch; 27 K-Q, Q-Kt8ch and wins; if in this 25 K-Kt, Qx Rch etc.), B-K6; 24 R-QB2, Q-Kt4ch; 25 K-R, QxKt∓.

IX 20 QR-Kt (or R-R), P-R3; 21 Kt-B3, Kt-Q5 and should win.

X 20 R-K, BxP! 21 QxR, Ktx Bch; 22 K-Kt2, BxR; 23 Q-B2, Kt-B5ch winning.

XI 20 R-B, BxP! 21 QxR, Ktx Bch; 22 K-Kt2, KtxR; 23 KxB, RxQ; 24 RxRch, Kt-B; 25 BxKt, P-KKt3 and White has no compen-sation for his material disadvantage.

XII 20 KR-Kt, KtxBch; 21 Rx Kt, BxP; 22 QxR, BxR; 23 Q-B2, BxP and White must resign.

XIII 20 K-Kt, BxPch! 21 Q xB, RxR and wins.

XIV 20 K-Kt2, Kt(R4)-B5ch; 21 K-R (if 21 K-Kt, BxPch; 22 Q xB, Kt-R6ch; or 21 K-B, Q-R6ch; 22 K-K, BxPch! 23 QxB, RxR; 24 RxR, KtxBch etc.), BxP; 22 Q xR, BxB; 23 Q-B2 (forced), Ktx B; 24 RxKt, BxP; 25 R(B)-Q, B -B5 dis ch; 26 K-Kt, Q-Kt4ch; 27 Q-Kt2, QxKt with a decisive material advantage.

19 QR-Q   R-B!

Now that Lasker has prevented Steinitz from achieving a harmoni-ous development, he regroups his own pieces. The same maneuver also appears in his game with Janowski at St. Petersburg 1914 (Game No. 70) as well as in his encounter with Rubinstein at Moscow 1925.

| 20 Q-Kt3 | P-R3 |
| 21 Kt-B3 | Kt-Q5! |

Sacrificing a P to initiate an attack which should at least draw.

22 QxP   KtxBch

In order to be able to attack the Q, and also to clear the seventh rank.

23 PxKt	R-Kt
24 QxP	R-Kt3
25 Q-B4	RxP
26 P-KR4?	

Probably fearing the pin after 26 Kt-K2, which would however have drawn:

I 26 . . . KtxKt; 27 BxKt, B-Q3 (or 27 . . . Q-K6; 28 B-Q3, R-K; 29 B-K4); 28 P-B4, R-K; 29 R-B2 followed by R-Kt2 and B-B3.

II 26 . . . B-Kt3; 27 Q-B! drawing easily.

III 26 . . . Q-R4; 27 P-Kt4, Q-R5? 28 QxB, KtxKt; 29 Q-KB2±.

After the text White seems to have a safe position, and it is by no means easy to see that Black's attack will prove decisive. Perhaps Steinitz was playing to win, and rejected 26 Kt-K2 on the ground that it would only suffice to draw.

26 . . . .   B-R2
27 B-K4

Kt-K2 could still be played.

27 . . . .   Q-Q3

But now 28 Kt-K2 would be answered by 28 . . . R-Q and White is lost, for if 29 Kt-B4, Kt-B4!! threatening . . . KtxP mate as well as . . . QxR; a beautiful conception.

28 P-B4

The text is forced, for if 28 KR-Kt, Q-Q2; 29 P-Kt4, R-B; 30 Q-Q5, Q-K2 winning a piece.

28 . . . .   Q-Q2
29 B-Kt2

If 29 P-B5, R-B; 30 Q-Q5, Q-B2; 31 Kt-R4, QxP; 32 KtxR, Q-R6ch; 33 K-Kt, Kt-K7 mate.

29 . . .   Q-Kt5!

Very pretty! If now 30 RxKt, QxKtP; 31 Kt-K2, QxPch; 32 K-Kt, RxKt; 33 QxR, BxRch winning the exchange.

30 Q-Q3

Better than 30 R-Q3, Kt-B4; 31 Kt-K4, KtxP.

30 . . . .   Kt-B4
31 Kt-K4

Steinitz is playing the best defense available, but against Lasker's forceful and elegant attack there are no longer any adequate replies.

31 . . . .   B-K6

This accurately calculated move quickly forces the win. 31 . . . KtxP; 32 R-Q2, KtxB; 33 KxKt wins a P but leaves White with a tenable game; while 31 . . . Kt-K6 wins the exchange, but leaves Black with a difficult game to win.

32 R-B3

If 32 QR-K, KtxPch; 33 KtxKt, QxPch.

32 . . . .   RxB!

33 KxR	KtxPch
34 K-R2	KtxRch
35 K-Kt2	Kt-R5ch
36 K-R2	Kt-B4
37 R-QKt	P-R4
38 R-Kt5	R-R
39 P-R3	RxP!

White resigns, for if 40 QxR, Black mates in four moves; while after 40 Q-Q8ch, K-R2; 41 Kt-Kt5ch, K-Kt3; 42 R-Kt6ch, BxR; 43 QxBch, P-B3.

Rarely does one game contain so many combinations!

GAME No. 21

St. Petersburg 1895-6

Queen's Gambit Declined

White	Black
H. N. Pillsbury	**Dr. E. Lasker**
1 P-Q4	P-Q4
2 P-QB4	P-K3
3 Kt-QB3	Kt-KB3
4 Kt-B3	

Pillsbury usually played B-Kt5 at this point.

4	P-B4
5 B-Kt5	

The most aggressive continuation. If 5 BPxP, KtxP with approximate equality.

5	BPxP
6 QxP	

An alternative line is 6 KKtxP, P-K4; 7 KKt-Kt5, P-Q5; 8 BxKt, PxB; 9 Kt-Q5, Kt-R3; 10 Q-R4 ±.

6	Kt-B3

Much safer is 6 . . . B-K2.

7 Q-R4

Here, however, White misses the best line. Pillsbury subsequently subjected the variation to rigorous analysis for many years and found that 7 BxKt gives White the better game. This he demonstrated conclusively in his Cambridge Springs encounter with Lasker.

7	B-K2
8 O-O-O	

A risky move which is difficult to avoid, for if 8 P-K3, Q-Kt3; 9 QR-Kt (or now O-O-O), P-KR 3; 10 B-Q3, PxP; 11 BxBP, O-O ∓ (12 BxRP, PxB; 13 QxP, Q-B4!).

8	Q-R4
9 P-K3	

The alternative is 9 PxP, Ktx P; 10 KtxKt, PxKt; 11 BxB, Ktx B; 12 K-Kt, B-B4ch; 13 K-R, Kt-B3∓.

9	B-Q2
10 K-Kt	P-KR3!

An excellent move; the Q must now remain at KR4 until the B is exchanged.

11 PxP	PxP
12 Kt-Q4	

If 12 B-Q3, O-O-O would win at least a P and expose White's K to attack.

12	O-O
13 BxKt	

If 13 BxP, PxB; 14 QxP, Kt-K4; 15 B-K2, KR-B and Black, with an extra piece, should have no difficulties.

13	BxB
14 Q-R5	

White is pursuing a will o' the wisp (K side attack!). The sequel clearly reveals the inadequacy of this plan. Either 14 Q-B4 or Q-Kt 3 would therefore be better.

14	KtxKt
15 PxKt	B-K3
16 P-B4	

Intending P-B5, P-KKt4, P-KR 4, followed by B-R3 and P-Kt5.

| 16 . . . . | QR-B |
| 17 P-B5 | |

He can hardly be blamed for overlooking Lasker's magnificent combination, but here 17 Q-B3 was in order.

| 17 . . . . | RxKt! |
| 18 PxB | |

Best: if 18 PxR, QxP;

I 19 PxB, Q-Kt5ch; 20 K-B2 (or 20 K-R, R-B; 21 Q-Kt4, R-B7 etc.), R-Bch; 21 K-Q3, QxPch; 22 K-K2, R-B7ch; 23 K-B3, R-B7 ch; 24 K-Kt3, Q-K6ch; 25 Q-B3, B-K4ch; 26 K-Kt4, P-R4ch win-ning.

II 19 Q-B3, Q-Kt5ch; 20 Q-Kt 3, BxPch; 21 B-Q3, QxQch; 22 P xQ, B-Kt5; 23 R-Q2, BxP; 24 B-B2, B-B3; 25 RxP, B-K3. Black has two Ps for the exchange, White's QKtP is weak and his K exposed; so that White can only hope for a draw at best.

Position after White's 18th move

18 . . . .   R-QR6!!
19 PxPch

Alternatives are:

I 19 PxR, Q-Kt3ch; 20 K-R, BxPch; 21 RxB, QxRch; 22 K-Kt, PxP; 23 B-K2, Q-K5ch; 24 K any, R-B7 and Black should win.

II 19 P-K7, R-K; 20 PxR, Q-Kt3ch; 21 K-B2, R-Bch; 22 K-Q2, BxP; 23 P-K8=Qch, RxQ; 24 B -Q3, Q-R4ch; 25 K-B, R-Bch; 26 B-B2, RxBch and wins. This vari-ation was given by the players in post-mortem analysis.

19	RxP
20 PxR	Q-Kt3ch
21 B-Kt5	

Forced:

I 21 K-R, BxPch; 22 RxB, Qx Rch; 23 K-Kt, Q-K5ch; 24 K-B, R-B7 and wins.

II 21 K-B2, R-B2ch; 22 K-Q2, QxPch; 23 K-K, Q-B6ch; 24 R-Q2 (if 24 K-K2, R-K2ch, while if 24 K-B2, B-Q5ch; 25 RxB, QxR ch; 26 K-K, Q-K6ch and mate next move), R-K2ch; 25 B-K2, B-Kt4 and wins. Note that if 23 B-Q3, Q-B7ch! wins.

| 21 . . . . | QxBch |
| 22 K-R | R-B2 |

. . . Q-B5 would have regained the exchange, for if 23 Q-Kt4, R -K2; 24 KR-K? BxPch. But there is no hurry: Black maintains his grip on the position.

23 R-Q2

Black was threatening mate in three beginning with . . . R-B8 ch!

| 23 . . . . | R-B5 |
| 24 KR-Q | R-B6 |

The concluding moves were played under fearful time-pressure.

25 Q-B5

The alternative 25 Q-K2 would be refuted by 25 . . . R--B8ch! (but not 25 . . . BxP? 26 Q-K6 ch!) ; 26 RxR, BxPch; 27 RxB, Q xQ; 28 R-KKt, Q-KB7! 29 R (Q4)-Q, P-Q5 and Black has good winning chances. In any case it is not easy to see that after the text White must lose.

25 . . . .   Q-B5

If 25 . . . RxP; 26 Q-B8ch, K -B2; 27 R-Kt2 etc.

26 K-Kt2

Losing quickly, but there was no longer any adequate defense:

I 26 K-Kt, RxP; 27 Q-B2, R-B6; 28 Q-Kt2, P-QKt4.

II 26 Q-Kt, RxP; 27 Q-Kt2, R-B6; 28 K-Kt, P-QKt4.

In both cases Black has only one P for the exchange, but he should win because of his opponent's cramped position.

26 . . . .   RxP!
27 Q-K6ch   K-R2
28 KxR

Allows a forced mate, but if 28 K-Kt, BxP! 29 Q-B5ch, P-Kt3; 30 Q-B7ch, B-Kt2; 31 QxKtP, R-R5, and Black wins easily.

28 . . . .   Q-B6ch

and Black mates in four (29 K-R4, P-Kt4ch; 30 KxP, Q-B5ch; 31 K-R5, B-Qch; 32 Q-Kt6, PxQ mate).

Lasker's outstanding combinative game. So competent a judge as Amos Burn says of the combination begun on the 17th move: "One of the finest ever made."

GAME No. 22

St. Petersburg 1895-6

Ruy Lopez

White	Black
Dr. E. Lasker	**W. Steinitz**
1 P-K4	P-K4
2 Kt-KB3	Kt-QB3
3 B-Kt5	P-Q3
4 P-Q4	B-Q2
5 Kt-B3	KKt-K2
6 PxP	

Better than 6 B-QB4 as played by Lasker in the first match with Steinitz.

6 . . . .   PxP

6 . . . KtxP gives Black a freer game.

7 B-Kt5!

An excellent move which completely refutes Black's opening strategy; either he remains with a weak, doubled and isolated QBP or else he must weaken his K side with . . . P-B3.

7 . . . .   P-KR3
8 KBxKt   KtPxB

Else the KP falls.

9 B-K3

The attack on Black's weak QB4 will serve as the motif of the ensuing play.

9 . . . .   Kt-Kt3
10 Q-Q3   B-Q3
11 Kt-Q2   Kt-K2

Black has a bad game but this move makes it even worse; he should have played 11 . . . Kt-B5.

12 Kt-B4   Kt-B
13 O-O-O   Q-K2

Not 13 . . . O-O; 14 KtxP!

14 P-B4!

Opening the KB file as a basis for future operations.

14 . . . .   P-B3

If 14 . . . PxP; 15 KtxBch, Kt xKt (15 . . . PxKt; 16 BxBP and the QP is lost, or 15 . . . QxKt; 16 Q-R6, Q-Kt5; 17 P-QR3, Q-Kt; 18 BxBP±); 16 BxBP winning a P.

Position after Black's 14th move

15 PxP   PxP

The alternative . . . BxP would lose very quickly: 16 KtxB, PxKt; 17 B-B5! Q-K3; 18 Q-Kt3, R-KKt; 19 KR-B (threatening R-B5 or Qx KtP), Kt-K2 (or 19 . . . P-Kt3; 20 Q-R4, P-Kt4; 21 Q-R5ch, K-Q; 22 Q-B7 and wins); 20 BxKt, Qx B (if 20 . . . KxB; 21 R-B5); 21 Q-Kt6ch, K-Q; 22 R-B7 etc.

16 KR-B

By means of the foregoing ex-change, Lasker has not only opened another file for his pieces, but has induced a new weakness in Black's Pawn position.

16 . . . .   Q-K3
17 Kt-R4   Q-K2

Black is lost: he has no adequate defense to B-B5. If for example 17 . . . R-B; 18 Kt-B5, BxKt (or

18 . . . Q-K2; 19 RxRch, KxR; 20 KtxBch, QxKt; 21 KtxP); 19 BxB, RxR; 20 RxR, Kt-K2; 21 Q-QB3, Kt-Kt3? 22 KtxP!

Steinitz had, to be sure, the in-ferior game after the opening; but that his position should be def-initely lost on the 17th move is quite a tribute to Lasker's energetic play.

18 B-B5   BxB
19 KtxB   B-Kt5
20 R-Q2   Kt-Kt3

Threatening to capture White's Kt at B5.

21 Kt-R6   R-KB

Or 21 . . . R-Q; 22 QxRch, QxQ; 23 RxQch, KxR; 24 Ktx KP.

22 Kt-R5

The play with the Kts is very pretty.

22 . . . .   RxRch
23 QxR

And now Black must lose at least a P.

23 . . . .   R-Q

If 23 . . . P-B4; 24 Kt-B6 (Q -Kt5ch is also good), Q-B2; 25 QxQch, KxQ; 26 KtxPch winning.

There followed: 24 KtxP, Rx R; 25 KtxQ, R-Q8ch; 26 QxR, BxQ; 27 Kt-B6, B-K7; 28 Kt-B5, B-B8; 29 P-KKt3, Kt-B5; 30 Ktx RP, B-Kt7; 31 Kt-B6, Kt-Q3; 32 KtxP, KtxP; 33 KtxKt, BxKt; 34 Kt-Q3, K-Q2; 35 K-Q2, K-Q3; 36 K-K3, B-Q4; 37 K-Q4, P-Kt4; 38 P-B4, B-Kt7; 39 P-QKt4, P-R4; 40 P-Kt5, P-R5, 41 PxP, Px P; 42 P-B5ch, K-Q2; 43 P-R4, K-B; 44 P-B6, K-Kt; 45 Kt-K5,

K-R2; 46 K-B5, B-R6; 47 Kt-Q7, resigns.

Lasker's exploitation of weak squares — a "hypermodern" strategem—is once more in evidence in this elegant game.

GAME No. 23

St. Petersburg 1895-6
Queen's Pawn Opening

White	Black
Dr. E. Lasker	**M. Tchigorin**

1 P-Q4	P-Q4
2 Kt-KB3	Kt-KB3

Tchigorin generally favored . . . B-Kt5 at this stage.

3 B-B4	QKt-Q2

Black should first develop his QB: 3 . . . B-B4 and if 4 P-B4, PxP! (better than 4 . . . P-K3; 5 Q-Kt3, Q-B; 6 Kt-B3, P-B3; 7 P-K3) =.

4 Kt-B3	P-B3

Both sides play inexactly. First White plays indifferently, and then Black creates a number of weaknesses for which he will suffer later on. Here the threat of Kt-QKt5 should have been parried with 4 . . . P-QR3 so as to permit . . . B-Q3 later, or a thrust at the center with . . . P-B4.

5 P-K3	P-K3
6 B-Q3	B-Kt5?

The disappearance of this B will leave the black squares in a woeful state. Better was 6 . . . B-K2 and if 7 O-O, O-O; 8 P-K4, PxP; 9 KtxP, KtxKt; 10 BxKt, Kt-B3; 11 B-Q3, P-QKt3 etc.

7 O-O	P-KR3

If 7 . . . BxKt; 8 PxB, Kt-K5; 9 BxKt, PxB; 10 Kt-Kt5, Kt-B3; 11 P-B3 would open the game to White's advantage.

8 Q-K2	O-O

Tchigorin relinquishes his plan; for if 8 . . . BxKt; 9 PxB, Kt-K5; 10 BxKt, PxB; 11 Kt-Q2, P-KB4 (or 11 . . . Kt-B3; 12 P-B3 ±); 12 B-Q6, and Black's game is already hopeless.

9 P-K4!	BxKt
10 PxB	PxP
11 BxKP	KtxB
12 QxKt	Kt-B3
13 Q-Q3	Kt-Q4?

Throughout the whole game Tchigorin makes no attempt to develop his QB. Here . . . P-QKt3 followed by . . . B-Kt2 and . . . P-B4 would still have left him with a playable game.

14 B-Q2	Kt-K2
15 KR-K	Kt-Kt3
16 Kt-K5!	KtxKt
17 RxKt	P-B3

Another weakness!

18 R-K3	P-KB4
19 R-Kt3	Q-R5

White threatened BxP. If (instead of the text) 19 . . . Q-B3; 20 B-B4, R-B2; 21 B-K5, Q-K2; 22 R-Kt6, K-R2 (22 . . . B-Q2; 23 Q-R3, K-R2; 24 BxP! winning. If here 23 . . . K-B; 24 Q-Kt3 etc.); 23 Q-Kt3, B-Q2; 24 P-KR4 with an overwhelming position.

20 R-R3	Q-K2

not 20 . . . Q-Kt5? 21 BxP!

21 R-K	R-B3
22 B-B4	B-Q2

23 R-Kt3

Threatening B-K5, R-Kt6, Q-Kt3, P-KR4 etc. as in the note to Black's 19th move.

| 23 . . . . | B-K |
| 24 P-B4 | Q-Q2 |

He cannot even play . . .R-Kt3 because of 25 QxP.

25 R(Kt3)-K3   P-QKt3

To prevent P-B5 and B-Q6.

26 B-K5   R-Kt3?

A strategical error in a difficult position. At Kt3 the R is useful for defensive purposes only, where- as at B2 it would have been just as valuable for defensive purposes, and in addition would have guard- ed the Q side.

| 27 P-KB3 | B-B2 |
| 28 Q-R3 | |

Threatening 29 R-Kt, R-K; 30 Q-R6 with P-QR4-5 to follow.

28	P-Kt4
29 PxP	PxP
30 R-B3!	R-QB
31 R(K)-K3	

Of course not 31 RxRch, QxR; 32 QxP? QxP.

31 . . . .   R-B5

Losing a P; but there was al- ready no defense.

32 RxR	PxR
33 Q-Kt4!	Q-Q
34 QxP	Q-R4
35 R-B3	K-R2
36 P-KR3	B-K
37 P-R3	B-Kt4
38 Q-Kt4	Q-R3

Threatening 30 . . . RxPch! 40 KxR, B-B8ch; 41 K-Kt3 (not 41 K-Kt, Q-K7 and mate follows), Q-K7 with an attack which will at least draw.

Position after Black's 38th move

39 R-B7!   B-B3!

39 . . . B-B8 would have led to a brilliant pyrotechnical display resulting, however, in White's favor: 40 Q-B8! RxPch; 41 K-R, R-R7ch!? 42 BxR (but not 42 KxR? Q-K7ch; 43 K-Kt3, Q-Kt7 ch; 44 K-B4, Q-Kt4 mate), B-Kt7 ch!? 43 KxB, Q-K7ch; 44 K-Kt3, Q-K8ch (44 . . . P-B5ch; 45 Qx P); 45 K-B4, Q-Q7ch; 46 K-K5, QxBch; 47 P-B4 and wins.

40 P-QB4

40 Q-B8 would be a gross blunder: 40 . . . RxPch! 41 Kx R, Q-K7ch; 42 K-Kt3? QxPch and mate in three, or 42 K-Kt, Q-K8 ch with perpetual check.

40 . . . .   BxP

41 P-Kt3!

Lasker does not fall into the trap (41 Q-B8? RxPch; 42 K-B, K-Kt3! 43 RxPch, K-R4; 44 Rx R, QxPch; 45 K-Kt, BxR and Black may draw. But now Q-B8 is finally threatened.

41	Q-Kt3
42 K-B2	B-K5
43 QxQ	PxQ
44 P-QR4	P-R4
45 P-R4!	

To prevent . . . P-R5, whereby Black would get his R in play again, say 45 P-B5, PxP; 46 PxP, P-R5; 47 P-B6, PxPch; 48 BxP, P-K4!

| 45 . . . . | R-Kt5 |
| 46 K-K3 | B-Kt7 |

Not 46 . . . B-B7; 47 R-B6.

| 47 K-Q3 | K-Kt |
| 48 K-B3 | K-B |

Now Black threatens to play . . . P-KKt4.

| 49 B-B4 | K-K |

On 49 . . . P-KKt4; 50 PxP, P-R5; 51 B-Q6ch, K-K; 52 PxP etc.

50 R-R7!	P-KKt4
51 BxP	RxPch
52 K-Kt4	RxB

A desperate move; but he is helpless against the advance of the Q side Ps.

53 PxR	P-R5
54 R-R7	P-R6
55 P-Kt6	Resigns

For if 55 . . . K-B; 56 K-Kt5, P-B5; 57 P-B5, PxP; 58 PxP, P-B6; 59 P-B6, P-B7; 60 R-B7ch, K-Kt; 61 P-B7, B-Kt2; 62 RxP winning.

GAME No. 24

Nuremberg 1896

Ruy Lopez

| White | Black |
| **M. Porges** | **Dr. E. Lasker** |

1 P-K4	P-K4
2 Kt-KB3	Kt-QB3
3 B-Kt5	Kt-B3

Lasker's favorite defense, along with 3 . . . P-Q3.

4 O-O	KtxP
5 P-Q4	B-K2
6 Q-K2	Kt-Q3
7 BxKt	KtPxB
8 PxP	Kt-Kt2
9 P-QKt3?	

The fianchettoed B is not particularly well placed, as it exerts practically no pressure on Black's game. The strongest continuation is 9 Kt-B3, O-O; 10 Kt-Q4! B-B4; 11 R-Q, BxKt; 12 RxB, P-Q4; 13 Px P e.p. PxP; 14 P-QKt4! (Schlechter-Réti, Vienna 1914).

| 9 . . . . | O-O |
| 10 B-Kt2 | P-Q4 |

Enabling Black to equalize.

11 PxP e. p.

Or 11 QKt-Q2, Kt-B4; 12 Kt-Q4, B-R3; 13 P-QB4, Q-Q2 followed by . . . Kt-K3 with excellent prospects.

| 11 . . . . | PxP |
| 12 QKt-Q2 | R-K! |

Beginning White's punishment for his slipshod development. This move, which will soon threaten . . . B-QR6, is a very difficult one to meet adequately. If in reply 13 Q-Q3, . . . Kt-B4 drives the Q back to the K file.

| 13 KR-K | B-Q2 |

Protecting the R.

14 Kt-K4?

Relatively best was 14 Q-B, a sorry admission of White's helplessness. The text merely loses a tempo, thus helping Black in his plans.

| 14 . . . . | P-Q4 |
| 15 QKt-Q2 | |

15 Kt-Kt3, B-QKt5 would cost the exchange.

15	. . . .	B-QR6
16	B-K5	P-B3
17	Q-R6	PxB
18	QxB	

QxKt would be even worse, for after 18 . . . P-K5 he could not reply 19 Kt-Q4 because of . . . B-Kt7. White has maintained equality in material but at what a cost in position!

18	. . . .	P-K5
19	Kt-Q4	Q-B3!

Black has attained his objective. All his pieces are admirably placed for a K side attack, while White's pieces are disorganized and ineffective.

20	P-QB3	R-KB
21	P-B3	

Not 21 R-KB, Q-Kt4; 22 Q-B, B-R6.

21	. . . .	Q-Kt4!
22	Q-B	

The Kt cannot move because of 22 . . . P-B4 followed by 23 . . . PxP with a winning game; 22 QR-Q would likewise be answered by . . . P-B4.

22	. . . .	Kt-B4!

The Kt enters with powerful effect. 22 . . . P-B4 would not have been so good because of 23 Kt-B2, PxP; 24 KtxP.

23	Kt-B	Q-Kt3
24	R-K3	Kt-Q6
25	Q-Q	Kt-B5

(See diagram next column)

Threatening mate as well as . . . Kt-R6ch winning the Q.

Position after Black's 25th move

26	Kt-Kt3	P-KR4!
27	Kt(Q4)-K2	KtxP!
28	KxKt	PxPch
29	RxP	B-R6ch!
30	KxB	

Or 30 K-B2, B-Kt5; 31 RxR ch, RxRch; 32 K-K3 (32 K-Kt, P-R5; 33 Q-Q2, BxKt; 34 QxB, PxKt; 35 P-R3, R-B7), P-R5. 30 . . . P-R5 would also suffice to win after 30 K-B2.

30	. . . .	Q-Kt5ch
31	K-Kt2	QxRch
32	K-Kt	

If 32 K-R3, Q-Kt5ch; 33 K-Kt2, P-R5.

32	. . . .	P-R5
33	Kt-R	

If 33 Kt-B, P-R6..

33	. . . .	Q-K6ch

White resigns, for 34 K-Kt2 leads to a pretty mate by . . . P-R6.

GAME No. 25

Nuremberg 1896
French Defense

White | Black
W. Steinitz | **Dr. E. Lasker**

1 P-K4	P-K3
2 P-Q4	P-Q4
3 Kt-Q2	P-QB4

The simplest and best reply.

4 QPxP

In order to give Black an isolated QP, which will not trouble Black too much, however, as he obtains an excellent development.

4. . . .	BxP
5 Kt-Kt3	B-Kt3
6 PxP	Kt-KB3

6 . . . PxP is also good enough.

7 B-Kt5ch

Not 7 PxP? nor 7 B-Kt5? because of the reply . . . BxPch.

7. . . .	B-Q2
8 BxBch	QxB
9 P-QB4	

Loss of time; 9 Kt-B3 was in order.

9. . . .	PxP
10 P-B5	

Playing for the Q side majority, which does not turn out to be of any value; 10 PxP followed by Kt-K2 would have maintained equality.

10	B-B2
11 Kt-B3	Kt-B3
12 O-O	O-O
13 Kt(Kt3)-Q4	KtxKt
14 QxKt	

KtxKt was better; the text loses too much time.

14	KR-K
15 B-K3	R-K5
16 Q-Q3	QR-K
17 KR-Q	

If 17 B-Kt5, Kt-R4 followed by . . . P-KR3 saves the QP.

17 . . . . P-KR3

To prevent B-Kt5.

18 P-QR3

Better 18 B-Q4.

18	Q-Kt5
19 P-Kt4	P-KKt4!

Lasker's handling of the attack is energetic and well timed.

20 Q-B3

Useless; he might at least have continued the Q side advance.

20	Q-B4
21 Q-Q3	Q-Kt3
22 Q-Kt5	

Not 22 Kt-Q2? BxPch! etc.

22 . . . . Q-R4

Now if 23 P-R3, P-Kt5.

23 QxP

Position after White's 23rd move

23 . . . . BxPch!
24 KtxB

K-B was slightly better.

24 . . . . R-R5

The point: if now 25 Q-B7, Kt-Kt5!

| 25 P-B3 | RxKt |
| 26 Q-B7 | |

Costs a piece; but he could not meet the threat of . . . Q-R5.

26	R-R8ch
27 K-B2	Q-R5ch
28 Q-Kt3	

Or 28 K-K2, RxR; 29 RxR, P-Q5.

28	QxQch
29 KxQ	RxR
30 RxR	RxB

There followed: 31 R-QB, Kt-K; 32 P-R4, R-R6; 33 P-Kt5, Rx P; 34 R-QKt, R-QB5; 35 P-Kt6, PxP; 36 PxP, R-B; 37 K-Kt4, Kt-Q3; 38 K-R5, K-Kt2; 39 P-Kt7, R-QKt; 40 R-Kt6, Kt-B4; 41 P-B4, PxP; 42 K-Kt4, Kt-K6ch; 43 KxP, Kt-B5; 44 R-Kt4, K-B3; White resigns.

GAME No. 26

Nuremberg 1896
Ruy Lopez

White	Black
S. Winawer	**Dr. E. Lasker**
1 P-K4	P-K4
2 Kt-KB3	Kt-QB3
3 B-Kt5	Kt-B3
4 O-O	KtxP
5 P-Q4	B-K2
6 Q-K2	Kt-Q3
7 BxKt	KtPxB
8 PxP	Kt-Kt2
9 Kt-Q4	

In order to prevent . . . P-Q4.

| 9 . . . . | O-O |
| 10 Kt-QB3 | B-B4 |

11 Kt-B5

White plays inconsistently. His attempt to attack is premature and ill-judged, for after the text, . . . P-Q4 gains a tempo.

For the correct line of play, see Game No. 24.

11	P-Q4
12 Q-Kt4	BxKt
13 QxB	R-K
14 B-B4	B-Q5

Threatening to win a P by 15 . . . P-Kt3.

| 15 KR-K | Kt-B4 |

Black has already obtained a superior game. Should White try to avoid the doubling of his QBP by 16 Kt-Q, he would lose a P after 16 . . . Kt-K5; 17 P-B3, P-Kt3; 18 Q-Kt4, BxKP; 19 BxB, RxB; 20 P-B3, Kt-B3.

16 QR-Q?

Winawer stakes everything on his attack: again showing faulty judgment. 16 B-Q2 was relatively better.

16	BxKt
17 PxB	Q-B
18 Q-R5	

18 QxQ, RxQ; 19 R-Kt should have been played.

18	Q-R3
19 R-K3	QxP
20 R-QB	Q-B5

Lasker intends to defend himself by advancing his QRP: a *reductio ad absurdum* of White's attack.

21 R-B3

If 21 R-R3, then simply . . . QxB.

| 21 . . . . | Kt-K3 |

22 B-Q2   R-K2
23 R-R3   Q-K5

Position after Black's 23rd move

If now 24 P-KB4, Q-Kt3; 25 Q-R4, R-Q2; 26 P-Kt4, Q-K5; 27 P-B5, Kt-B; 28 R-K, QxQBP; 29 P-K6, PxP; 30 PxP, R-Q3; 31 P-K7, Kt-K3; 32 R(R3)-K3 (if 32 B-B4, KtxB; 33 P-K8=Qch, RxQ; 34 RxRch, K-B2; 35 Q-K7 ch, K-Kt3; 36 R-Kt3, P-Q5! and Black should win), Q-Kt3; 33 Q-R5, QxQ; 34 PxQ, K-B2; 35 R-B3ch, KxP; 36 B-B4, R-K; 37 B xRch, KxB with a winning ending: Black has three Ps for the ex-change, while in addition White's Ps are weak.

24 P-B3   Q-Kt3
25 Q-R4   R-Q2
26 P-KB4   Q-K5
27 P-Kt4   Kt-B

Temporarily preventing P-B5.

28 Q-B2   P-QR4
29 R-K3   Q-B5
30 P-B5   P-R5

30 . . . QxPch; 31 R-Kt3 would only strengthen White's attack (Tarrasch).

31 R-B

Or 31 P-K6, PxP; 32 PxP, Ktx P; 33 RxKt, QxPch etc.

31 . . . .   P-R6!

Lasker's cold-bloodedness is com-mendable.

32 R(K3)-K

32 P-R3 (intending P-K6) would be met by . . . P-R7.

32 . . . .   P-R7
33 P-R3   P-B4

White's Rs are now tied to the first rank by the passed P, and Lasker has things his own way.

34 K-R2

If 34 P-K6, PxP; 35 PxP, Ktx P; 36 RxKt, P-R8=Q.

34 . . . .   P-Q5
35 Q-B3   P-QB3!

In order to double the Rs on the R file. The P cannot be captured because of 36 . . . P-R8=Q; 37 RxQ, Q-K7ch etc.

36 P-K6   PxP
37 PxP   KtxP
38 QxP   R(Q2)-R2
39 R-QR   R-KB

Switching the attack to the other wing.

40 KR-K   Kt-Q
41 Q-Kt6   (R(R2)-KB2
42 B-Kt5   R-B7ch
43 K-Kt3

Not 43 K-Kt, Q-Q4 etc.

43 . . . .   QxPch

White resigns, for 44 K-R4 would lead to mate in three (44 . . . QxPch etc.). "A faultless game on Lasker's part." (Tarrasch)

GAME No. 27
Nuremberg 1896
Ruy Lopez

White   Black
Dr. E. Lasker   Dr. S. Tarrasch

1	P-K4	P-K4
2	Kt-KB3	Kt-QB3
3	B-Kt5	P-QR3
4	BxKt	QPxB
5	Kt-B3	

For once Lasker does not adopt his favorite exchange of Qs.

5 . . . .   B-QB4

5 . . . P-B3 is correct at this stage, the model continuation (from Black's point of view) being 6 P-Q3, B-Q3; 7 B-K3, Kt-K2; 8 Q-Q2, P-QB4; 9 Kt-K2, Kt-B3 (Colle-Dr. Alekhine, Scarborough 1926).

| 6 | P-Q3 | B-KKt5 |
| 7 | B-K3 | Q-Q3 |

This is about the best move at Black's disposal. 7 . . . BxB would open the KB file, thereby providing Black with a valuable basis for future operations.

8 BxB

Lasker's readiness to exchange is accounted for by the fact that this game was played in the next to last round, so that taking a risk of any sort was naturally out of the question.

| 8 | . . . . | QxB |
| 9 | Q-Q2 | BxKt |

After this Black's difficulties mount steadily. As Tarrasch points out, the threat of Q-Kt5 could very easily have been parried by 9 . . . P-B3.

10 PxB   Kt-K2

| 11 | O-O-O | Kt-Kt3 |
| 12 | Q-K3! | |

An excellent maneuver which brings out all the weak points of Black's ninth move.

12 . . . .   QxQch

"This is not good as it strengthens White's center. But after 12 . . . Q-K2 Black would be unable to play . . . O-O-O because of White's subsequent Q-R7. At the same time castling on the other wing would be dangerous in view of the open Kt file." (Tarrasch)

13 PxQ

The foregoing exchange has also enabled White to prevent the hostile Kt from occupying a beautiful square at KB5.

| 13 | . . . . | R-Q |
| 14 | Kt-K2 | |

The indicated strategy for White is to play P-KB4.

| 14 | . . . . | P-B3 |
| 15 | KR-Kt | K-B2 |

The K is too exposed here, in view of the prospective opening of the KB file. Hence castling would have been preferable.

16 QR-B   KR-K

Black takes steps to guard against the advance of White's center Ps after the eventual P-KB4.

17 Kt-Kt3!   Kt-B

Hoping to prevent White's Kt from assuming a dominating position, but this does not prove feasible.

18 P-KB4   P-QB4

See the note to Black's 16th move. Black fears 19 PxP, Rx

KP; 20 P-Q4, KR-K; 21 P-K5, for example 21 . . . P-QB4; 22 P-B3, PxP; 23 KPxP, P-QB4; 24 Kt-K4 winning; or 20 . . . R-K3; 21 P-K5 with the strong threat of Kt-K4.

19 Kt-R5

Lasker has played admirably from his 12th move on and now forces a decisive gain in material.

19 . . . .   P-KKt3

Black has nothing better, for if 19 . . . Kt-Kt3; 20 P-B5; or 19 . . . Kt-K3; 20 P-B5, Kt-Kt4; 21 P-KR4.

Position after Black's 19th move

20 PxP!   RxKP

Capturing the Kt would lead to mate in two.

21 KtxP   K-Kt2
22 R-B2   P-KR4

Threatening to cut off the Kt's retreat with . . . P-B3.

23 Kt-Q5   P-B3
24 Kt-B4   P-B5
25 R(B2)-Kt2   R-Q3

In addition to his material advantage White has a vastly superior position.

There followed: 26 P-KR4, Px

P; 27 PxP, K-B2; 28 R-Kt5! Rx R; 29 RxR, R-B3; 30 P-K5, R-B4; 31 RxR, PxR; 32 P-Q4, K-K2; 33 K-Q2, P-B4; 34 K-Q3, PxP; 35 PxP, K-Q; 36 P-Q5, K-Q2; 37 K-Q4, K-B2; 38 P-Kt4, K-Q2; 39 K-B5, K-B2; 40 P-Q6 ch, K-Q2; 41 K-Q5, resigns.

GAME No. 28

Match 1896-7

Ruy Lopez

White	Black
Dr. E. Lasker	**W. Steinitz**
1 P-K4	P-K4
2 Kt-KB3	Kt-QB3
3 B-Kt5	B-B4

A defense often played by Steinitz.

| 4 P-B3 | KKt-K2 |
| 5 O-O | |

Stronger is 5 KtxP, KtxKt; 6 P-Q4.

5 . . . .   Kt-Kt3

. . . B-Kt3 gives Black a good game, for if 6 P-Q4, PxP; 7 Px P, P-Q4; 8 PxP, KtxP; 9 R-Kch, B-K3; 10 Kt-K5, Q-Q3 (Chajes-Bogoljubow, Carlsbad 1923).

6 P-Q4	PxP
7 PxP	B-Kt3
8 Kt-B3	O-O
9 P-QR4	P-QR3
10 B-QB4	P-R3

Probably played to prevent Kt-KKt5, which is however not a threat at this point. 10 . . . P-Q3 would be better, and if then 11 Kt-KKt5, P-R3; 12 Q-R5, Px Kt; 13 QxKt, KtxP; 14 BxP, Kt-K3! 15 BxKt, BxB with a good game.

11 P-R3	P-Q3
12 B-K3	QKt-K2
13 R-K	P-B3
14 Q-Kt3	B-B2
15 Kt-Q2	R-Kt
16 QR-B	P-Kt4
17 PxP	RPxP

Black has only succeeded in weakening his QBP.

18 B-Q3	K-R

In order to play . . . P-KB4; but since this move allows the White Q to enter at K6 after the Bs have been exchanged, it would have been wiser to play 18 . . . B-K3; 19 Q-B2, B-Kt3, or possibly 19 . . . P-KB4, while if (after 18 . . . B-K3) 19 P-Q5, Kt-K4! 20 B-B, PxP; 21 PxP, B-Q2 with a fair game, for if 22 Kt xP, B-R4 (threatening . . . Q-K), or 22 BxP, B-R4 and wins.

19 Kt-K2

Intending P-Kt4 followed by Kt-Kt3-B5.

19	P-KB4
20 PxP	BxP
21 BxB	RxB
22 Kt-Kt3	R-KB
23 Q-K6	Q-B

If 23 . . . R-B3; 24 Q-Kt4 and Black must play 23 . . . Q-QB to prevent QKt-K4 followed by P-R4-R5 with a strong K side attack.

24 QxQ	KRxQ
25 Kt-Kt3	K-Kt
26 Kt-K4	K-B2
27 P-Kt3	K-K

White is systematically restricting the scope of the hostile pieces. The QBP, being fixed, is a permanent weakness. With the text

White plans P-R4-R5 at a suitable moment, and at the same time he prevents occupancy of his KB4 by the Black pieces. Finally, the QB can now play to B4, and the importance of this consideration will soon become evident.

28 R-K2!	K-Q2
29 QR-K!	

Position after White's 29th move

Lasker has conjured up some very pretty mating threats out of an apparently simple position. If Black should now play 29 . . . Kt -Q4; 30 BxP!! wins at least a P, for if 30 . . . PxB; 31 Kt(K4)- B5ch, PxKt; 32 KtxPch and mate follows! Black could have held the position, temporarily at any rate, with 29 . . . Kt-B4; 30 B- Q2, R-B (but not 30 . . . B-Kt3; 31 KtxP! KtxKt; 32 R-K6, Kt-B; 33 R-K7ch, K-Q; 34 B-B4, B-B2; 35 RxP and Black has no adequate defense against R-Kt8. If in this 32 . . . Kt-R; 33 R-K7ch, K-Q; 34 RxP, Kt(R)-B2; 35 Kt-B5, B xKt; 36 PxB, Kt-B5; 37 B-B4, R- Kt2; 38 P-Kt3, Kt-R4; 39 R-Kt8 ch, K-Q2; 40 R-Qch etc.); 31 B- Kt4, QR-K. White has the initiative and a decided advantage in terrain, but the win is still far off.

| 29 . . . . | B-Kt3 |
| 30 B-B4 | B-B2 |

30 . . . KtxB would allow a catastrophe on the K side: 31 Kt-B6ch! PxKt; 32 RxKtch, K-Q; 33 R-K8ch, K-Q2; 34 R(K)-K7 mate. The text is forced, for if 30 . . . Kt-B4; 31 BxQP! KtxB; 32 KtxKt, KxKt; 33 R-K6ch followed by RxKt.

| 31 P-R4 | P-R4 |
| 32 B-Kt5 | |

The threat of P-R5 has enabled White to gain this valuable post for his B. 32 . . . Kt-B4 would no longer be an adequate defense, for then 33 P-Kt4! PxP; 34 P-R5, Kt-B (34 . . . Kt(Kt3)-R5? 35 BxKt, KtxB; 36 Kt-B6ch! and mate in three); 35 P-R6! R-K; 36 PxP, Kt-R2; 37 Kt(K4)-B5ch! and wins.

| 32 . . . . | B-Q |

If 32 . . . R-K; 33 P-Kt4! PxP; 34 P-R5, Kt-B; 35 Kt(K4)-B5 ch! PxKt; 36 RxKtch etc.

33 P-Kt4!	PxP
34 P-R5	Kt-B
35 Kt(K4)-B5ch!	PxKt
36 KtxPch	K-Q3

36 . . . K-B2; 37 BxKt, BxB; 38 RxBch, K-Kt3; 39 RxP would prevent mate but not ultimate defeat.

| 37 B-B4ch | K-Q4 |
| 38 R-K5ch | K-B5 |

38 . . . KxP; 39 R-Qch, K-B5; 40 R-K4ch, KxKt; 41 B-K3 mate is hardly more appetizing.

| 39 R-Bch | KxP |

Or 39 . . . K-Kt5; 40 B-Q2 mate.

| 40 Kt-Kt3ch | K-Q6 |
| 41 R-K3 mate | |

Lasker has played the concluding phase with great artistry.

GAME No. 29

Match 1896-7

Giuoco Piano

White	Black
W. Steinitz	**Dr. E. Lasker**
1 P-K4	P-K4
2 Kt-KB3	Kt-QB3
3 B-B4	B-B4
4 P-B3	Kt-B3
5 P-Q4	PxP
6 PxP	B-Kt5ch
7 Kt-B3	

The usual line of play hereabouts is 7 B-Q2, BxBch; 8 QKt xB, P-Q4; 9 PxP, KKtxP; 10 O-O, O-O; 11 Q-Kt3, QKt-K2 etc.

| 7 . . . . | KtxKP |

If instead 7 . . . P-Q4; 8 PxP, KKtxP; 9 O-O, B-K3; 10 B-KKt5, B-K2; 11 BxKt, BxKB; 12 Ktx B, QxKt; 13 BxB, KtxB; 14 R-K± as in the celebrated game Steinitz-Von Bardeleben, Hastings 1895.

| 8 O-O | BxKt |

Undoubtedly stronger than 8 . . . KtxKt; 9 PxKt, BxP; 10 Q-Kt3, P-Q4! 11 BxP, O-O; 12 BxPch, K-R; 13 QxB, RxB = (Dr. Bernstein's analysis).

| 9 PxB | |

The alternative 9 P-Q5 leads to the well-known Möller Attack, whereby White at least obtains some compensation for the sacrificed P. The refutation of the text

is rather obvious—but not to a
Steinitz!

    9 . . . .   P-Q4
  10 B-R3?

This sacrifice of a piece is un-
sound, as Lasker had already demonstrated in the 1st game of the
match. 10 B-QKt5, O-O; 11 Bx
Kt, PxB; 12 B-R3 is certainly
better, although Black still retains
the advantage.

  10 . . . .   PxB
  11 R-K   B-K3!

Black can safely hold the piece
by 11 . . . P-B4; 12 Kt-Q2, K-
B2; 13 KtxKt, PxKt; 14 RxP, Q-
B3!∓ as played in the game quoted above. Lasker was perhaps
afraid that Steinitz had discovered
an improvement on his previous
play. With the text he avoids all
traps and emerges a P ahead with
the better position. Furthermore,
Steinitz, playing the White pieces,
is forced to defend himself after
twelve moves: an important *psychological* consideration.

  12 RxKt   Q-Q4
  13 Q-K2   O-O-O

By no means dangerous, for
after . . . P-QKt3 the Black K is
perfectly safe.

  14 Kt-K5   KR-K
  15 KtxKt

15 P-B4 would weaken the K
side, as the Kt cannot be permanently maintained at K5.

  15 . . . .   QxKt
  16 R-K   R-Kt

White's massing of his heavy
artillery is thus rendered pointless.

  17 R-K5   P-QKt3

  18 B-B   P-KKt4!
  19 RxP

Steinitz foresees that the opening of the KKt file will probably
prove decisive; but there is not
much else to be done against the
threat of 19 . . . P-Kt5 followed
by . . . B-Q4.

  19 . . . .   RxR
  20 BxR   R-Kt
  21 P-B4

Forced: if 21 P-KR4, P-KR3
and the B is lost.

  21 . . . .   B-Q4

Threatening . . . P-B3.

  22 P-Kt3

White has defended himself
against all his opponent's threats
for the time being, but the weakness of the white squares persists
and must eventually lead to the
loss of the game. Here we see
Lasker playing hypermodern chess
in 1896!

  22 . . . .   K-Kt2
  23 P-KR3   Q-Kt4!

In order to transpose the res-
pective positions of B and Q; Black
will then have definite mating
threats at his disposal.

  24 K-R2

White is helpless: if for example
24 Q-K5, P-KB3! 25 QxP, Q-Kt7
and wins.

  24 . . . .   R-Kt3
  25 Q-QB2   P-KB3
  26 B-R4   B-B3
  27 P-Kt4

Now Black can advance his
KRP to R5 and completely cripple
White's game. But Black was al-
ready threatening . . . Q-Q4 and

. . . R-Kt followed by . . . R-K.

27	. . . .	Q-Q4
28	Q-B2	P-KR4
29	P-Kt5	PxP
30	BxP	

If 30 PxP, R-Kt2; 31 R-K5, Q-R8ch; 32 K-Kt3, R-B2! 33 R-KB5, RxR; 34 QxR, Q-K8ch; 35 Q-B2, QxPch; 36 K-R2, Q-Q6 with a winning ending.

30	. . . .	P-R5!
31	R-KB	R-Kt
32	Q-Q2	P-R4!

A very fine conception which allows Black to win in the most efficacious manner. 32 . . . R-K would also win, but less quickly.

33	P-R4	R-K
34	P-B5	

If 34 BxP, R-K6! 35 B-Kt3 (or 35 P-B5, Q-Q3ch; 36 K-Kt, R-Kt6ch; 37 K-B2, R-Kt7ch), RxP; 36 P-B5, R-Q6; 37 Q-K2, P-B6! and wins.

34	. . . .	R-KKt!

White is in *Zugzwang!*

The B cannot move because of . . . R-Kt7ch; the Q must remain at Q2 to defend the B and guard mate; P-B6 would leave the B undefended; and K-Kt would lose the B. If the R moves anywhere but to KKt, Black plays . . . Qx BP and the RP cannot be captured. The only move that remains is 35 R-KKt, which would lose quickly after 35 . . . RxB! 36 QxR, Q-Q3ch; 37 R-Kt3, PxRch; 38 QxP, B-K; 39 P-R4, QxQch; 40 KxQ, P-Kt4! (the point of Black's 32nd move); 41 PxP, P-R5! and Black queens first. Therefore White resigns.

Final position

GAME No. 30

Match 1896-7

Ruy Lopez

White	Black
Dr. E. Lasker	**W. Steinitz**

1	P-K4	P-K4
2	Kt-KB3	Kt-QB3
3	B-Kt5	B-B4
4	P-B3	KKt-K2
5	P-Q4	PxP
6	PxP	B-Kt5ch

Unsatisfactory, for later on Black's QB4 becomes weak; but 6 . . . B-Kt3 would be even worse: 7 P-Q5, Kt-QKt; 8 P-Q6, PxP; 9 B-KB4, O-O; 10 Kt-B3 ±.

7	B-Q2	BxBch
8	QxB	P-Q4

If 8 . . . P-QR3; 9 B-R4, P-Q4; 10 PxP, QxP; 11 Kt-B3, Q-K3ch; 12 K-B, Q-B5ch; 13 K-Kt ± (Alekhine - Bogoljubow, All-Russian Tournament 1914).

9	PxP	KtxP
10	BxKtch	PxB

In his notes to the game Réti-Marshall in the monumental New York 1924 Tournament Book,

Alekhine comments on the remarkable similarity of the two games
up to this point.

| 11 O-O | O-O |
| 12 Kt-B3 | P-B3 |

Sooner or later the possibility
of Kt-K5 will force this move.

13 KR-K

13 P-KR3 would have been more
precise, for now Black could have
obtained a good game by 13 . . .
B-Kt5; 14 Q-Q3 (or 14 Kt-KR4,
P-KB4; 15 P-KKt3, P-B5), BxKt;
15 QxB, Q-Q2.

13	R-Kt
14 P-KR3	B-B4
15 QR-B	Q-Q3
16 Kt-KR4	B-Q2
17 Kt-K4	Q-B5

A weak reply; 17 . . . Q-Kt5
would have given Black counter-
play.

18 QxQ	KtxQ
19 Kt-QB5	B-B
20 P-QKt3	K-B2
21 Kt-B3	R-K

The exchange of Rs is ill-advised,
for White is enabled to obtain
control of the K file. 21 . . . R-
Q would have set White a more
difficult problem. Lasker's handling of this end-game is classic
throughout.

22 RxR	KxR
23 R-Kch	K-B2
24 Kt-Q2	Kt-K3?

A strategical blunder: Black rids
himself of his only active piece.
Correct was 24 . . . R-Kt5; 25
Kt-B4, B-K3! with good chances.

| 25 KtxKt | BxKt |
| 26 Kt-K4 | B-Q4 |

27 Kt-B5	R-Kt5
28 R-Q	K-K2
29 P-B3	K-Q3
30 K-B2	R-Kt

Black's inelastic Pawn position
cramps his position badly;and his B
can force no weakness in White's
Pawn structure.

| 31 R-K | B-B2 |
| 32 Kt-K4ch | |

Position after White's 32nd move

| 32 . . . . | K-Q2 |

If 32 . . . K-Q4; 33 K-K3, R-
K; 34 R-QB, P-KB4? 35 R-B5ch,
K-K3; 36 R-K5ch, K-Q2; 37 Rx
KBP.

33 K-K3	B-Q4
34 Kt-B5ch	K-Q3
35 K-Q3	P-KR4?

The Q side was already weak;
now he ruins the K side as well.
Passive resistance was in order.

36 P-KR4	R-KR
37 K-B3	R-QKt
38 P-B4	R-Kt

If 38 . . . BxKKtP; 39 R-K6
ch, K-Q4; 40 R-K7 or 39 R-KKt,
regaining the P with advantage in
either case.

39 P-Kt3   P-Kt4?

Again Steinitz misjudges the position. There was no direct threat and hence no need for immediate action. Against passive resistance White would probably have played P-B5 and Kt-Q3-B4.

40 BPxP	PxP
41 R-K5	PxP
42 PxP	R-Kt6ch
43 K-Kt4	R-Kt5

Black's moves are all forced; if 43 . . . B-B6; 44 RxP! BxR; 45 Kt-K4ch.

44 Kt-Kt7ch	K-Q2
45 RxP	RxPch
46 K-R5	B-B2

White is virtually a P ahead, Black's doubled QBP being useless.

47 R-R6	R-Q7
48 Kt-B5ch	K-K2

48 . . . K-Q; 49 P-R4, B-K; 50 R-R8 is no better.

49 P-R4	R-Q3
50 R-R8	R-Q4
51 P-Kt4	B-K

To prevent R-R8; if 51 . . . R-Q; 52 RxR, KxR; 53 K-R6 with an easy win.

52 R-R6	R-B4

If 52 . . . R-K4; 53 K-R6; whereas 53 K-R6 is now answered by . . . R-B5.

53 R-K6ch	K-Q

The Black K must go to the Q side, for it is obvious that White will soon win the QRP.

54 R-K4	B-B2
55 K-R6	B-Q4
56 R-Q4	K-B
57 KxP	R-R4

58 R-KB4	R-R
59 P-KR5	B-R7

The ending is pretty; if 59 . . . K-Q; 60 K-Kt7, RxP; 61 P-R5 followed by P-R6-R7-R8=Q.

60 P-R6	B-Q4
61 P-R7	B-R7
62 R-K4	B-B2
63 R-R4	B-R7
64 Kt-K4	B-Kt6
65 P-R5	B-B7

Or 65 . . . B-Q4; 66 Kt-B6.

66 R-Kt4!	Resigns

For if 66 . . . RxP; 67 R-Kt8 ch, K-Q2; 68 Kt-B6ch etc., or 66 . . . B-Kt6; 67 Kt-B6.

A much admired end-game.

GAME No. 31

Match 1896-7

Giuoco Piano

White	Black
Dr. E. Lasker	**W. Steinitz**

1 P-K4	P-K4
2 Kt-KB3	Kt-QB3
3 B-B4	B-B4
4 Kt-B3	P-Q3
5 P-Q3	Kt-B3
6 B-K3	BxB

In the 17th game of the first match, Steinitz had played 6 . . . B-Kt3 with the continuation 7 Q-Q2, Kt-QR4; 8 B-Kt5ch (better B-Kt3), P-B3; 9 B-R4, BxB; 10 PxB, P-QKt4; 11 B-Kt3, Q-Kt3; 12 O-O, Kt-Kt5; 13 QR-K, P-B3 with a slight advantage to Black.

7 PxB	Kt-QR4

Not the best; . . . B-K3 would equalize easily.

8 B-Kt3	KtxB
9 RPxKt	Kt-Kt5
10 Q-K2	P-KB3
11 P-Q4	

Now White has a definite advantage: if Black wishes to free his
game by . . . P-Q4 or . . . P-
KB4, he must first play . . . PxP;
but then White can recapture and
maintain a strong P center which
cannot be attacked easily.

| 11 . . . . | P-B3 |
| 12 O-O-O | Q-K2 |

White threatened 13 P-R3, Kt-
R3; 14 PxP, BPxP; 15 KtxP.

13 P-R3	Kt-R3
14 P-KKt4	B-Q2
15 Kt-KR4	

In order to force a weakening
of Black's KBP. Lasker is evidently of the opinion that after 15 . . .
P-KKt3; 16 Kt-B3, P-KB4; 17 KtP
xP, KtPxP; 18 QPxP, QPxP; 19
Q-R2, Kt-B2; 20 PxP, BxP; 21
KR-Kt Black's position would be
too exposed.

| 15 . . . . | P-KKt3 |
| 16 Kt-B3 | |

Black was threatening to win a
P by . . . P-KB4. Lasker, per-
ceiving that . . . P-KB4 cannot
be prevented (16 Q-B2, O-O-O;
17 QR-B, QR-B; 18 Q-Kt3, P-
KB4), plays to give the impression
that the advance is not desirable
for Black. The ruse is successful
and Steinitz delays . . . P-KB4
until Lasker has had time to prevent the move.

16	Kt-B2
17 QR-Kt	O-O-O
18 P-Kt4	K-Kt

If 18 . . . P-Q4; 19 KPxP, Qx
P; 20 PxKP, PxKP; 21 P-K4±.

| 19 Q-B2 | QR-KB |
| 20 Q-Kt3 | P-KR3 |

A superfluous defensive move,
but it is already difficult to find
a satisfactory move for Black.

21 R-B	Kt-Q
22 R(R)-Kt	Kt-K3
23 R-B2	Kt-B2
24 R(Kt)-B	

Now that White has permanently prevented . . . P-KB4, he proceeds to build up an attack on the
Q's wing.

| 24 . . . . | R(B)-Kt |

"The wrong Rook": he should
have played R(R)-Kt, so that if
25 Kt-KR4, Kt-K3 (in the game
this is impossible, the KBP being
unprotected).

| 25 Kt-KR4 | Kt-K |
| 26 P-QKt5! | |

The P cannot be taken because
of Kt-Q5.

| 26 . . . . | K-R |
| 27 KtPxP | KtPxP |

After 27 . . . BxBP; 28 P-Q5,
B-Q2; 29 P-Kt3 Black's position
cannot be freed. Lasker's precise
handling of this game is note-
worthy.

| 28 Kt-B3 | P-Kt4 |

In order to play . . . P-KR4
without allowing P-Kt5 in reply.

| 29 R-Kt2 | P-KR4 |
| 30 P-Kt3 | |

He can afford to ignore Black's
imaginary threats.

30	R-R3
31 K-Kt2	R(Kt)-R
32 Q-B2	Kt-B2

33 R-QR   R-QKt

Lasker's attack has been ac-curately timed. This retreat is necessary, for if 33 . . . Kt-K3; 34 P-Q5, Kt-B4; 35 Kt-Q2 and White's attack should strike home first.

34 Q-K2   R-Kt2
35 R(Kt2)-Kt   R(R3)-R
36 R(R)-Q   RPxP
37 RPxP   R-QB
38 Q-Q3   B-K3

White was threatening to win a P.

39 Kt-Q2   Kt-Kt4
40 Kt(Q2)-Kt! R(Kt2)-B2
41 Kt-R4   R-Kt2
42 K-B   R(B)-QKt
43 R-Kt2   R-Q2
44 Kt(Kt)-B3   Kt-B2
45 P-Q5

After an interval of irrelevant maneuvering, Lasker proceeds to a direct attack on the Black K.

45 . . . .   PxP
46 PxP   B-Kt
47 Q-B4   R-QB
48 K-Kt2   R-Kt

The meaningless moves here-abouts are due to time-pressure. Steinitz overstepped the time limit at this point, but Lasker, who was unwilling to win the game in this way, allowed him to play on.

49 P-K4   R(Q2)-Q
50 R-B2   R-KB
51 R(Q)-KB   B-R2
(See diagram next column)
52 RxP!

Position after Black's 51st move

A neat final combination which decides the game in a few moves.

52 . . . .   RxR
53 RxR   QxR
54 QxKt   Q-R

If 54 . . . B-Kt3; 55 Q-B6ch, R-Kt2; 56 Kt-Kt5, K-Kt; 57 Kt xQP, R-QB2; 58 Q-Kt5ch, K-R; 59 Kt-Kt6ch! PxKt; 60 Q-R6ch, K-Kt; 61 QxPch etc.; or 54 . . . R-Kt2; 55 Q-B8ch, R-Kt; 56 Q-B6ch transposing into the same variation.

55 Q-B6ch   R-Kt2
56 Kt-Kt5   K-Kt
57 QxPch   K-B
58 Q-B6ch   Resigns
For if 58 . . . K-Kt; 59 Kt-B5.

GAME No. 32

Match 1896-7

Ruy Lopez

White	Black
Dr. E. Lasker	**W. Steinitz**

1 P-K4	P-K4
2 Kt-KB3	Kt-QB3
3 B-Kt5	P-QR3
4 BxKt	QPxB
5 Kt-B3	B-KKt5

Better would be 5 . . . P-B3, a move generally attributed to Dr. Bernstein, but played by Steinitz in the '80s.

| 6 P-KR3 | BxKt |
| 7 QxB | Kt-K2 |

7 . . . Q-Q2 followed by . . . O-O-O seems preferable; while 7 . . . Q-B3 could certainly be played without disadvantage.

| 8 P-Q3 | P-QB4 |
| 9 Q-Kt3 | Kt-Kt3? |

The logical continuation of his previous move was 9 . . . Kt-B3 and if 10 P-B4, P-B3=.

| 10 B-K3 | B-Q3 |
| 11 O-O-O | O-O? |

11 . . . Q-Q2 followed by . . . O-O-O would have been far safer.

| 12 P-KR4 | Kt-B5 |
| 13 K-Kt | |

If 13 BxKt, PxB; 14 Q-Kt4 (threatening Kt-Q5), Q-B! followed by . . . P-B4 with a good game for Black.

| 13 . . . . | Kt-K3 |
| 14 Q-Kt4 | Q-K |

To play the Q to the K side, but this plan is never carried out.

| 15 Kt-K2 | Kt-Q5 |
| 16 KtxKt | KPxKt |

Unfortunately forced, for 16 . . . BPxKt; 17 B-R6! would cost Black the exchange.

| 17 B-R6 | B-K4 |
| 18 B-B! | |

Best: if 18 P-KB4, Q-K3!

18	Q-K3
19 Q-K2	P-B4
20 P-KB4	B-Q3
21 P-K5	B-K2
22 P-R5	

Preparing P-KKt4 by preventing Black from playing . . . Q-KKt3.

| 22 . . . . | QR-Q |
| 23 P-KKt4 | P-QKt4 |

The opening of the QB file only helps White, since his pieces are posted to better advantage. Preferable was 23 . . . PxP; 24 QR-Kt, R-B4; 25 RxP, B-B; 26 KR-Kt, R-Q2; 27 R-Kt5, R(Q2)-B2 and White's win is by no means easy (Tarrasch).

24 QR-Kt	P-B5
25 R-Kt2	PxQP
26 BPxP	PxP
27 RxP	R-B4
28 KR-Kt	B-B
29 R-Kt5	RxR

He can no longer blockade the BP; if 29 . . . R-Q2; 30 RxR, QxR; 31 R-Kt5 followed by P-B5 etc.

| 30 RxR | R-Q4 |

Preventing P-B5.

31 Q-B3

Threatening P-B5 and if . . . QxKP? in reply, P-B6 will win.

Position after White's 31st move

| 31 . . . . | R-Q2 |
| 32 Q-K4 | R-Q4 |

33 R-Kt2

Intending R-K2 and finally P-B5.

| 33 . . . . | P-B3 |
| 34 R-K2 | Q-Kt5 |

If 31 . . . P-Kt3; 32 PxP, PxP; 33 R-Kt2, K-B2; 34 R-Kt5 with a winning position.

35 P-K6	B-K2
36 R-QB2	QxRP
37 RxP	R-Q
38 RxP	Q-K
39 R-R7	P-R4
40 P-B5	P-R5
41 Q-Kt4	Resigns

Black is helpless against the threat of B-R6 or B-Kt5.

GAME No. 33

Moscow 1899

Four Knights' Game

White	Black
	—.Bobrow
	—.Gontscharow
Dr. E. Lasker	—.Grigoriew
	V. Nenarokow
1 P-K4	P-K4
2 Kt-QB3	Kt-QB3
3 Kt-B3	Kt-B3
4 B-Kt5	B-Kt5
5 P-Q3	

A temporary deviation from the book line; but the game soon turns into the usual channels.

5	P-Q3
6 O-O	BxKt
7 PxB	O-O
8 B-Kt5	Kt-K2

Not good after the exchange on the 6th move. . . . Q-K2 is preferable.

| 9 Kt-R4 | P-B3 |
| 10 B-QB4 | P-Q4 |

| 11 B-Kt3 | PxP |
| 12 PxP | QxQ? |

The *Deutsche Schachzeitung* recommends 12 . . . B-Kt5; 13 P-B3, Q-Kt3ch; 14 K-R, QR-Q, but then 15 Q-K! B-R4; 16 Q-Kt3 would win a P. The way in which Lasker refutes the text is remarkable for its simplicity and refinement.

13 QRxQ	Kt-Kt3
14 KtxKt	RPxKt
15 BxKt	PxB
16 R-Q6!	

Enabling White to turn his positional advantage (the open Q file) into material advantage.

16 . . . .   K-Kt2

Forced (16 . . . P-KB4; 17 Rx Pch).

| 17 P-KB4! | PxP |
| 18 KRxP | B-K3 |

If instead 18 . . . P-KB4; 19 PxP, BxP; 20 P-Kt4, B-B; 21 R (Q6)-B6, B-K3; 22 BxB, PxB; 23 RxR! RxR; 24 RxR, KxR; 25 P-KR4 and wins; or 19 . . . PxP; 20 B-B4 followed by B-Q3 and the KBP is lost.

| 19 BxB | PxB |
| 20 RxKP | QR-Q |

Although White has won a P, his ultimate victory is questionable because his Ps are weak and the pieces left on the board offer Black excellent drawing chances.

(See diagram on next page)

21 P-K5!   PxP

If 21 . . . P-KB4; 22 R-Q4±.

22 RxR   RxR

The only chance consisted in . . . KxR. Now the game is re-

Position after Black's 20th move

duced to an arithmetic problem.

23 R-K7ch!   R-B2
24 RxRch   KxR
25 P-KR4!

The point of White's 21st move. He must obtain a remote passed P on the K side which will leave Black helpless.

25 . . . .   P-R4
26 P-Kt4   P-R5
27 K-B2   P-R6
28 K-K3   K-K3
29 K-K4   K-B3
30 P-B4   K-K3
31 P-B5   K-B3
32 P-R5

Even simpler would be 32 P-B4! K-K3; 33 P-R5.

32 . . . .   PxP
33 PxP   K-Kt4
34 KxP   KxP
35 K-Q6   K-Kt5
36 K-B7   K-B6
37 KxP   K-K7
38 KxP   K-Q7
39 K-Kt5   KxP
40 P-B6   K-Kt7
41 P-B7   KxP
42 K-Kt4   K-Kt7
43 P-B8=Q   P-R7
44 Q-R8ch

Simpler is 44 Q-B3ch, K-Kt8; 45 K-Kt3.

44 . . . .   K-Kt8
45 Q-Rch   K-Kt7
46 Q-Kt2ch   K-Kt8
47 K-B3!   P-R8=Qch
48 K-Kt3   Resigns

GAME No. 34

London 1899

Caro-Kann Defense

White   Black
Dr. E. Lasker   **F. J. Lee**

1 P-K4   P-QB3

In the '90s this was still something of a novelty.

2 P-Q4   P-Q4
3 Kt-QB3   PxP
4 KtxP   B-B4
5 Kt-Kt3   B-Kt3
6 Kt-B3   Kt-Q2
7 P-KR4

In order to force Black to exchange after 8 B-Q3.

7 . . . .   P-KR3
8 B-Q3   BxB
9 QxB   KKt-B3
10 B-Q2   P-K3
11 O-O-O   Q-B2
12 KR-K   O-O-O
13 Q-Kt3   B-Q3
14 Kt-K2   Kt-Kt5

Mieses suggests 14 . . . Kt-K5; 15 B-K3, QKt-B3 threatening . . . Kt-Kt5 or else 15 R-B, Ktx B etc., etc.

15 R-B   QKt-B3
16 Q-R4   K-Kt
17 P-B4

From this point Lasker steadily gains ground. He now threatens 18

P-B5, B-K2; 19 B-B4.

17 . . . .   Q-K2

Very timorous; he should have played 17 . . . P-K4 or else 17 P-B4; 18 Kt-B3, P-R3.

18 Kt-B3   Q-B2

Again . . . P-B4 was indicated: 19 Kt-QKt5, P-R3; 20 KtxB, Qx Kt; 21 PxP, QxP; or 18 . . . P-K4; 19 QR-K (19 P-B5, B-B2; 20 PxP, KtxKP; 21 KtxKt, BxKt; 22 KR-K, Q-B2! 23 RxB, RxB!), Q-Q2! 20 PxP, KtxKP; 21 KtxKt, BxKt; 22 RxB, QxBch.

19 P-KKt3!

Preventing . . . B-B5.

19 . . . .   Q-B

. . . P-K4 would not do because of 20 P-B5, B-K2 (. . . Px P? 21 PxB); 21 PxP, KtxKP; 22 KtxKt, QxKt; 23 B-B4. Nor can Black play 19 . . . P-B4; 20 Kt-QKt5, Q-Kt3; 21 KtxB followed by B-B4.

20 P-Kt4!   P-K4
21 PxP   KtxKP

Or 21 . . . BxKP; 22 KtxB, KtxKt; 23 B-B4, Q-B2; 24 KR-K, RxRch; 25 QxR, Kt(B3)-Q2; 26 Q-Q4, P-B3; 27 B-K3, P-QKt3; 28 P-B4, Kt-Kt5; 29 B-Q2 and Black's position will soon become untenable.

22 B-K3!

An accurately calculated winning move, as Lee soon learns to his sorrow.

(See diagram next column)

22 . . . .   KtxP

There is no longer any adequate defense:

I 22 . . . P-QKt3; 23 RxB,

Position after White's 22nd move

KtxKt; 24 RxP, Q-Kt2; 25 B-B4 ch, K-R; 26 R-B7, Q-Kt; 27 Q-B6ch and mate follows.

II 22 . . . P-QR3; 23 RxB, KtxKt; 24 B-B4, RxR; 25 Q-Q! Kt-R7; 26 QxRch, K-R2; 27 B-K3 ch, K-R (27 . . . P-Kt3; 28 R-Q, Kt(R7)-Kt5; 29 B-Q4, R-Q; 30 BxPch); 28 Kt-R4, Kt-Q2; 29 QxKt, QxQ; 30 Kt-Kt6ch, K-Kt; 31 KtxQch, K-B2; 32 R-R winning a piece.

III 22 . . . KtxKt; 23 QxP ch, K-B2; 24 B-Kt6ch, K-Q2; 25 BxR winning easily.

23 BxPch   K-B2
24 R-Q4!   P-QKt4

The Kt cannot move (24 . . . Kt-Kt3; 25 BxKtch! or 24 . . . Kt-K4; 25 KtxKt etc.).

25 KtxPch!

This breaks Black's defense very quickly.

25 . . . .   PxKt
26 QxP   Kt-R6
27 Q-R5ch   K-Kt2 dis ch
28 B-B5!   BxB
29 PxB   RxR

White threatened mate in two; . . . Q-B2 would lose after 30 R-

Kt4ch, K-B; 31 Q-R6ch, K-Q2; 32 R-Kt7.

30	KtxR	Q-Q
31	P-B6ch!	K-B
32	Q-R8ch	K-B2
33	Q-R7ch	K-Q3

Black has no choice.

34	QxKtch	K-Q4
35	R-Q	Q-Kt3
36	Kt-B3 dis ch	K-K3

Or 36 . . . K-K5; 37 Q-Q3 mate!

37	Q-Q6ch	K-B4
38	Q-Q3ch	K-Kt5
39	Kt-K5ch	Resigns

For if 39 . . . K-R6; 40 Q-B ch, K-R7; 41 Q-R or Kt-B3 mate!

GAME No. 35

London 1899

Queen's Pawn Opening

White   Black

J. H. Blackburne   Dr. E. Lasker

1	P-Q4	P-Q4
2	Kt-KB3	Kt-KB3
3	P-K3	P-K3
4	B-Q3	QKt-Q2
5	QKt-Q2	B-Q3
6	P-K4	PxP
7	KtxP	P-QKt3
8	O-O	B-Kt2
9	KtxBch	PxKt

The position is now perfectly even, but Blackburne (who had defeated Lasker very brilliantly earlier in the tournament) imperceptibly drifts into an inferior position.

10	R-K	O-O
11	B-KKt5	Q-B2
12	P-B3	KR-K

Intending . . . P-K4.

13 B-Kt5   B-B3

More or less forced if Black is to avoid the doubling of his Ps which would result from QBxKt etc.

14	BxB	QxB
15	Q-Q3	P-KR3
16	B-R4	

BxKt was indicated, as the B will turn out to be useless for the rest of the game.

| 16 | . . . . | QR-B |
| 17 | QR-Q | Kt-Q4! |

In this game Lasker shows himself a precursor of the Hypermodern School — particularly in controlling White's center squares with his KKt, instead of advancing . . . P-Q4.

18 B-Kt3   P-QKt4!

A stratagem which was a great favorite with Nimzowitsch: paralyzing the adversary's majority of Ps on either wing. Now White's Q side Ps are fixed, while Black is soon free to advance his Ps on the other flank.

| 19 | Kt-Q2 | Kt(Q2)-Kt3 |
| 20 | P-QR3 | |

A further weakening of the position which Lasker promptly utilizes by

20	. . . .	P-QR4!
21	R-QB	P-R5
22	P-R4	

Evidently fearing the advance of Black's Ps, but the RP turns out to be a welcome target later on.

22 . . . .   P-B4!

Shifting the attack to the K side with decisive effect.

23 B-R2

After 23 P-KB4 the B would be

buried alive, and sooner or later Black would break through with . . . P-KKt4 or . . . P-K4.

23	Q-Q2
24 Q-Kt3	P-B5
25 Q-Q3	P-K4
26 P-B4?	

This attempt to simplify the position is faulty because it relinquishes command of K4. It was essential for White to prevent the advance of the hostile KP as long as possible—though there could be little doubt as to the outcome, White being practically a piece down.

| 26 . . . . | KtPxP |
| 27 KtxP | |

Position after White's 27th move

| 27 . . . . | P-K5! |

The most forceful continuation: Marco gives the following interesting variations after the alternative 27 . . . Q-B3:

I 28 Kt-Q2, QxR; 29 RxQ, RxRch; 30 Kt-B, PxP with the fatal threat of . . . R(K)-K8.

II 28 Kt-K3, QxR; 29 RxQ, RxRch; 30 Kt-Q, PxP; 31 K-B! Kt-B5; 32 QxP, KtxKtP! 33 Qx Ktch, K-R with decisive advantage for Black.

III 28 KtxKt, QxR; 29 Q-B! QxR; 30 QxQ, KtxKt∓.

28 Q-B

On 28 KtxKt? Lasker intended . . . RxR; 29 RxR, PxQ! 30 Kt xQ, P-Q7! etc. or else 28 RxP, R xR; 29 QxR, Q-Kt4 and wins.

| 28 . . . . | KtxKt |
| 29 RxKt | R-Kt! |

An important gain of time.

| 30 R-B2 | K-R! |

In order to be able to answer 31 Q-B4 with . . . KR-B.

| 31 KR-B | Q-Kt5! |

To this move there is no adequate reply.

32 P-B3	QxRP
33 PxP	KRxP
34 R-B8ch	RxR
35 RxRch	K-R2
36 Q-Kt	Kt-B3

If now 37 R-K8, P-Q4! followed by . . . Kt-Kt5.

| 37 P-Q5 | P-Kt3 |

In order to prevent R-K8.

| 38 R-B7ch | K-R! |

A little finesse: after 38 . . . K-Kt Black would be unable to move his R.

39 R-B

Or 39 R-B8ch, K-Kt2; 40 R-B 7ch, K-B; 41 R-B8ch, K-K2; 42 R-B7ch, K-Q etc.

| 39 . . . . | R-K7 |
| 40 K-R | |

If 40 R-B, P-B6!

40	Kt-Kt5
41 R-B8ch	K-Kt2
42 R-B7ch	K-B3
Resigns	

GAME No. 36

London 1899
French Defense

White | Black
M. Tchigorin | **Dr. E. Lasker**

1 P-K4   P-K3
2 Q-K2

Tchigorin's favorite continuation, which has the purely subjective merit of throwing the players
on their own resources—an unfortunate proceeding against a
Lasker!

2 . . . .   Kt-QB3

An equally good line of play
would be 2 . . . P-QB4 followed
by 3 . . . Kt-QB3.

3 Kt-QB3

P-KB4 first is more in the spirit
of this variation.

3 . . . .   P-K4

Now we have a Vienna Game,
which renders White's Q move
quite useless.

4 P-KKt3   Kt-B3
5 B-Kt2   B-B4
6 P-Q3   P-Q3
7 B-Kt5

Tchigorin artlessly follows out
his usual policy of exchanging Bs
for Kts. In the present game this
procedure is faulty, because the
Kts have no good squares at their
disposal.

Schlechter suggests 7 Kt-R4 as
a better move; even 7 B-K3 was
preferable to the text.

7 . . . .   P-KR3
8 BxKt

It was still possible to play B-
K3.

8 . . . .   QxB

If now 9 Kt-R4 the continuation
might be 9 . . . B-Q5; 10 P-QB
3, QxPch; 11 QxQ, BxQch; 12 K
xB, P-QKt4; 13 P-Kt3, PxKt; 14
PxP, R-QKt $\mp$ (Schlechter).

9 Kt-Q5   Q-Q
10 P-QB3   Kt-K2
11 KtxKt   QxKt
12 O-O-O   B-Q2
13 P-KB4   O-O-O
14 Kt-B3   B-B3

The position has the appearance
of being quite even: actually
Black's position is already superior,
as his pieces have more of a future
than White's. Furthermore, the
advance of the KBP has provided
a potential target for Lasker's
attack.

15 KR-B   P-B3
16 K-Kt   KR-K

Threatening 17 . . . PxP; 18
PxP, P-Q4 etc. Nor can White
very well forestall this maneuver
by 17 PxP, QPxP because of the
resulting backward QP.

17 P-B5   B-R5
18 R-B

The advance of the KtP would
only help Black later on in working up an attack.

18 . . . .   K-Kt
19 Kt-Q2

Tchigorin is so dissatisfied with
his position that he is even willing
to cast his principles overboard
and play 20 P-QKt4, B-Kt3; 21
Kt-B4 in order to rid himself of
one of the bothersome Bs.

19 . . . .   P-R3

Parries White's threat.

20 B-B3   B-R2

21 P-R4?

Possibly with the idea of playing P-KKt4-5 later on; but either B-R5 or else Q-K followed by B-Q was better. In that event, however, Black would maintain his superiority by . . . P-Q4!

21	R-QB
22 Kt-B4	R(K)-Q
23 Kt-K3	B-K!
24 KR-Q	

Now White is in a position to play R-Kt followed by the advance of his KKtP; but instead of carrying out one bad plan consistently he prefers to vacillate among several bad ones.

| 24 . . . . | B-B2 |
| 25 P-B4? | |

A further weakening that creates a hole which can be occupied by Black's KB, and allows Black to open a file in short order.

| 25 . . . . | P-B3 |
| 26 R-B2 | |

White should reserve this square for his Kt.

26	B-Q5!
27 R(Q)-QB	Q-B2
28 Kt-Q	Q-R4
29 Kt-B3	P-QKt4!
30 P-Kt3	R-Q2
31 PxP	

White could at least prolong his resistance by 31 Q-K with the threat (in some variations) of Kt-K2.

| 31 . . . . | RPxP |
| 32 Kt-Q5 | K-Kt2 |

If now 33 P-QKt4, Q-R6; 34 Q-Q2, P-B4! etc.

33 P-KKt4

An afterthought . . .

| 33 . . . . | R(Q2)-Q |
| 34 Kt-K7 | |

Or 34 Kt-B3, R-QR and White is helpless against the threat of . . . BxP.

Position after White's 34th move

| 34 . . . . | BxP! |
| 35 KtxR | |

If 35 KtxP, RxKt! 36 RxR, Q-Kt5! 37 R-B7ch, K-Kt; 38 R(B)-B2 (if the other R returns to B2, then Black has a mate in three), BxR dbl ch; 39 KxB, Q-Kt7ch winning easily.

35	RxKt!
36 Q-Q2	Q-R6!
37 R-R	R-QR

Black's position has now reached its maximum power.

38 R-R2	BxPch!
39 RxB	Q-Kt6ch
40 K-B	

Or else 40 R-Kt2, BxR; 41 Qx B, QxPch, etc.

40	RxR
41 QxR	B-K6ch
42 Q-Q2	QxP
Resigns	

Lasker's play in this game (particularly the handling of the Bs) is a model of first-class strategical maneuvering. Equally pleasing is his forceful conduct of the final phase of the game beginning with his 26th move.

GAME No. 37

London 1899

Queen's Pawn Opening

White	Black
Dr. E. Lasker	**H. N. Pillsbury**

1 P-Q4	P-Q4
2 Kt-KB3	P-QB4
3 P-K3	Kt-QB3
4 P-B4	BPxP

Simpler is 4 . . . P-K3, transposing into the "Normal Variation" of Tarrasch's Defense.

5 BPxP	QxP
6 Kt-B3	Q-QR4
7 KtxP	KtxKt
8 QxKt	P-K4

If 8 . . . Kt-B3; 9 B-Kt5ch, B-Q2; 10 BxBch, KtxB; 11 O-O, P-K4; 12 Q-K4±.

9 Q-Q5

Not 9 B-Kt5ch, QxB; 10 KtxQ, PxQ; 11 Kt-B7ch, K-Q; 12 KtxR, P-QKt3 and the Kt cannot escape.

9	QxQ
10 KtxQ	B-Q3
11 B-B4	Kt-K2
12 O-O	

K-K2 was more natural.

12	B-K3
13 R-Q	BxKt
14 BxB	KtxB
15 RxKt	O-O-O

If 15 . . . K-K2; 16 R-Kt5, P-QKt3; 17 B-Q2 and White has some initiative.

16 B-Q2	B-B2
17 RxRch	RxR
18 B-B3	P-B3

Unnecessary and bad. 18 . . . K-Q2! 19 R-Qch, K-K3 = was indicated.

19 R-QB   P-QKt3

A further weakness. 19 . . . K-Q2 was preferable.

20 K-B   K-Kt2

20 . . . K-Q2 was still in order.

21 K-K2   P-QR4

Pillsbury may have been playing to win, but the P moves have only weakened his position.

22 P-QR4   P-QKt4

Likewise undesirable.

23 PxP   R-Q4

Not 23 . . . K-Kt3? 24 BxP ch!

24 R-QR!

Up to this point Pillsbury's weakening moves have been voluntary; from now on they will be forced. Lasker's utilization of the slight weaknesses in the hostile position is worth careful study.

24	RxP
25 R-R4!	

To force a weakening of Black's K side Ps. A similar maneuver occurs in Game No. 49.

25 . . . .   K-Kt3

If 25 . . . R-Q4 (to avoid . . . P-Kt4); 26 R-R4, P-R3; 27 R-KKt4, R-Q2; 28 K-B3, P-B4; 29 R-Kt6±.

26 R-R4	P-R3
27 R-KKt4	P-Kt4
28 R-QB4	

Intending to invade the weak white squares with his K.

28 . . . .   P-B4

Practically forced, to prevent the entrance of White's K. If for example 28 . . . R-B4; 29 RxR, KxR; 30 K-B3, P-B4; 31 P-K4! P-Kt5ch; 32 K-Kt3 and White should win.

29 P-KKt4   PxP
30 RxP   K-B4

To answer 31 K-B3 with . . . K-Q4.

31 P-R4   PxP
32 RxP   R-Kt3
33 K-Q3   R-Q3ch

If instead 33 . . . K-Q4; 34 R-R5, R-K3; 35 P-B4 winning a P.

34 K-K4   R-KKt3

Position after Black's 34th move

35 P-Kt4ch

More direct—but also more risky —was 35 BxP, BxB (or 35 . . . R-K3; 36 R-R5); 36 KxB, R-Kt 3; 37 P-B4, RxP; 38 RxP, P-R5; 39 R-R6, K-Kt5; 40 P-B5, P-R6; 41 P-K4, P-R7; 42 K-B6, K-Kt6; 43 P-K5, R-Kt8; 44 P-K6, P-R8 =Qch; 45 RxQ, RxR; 46 P-K7, R-K8; 47 K-B7, K-B5; 48 P-K8 =Q and wins. But since this win-ning process must be calculated to a nicety (Black loses by only one move), and since the text leaves

White with a win which is only a question of time, Lasker cannot be blamed for avoiding 35 BxP.

35 . . . .   PxP
36 BxPch   K-B3

Of course not 36 . . . KxB? 37 K-B5 dis ch and wins.

37 B-B3   R-Kt7

The P cannot be held, for if 37 . . . R-K3; 38 R-R5 etc.

38 RxPch   K-Q2
39 R-R7ch   K-Q

Best. If 39 . . . K-B3; 40 Bx P, BxB; 41 KxB, RxP; 42 P-K4 with a book win, whereas after the text, 40 BxP, BxB; 41 KxB, RxP; 43 P-K4, R-K7 draws.

40 P-B3   R-K7
41 B-Kt4

Again BxP would lead to a theoretical draw. The move actu-ally made provides an answer to the threat of . . . B-Kt3.

41 . . . .   B-Kt3
42 B-K7ch   K-B
43 B-Kt5   B-B2
44 R-R5   K-Q2
45 R-R7ch   K-B3
46 R-B7   R-K8
47 B-R6   R-K7
48 K-B5   B-Q3
49 K-K6   R-KKt7
50 B-Kt7   R-Kt3ch
51 K-B5   R-Kt6
52 K-K4

Finally threatening BxP.

52 . . . .   R-Kt4
53 B-B6   R-R4
54 R-KKt7

Planning R-Kt5.

54 . . . .   B-B4!

After this 55 BxP, BxP would only draw for White.

55 R-Kt6	K-Q2
56 B-Kt5	B-K2
57 K-B5	

Not 57 R-Kt7? RxB. The text threatens R-Kt7.

57	B-B4
58 R-Kt7ch	K-B3
59 K-K6	R-R6
60 R-B7	R-Kt6

Or 60 . . . P-K5; 61 PxP, Bx P; 62 BxB, RxB; 63 P-K5 and again White has a book win.

61 R-B5	B-Q3
62 P-K4	

If 62 B-B6, P-K5! 63 PxP, Rx P draws.

62	R-R6
63 B-K7	B-B2
64 B-Kt4	

Better than 64 B-B6, R-R3.

64	R-R3ch
65 R-B6	R-R4
66 K-K7 dis ch	K-Kt4
67 B-Q6	R-R2ch

The KP must fall! If 67 . . . B-Kt3; 68 R-B5.

68 K-K6	B-Q
69 R-B8	B-R5
70 BxP	K-B3
71 R-B8ch	K-Kt2
72 R-KR8	R-K2ch
73 K-Q6	RxB
74 KxR	B-K8
75 K-K6	Resigns

GAME No. 38

London 1899

French Defense

White   Black

Dr. E. Lasker   J. W. Showalter

1 P-K4	P-K3
2 P-Q4	P-Q4
3 Kt-QB3	Kt-KB3
4 B-Kt5	B-Kt5
5 P-K5	P-KR3
6 B-Q2	BxKt
7 PxB	Kt-K5
8 B-Q3	

An old continuation which has now been generally replaced by Q-Kt4.

8	KtxB
9 QxKt	P-QB4
10 P-KB4	Q-R4
11 P-B4!	

A deeply-considered move which yields White a superior end-game.

11	QxQch
12 KxQ	QPxP
13 BxP	PxP
14 Kt-B3	Kt-B3
15 B-Kt5	B-Q2
16 BxKt	BxB
17 KtxP	

The position now arrived at is somewhat in White's favor, as the nature of the P configuration renders the Kt superior to the B.

17	BxP?

But this is a blunder which magnifies White's advantage considerably. It would have been better to continue with . . . QR-B followed by . . . K-K2 etc.

18 KR-KKt	B-K5
19 RxP	

Showalter was evidently under the impression that this capture was impossible because of 19 . . . B-Kt3 with 20 . . . K-B to follow.

19	K-K2

To his sorrow Black discovers that 19 . . . B-Kt3 would not do because of 20 R-KKt! (not 20 Kt xP, K-K2), K-B; 21 KtxPch and wins, or else 20 . . . O-O-O; 21 K-K3, B-R4; 22 Kt-Kt5, K-Kt; 23 Kt-Q6± (Marco).

| 20 K-K3 | B-R2 |
| 21 QR-KKt | QR-QB |

With the idea of tying White's pieces to the defense of the BP, but this proves to be a vain hope. 21 . . . QR-KKt would be answered by 22 RxB!

Position after Black's 21st move

22 Kt-Kt5!

For Black cannot reply 22 . . . RxP because of 23 Kt-Q6, nor 22 . . . BxP; 23 Kt-Q6, QR-B; 24 R-QB followed by R-B7ch.

22	P-Kt3
23 Kt-Q6	QR-B
24 P-B4	KR-Kt
25 RxR	

Taking advantage of the fact that 25 . . . RxR would cost a P after 26 RxR, BxR; 27 Kt-B8ch. The removal of one pair of Rs greatly simplifies matters and makes the win quite easy.

| 25 . . . . | BxR |
| 26 P-KR4! | |

Marco comments admiringly on Lasker's cogent play hereabouts. The text is intended to hem in the B still further by preventing a subsequent . . . B-Kt3.

26	R-Q
27 P-R5	K-B
28 P-R4	B-R2
29 P-R5!	

It is clear that the capture of the P would soon turn out to be fatal for Black.

| 29 . . . . | R-Kt |
| 30 PxP | RxP |

This allows the BP to become passed, but after 30 . . . PxP; 31 R-QR-R7, Black's pieces are paralyzed.

31 P-B5	R-B3
32 K-Q4	B-B7
33 R-QB	B-Kt6
34 R-QKt	B-Q4
35 P-B5	B-B6
36 PxP	

P-B6 would be equally conclusive.

36	BxP
37 PxP	BxP
38 R-KB	Resigns

GAME No. 39

London 1899

Ruy Lopez

White	Black
F. J. Lee	**Dr. E. Lasker**
1 P-K4	P-K4
2 Kt-KB3	Kt-QB3
3 B-Kt5	P-QR3
4 B-R4	Kt-B3
5 P-Q3	P-Q3
6 P-B3	P-QKt4
7 B-B2	

White's play is so timorous that Lasker is soon enabled to seize the initiative without difficulty.

7 . . . .   P-Kt3

This is much better than deploying the B at K2.

8 P-QR4   B-QKt2

As a rule this move is not good because it allows White to plant a Kt at KB5; in the present instance, however, it is unobjectionable because White does not have access to this square.

9 QKt-Q2   B-Kt2
10 Kt-B   P-Q4

Black's position is already superior.

11 Q-K2   O-O
12 Kt-Kt3

Here White might first have interpolated 12 RPxP, RPxP; 13 RxR etc.

12 . . . .   Q-Q3
13 O-O   KR-K
14 P-R3   Kt-QR4

Having obtained an advantageous opening, Lasker commences the middle-game operations by rounding off his Pawn formation.

15 B-Q2

After this move Black's command of the board becomes really formidable. Unfortunately 15 P-QKt4 would not do because of . . . Kt-B3 followed by 16 . . . P-Q5!

15 . . . .   P-B4
16 KR-Q

If 16 P-B4, PxKP; 17 Kt(Kt3) xP, BxKt; 18 BxKt, BxKt; 19 Q xB, P-Kt5∓.

16 . . . .   Q-B2

Preparing for the advance of the BP.

17 Q-K

It would have been better to retreat to B, in order to avoid the unpleasant *vis-a-vis* on the K file, as the next note shows. But even then . . . P-B5 would be a formidable move to meet.

17 . . . .   P-B5!

Parrying the transparent threat of P-B4 and at the same time disorganizing White's game still further.

18 P-Q4

Losing a P. 18 KPxP would likewise be bad because of 18 . . . BPxP; 19 BxP, P-K5 winning a piece. Perhaps QPxP would have been best.

18 . . . .   KtxP
19 KtxKt   PxKt
20 KtxP   BxKt
21 PxB   QxP
22 B-K3

White has lost a P without any compensation. The rest requires only technical skill.

22 . . . .   Kt-B3
23 P-QKt3   Kt-R4

In order to force White's reply.

24 P-QKt4   Kt-B3
25 R-Q7

White's belated efforts to obtain counter-play only assist Lasker in his objectives: gaining control of the Q file and undertaking a general K side advance.

25 . . . .   R-K2
26 R(Q7)-Q   R-Q
27 RxRch   KtxR
28 PxP   PxP
29 Q-Q2   Kt-K3
30 P-R4   B-Q4
31 R-R6   R-Q2
32 Q-K   B-Kt2
33 R-R5   P-B4!

34	P-Kt3	P-B5
35	PxP	KtxP
36	B-Q4	Q-KB4
37	Q-K3	

Position after White's 37th move

37	. . . .	RxB!

Beginning an accurately calcu-lated combination which leads to a piquant finish. All of White's moves are forced. (Subsequently Dr. Tarrasch pointed out the following elegant win; 37 . . .Q-Kt5 ch; 38 K-B, Q-Kt7ch; 39 K-K, Q-Kt8ch; 40 K-Q2, Kt-Kt7; 41 Q-K2, P-K6ch! 42 PxP, B-B6!)

38	PxR	Q-Kt5ch
39	K-B	Q-Kt7ch
40	K-K	Q-Kt8ch
41	K-Q2	P-B6ch!
42	QxP	QxPch
43	K-Q	P-K6
44	B-Kt3ch	K-Kt2
45	P-Q5 dis ch	K-R3
46	Q-K	B-B!

This was the move on which Lasker relied when he played his 37th move.

White resigned.

GAME No. 40

London 1899
(*1st brilliancy prize*)
Vienna Game

White	Black
W. Steinitz	**Dr. E. Lasker**
1 P-K4	P-K4
2 Kt-QB3	Kt-KB3
3 P-B4	P-Q4
4 P-Q3	

This unusual move was a great favorite with Steinitz, although in his later years he was uniformly unsuccessful with it.

| 4 . . . . | Kt-B3 |

Steinitz's opponents as a rule replied . . . P-Q5 at this point; in his game with Pillsbury from the same tournament, the continu-ation was 5 QKt-K2, Kt-B3; 6 Kt-KB3, B-Kt5; 7 P-B3, B-Q3; whereby Black sacrifices a P for a speculative attack.

5 BPxP	QKtxP
6 P-Q4	

This is the beginning of White's difficulties. Kt-B3 or PxP would have been better.

6	Kt-Kt3
7 PxP	

The *Handbuch* gives the follow-ing variation after 7 P-K5: . . . Kt-K5; 8 KtxKt, PxKt; 9 B-QB4, P-QB4! 10 P-B3, PxP; 11 PxP, B-Kt5ch; 12 B-Q2, BxBch; 13 Q xB, O-O; 14 Kt-K2, B-K3; 15 P-QKt3, Q-Kt3!∓.

7	KtxP
8 KtxKt?	

There was no good reason for thus flinging away several tempi and facilitating Black's develop-ment, all the more so since 8 B-QB4, KtxKt; 9 PxKt, Q-R5ch; 10 P-Kt3, Q-K5ch; 11 Q-K2, Qx Qch; 12 KtxQ, B-KB4; 13 B-Kt3 leads to an ending with only a minimal disadvantage for White.

8	QxKt
9 Kt-B3	B-Kt5
10 B-K2	O-O-O
11 P-B3	

Schlechter points out that this move is sheer waste of time and recom-mends castling instead. If then 11 . . . BxKt; 12 RxB! QxPch(12 . . . Kt-R5; 13 R-B2, P-QB4? 14 Q-Q3! threatening Q-R3ch); 13 QxQ, RxQ; 14 RxP=.

11	B-Q3
12 O-O	KR-K!

Lasker has obtained a beautiful position while Steinitz has not yet had an opportunity of completing his development.

13 P-KR3   B-Q2

If now 14 P-B4, Q-K3; 15 B-Q3, Kt-B5; 16 BxKt, BxB and White's center Ps are weak (Mieses).

14 Kt-Kt5

At first sight this move seems to usher in a decided change for the better in White's fortunes.

14 . . . .   Kt-R5!

But not 14 . . . P-KB3; 15 B-B3, Q-Kt; 16 Kt-K4 etc. The text is the prelude to a very fine com-bination.

(See diagram next column)

15 Kt-B3

I   15 R-B2, B-Kt6 winning the exchange.

Position after Black's 14th move

II   15 B-B3, KtxBch;

(a)   16 KtxKt, B-Kt4; 17 R-K, B-Kt6∓.

(b)   16 QxKt, QxQ; 17 RxQ, R-K8ch; 18 R-B (18 K-B2, QR-K), QR-K; 19 B-Q2, RxQR; 20 RxR, R-K7; 21 R-Q, B-B3; 22 Kt-B3, P-B3∓.

15	KtxP!!
16 KxKt	BxPch!

An elegant combination which reveals the point of the foregoing sacrifice, for if now 17 KxB, Q-B4ch; 18 K-Kt2, Q-Kt5ch; 19 K-R, Q-R6ch; 20 K-Kt, Q-Kt6ch; 21 K-R, R-K5; 22 B-KKt5, R-Kt5; 23 R-KKt, Q-R6ch and mate next move.

17 K-B2

One would now expect the plausible reply . . . BxR, but Lasker finds a much stronger con-tinuation which is far from obvi-ous.

17	P-KB3!
18 R-KKt	

White is helpless against the in-tended advance of the K side Ps. 18 R-R would be answered by . . . Q-KB4, threatening . . . B-Kt6ch! with fatal effect.

18 . . . .   P-KKt4
19 BxP

Else Black continues . . . P-K
R4 etc. 19 Kt-K (hoping to stop
. . . P-KR4) would be refuted by
. . . Q-B4ch.

19 . . . .   PxB
20 RxP   Q-K3
21 Q-Q3   B-B5

Winning the exchange, for if
22 R-R5, Q-Kt5! or 22 R-Kt7, B-
B4.

22 R-R   BxR
23 KtxB   Q-B3ch
24 B-B3   B-B4
25 KtxP   Q-KKt3

Trapping the Kt.

26 Q-Kt5

A desperate sortie to save his
self-respect before resigning.

26 . . . .   P-B3
27 Q-R5   R-K2!

Killing two birds with one stone,
for if now 28 QxP, R-Kt; 29 Q-
R8ch, K-B2; 30 Q-R5ch, K-Kt
and wins.

28 R-R5   B-Kt5
29 R-KKt5   Q-B7ch

Not 29 . . . QxKt? 30 BxBch.

30 K-Kt3   BxB
Resigns.

GAME No. 41

Paris 1900

Queen's Gambit Declined

White	Black
A. Burn	**Dr. E. Lasker**
1 P-Q4	P-Q4
2 P-QB4	P-K3
3 Kt-QB3	Kt-KB3
4 Kt-B3	P-B4
5 BPxP	BPxP

5 . . . KtxP is safer, for example 6 KtxKt, QxKt; 7 B-K3!
Kt-R3! 8 P-KKt3, PxP = (Kash-
dan-Alekhine, Folkestone 1933).

6 QxP   KtxP
7 P-K4

7 KtxKt is certainly better.
Burn is playing for a draw, and
this accounts for his allowing the
Q side Ps to be weakened.

7 . . . .   KtxKt
8 QxQch   KxQ
9 PxKt   B-B4
10 Kt-K5

Now White realizes the weakness of his position; but such artificial maneuvers only make his
game worse. 10 Kt-Q4 followed,
if 10 . . . K-K2, by 11 B-K3,
was preferable to the text.

10 . . . .   K-K2!

Since Black's 12th move is . . .
K-K, it may seem that this is mere
loss of time. Yet the move is only
another example of Lasker's remarkable precision; for if 10 . . .
K-K; 11 B-Kt5ch, Kt-Q2; 12 K-
K2, P-QR3; 13 BxKtch, BxB; 14
KtxB, KxKt; 15 B-K3. Now Black
must either exchange Bs, in which
case the ending is drawn, or else
he must avoid the exchange, allowing White to place his B excel-
lently for both attack and defense,
so that the game will probably end
in a draw, a possibility being 15
. . . B-R6; 16 KR-Qch, K-K2; 17
QR-Kt, P-QKt4; 18 P-B4! PxP;
19 R-Kt7ch, K-B3; 20 R(Q)-
Q7 and White has the better game,
for if 20 . . . KR-KB; 21 R(Kt7)-
B7, QR-B? 22 RxPch±.

11 Kt-Q3   B-Kt3
12 B-R3ch   K-K

13 Kt-K5

To play his Kt to Q6.

13 . . . .   Kt-Q2
14 B-Kt5

If 14 Kt-B4, B-B4; 15 Kt-Q6ch, K-K2; 16 BxB, KtxB; 17 P-K5, B-Q2; White's Kt does not accomplish much at Q6, while Black's superior Pawn position gives him the better game.

14 . . . .   B-B2!

Again very precisely played. If 14 . . . P-QR3; 15 BxKtch, Bx B; 16 Kt-B4 forces Bs of opposite color, so that Black's winning chances are slight.

15 Kt-Q3

15 BxKtch would be answered by . . . BxB; 16 KtxB, KxKt; 17 R-Qch,K-B3 and White's B is badly placed, while his Rs have no future on the Q file: Black retains the advantage. Other plausible moves are likewise inadequate for White:

I 15 BxKtch, BxB; 16 Kt-B4, B-B3; 17 P-B3, R-Q∓.

II 15 Kt-B4, P-QR3; 16 Bx Ktch, KxB! 17 R-Qch, K-B3; 18 Kt-Q6, P-B3!∓.

15 . . . .   P-QR3
16 B-R4   P-QKt4
17 B-Kt3   B-Kt2
18 P-B3   R-QB!

It is essential to prevent White from playing P-QB4. If now 19 P-QB4, PxP; 20 BxP, B-R4ch.

19 K-Q2   P-QR4
20 QR-QKt   B-B3

Prophylaxis! Black intends . . . Kt-Kt3 followed by . . . Kt-B5 (at the proper moment), . . . P-B3, . . . K-B2 etc. His last two moves were necessary to enable him to carry out this plan; for if White plays Kt-B5 after . . . Kt-Kt3, Lasker can simply reply . . . P-R5 and . . . Kt-B5ch. White therefore retreats voluntarily, but fares equally badly.

21 B-B2   P-B3
22 P-Kt3?

In order to be able to move the KR; 22 P-R3 would also weaken the K side. Better than the text is 22 Kt-B5 and if 22 . . . Kt-Kt3; 23 B-Q3; or 22 . . . KtxKt; 23 BxKt, B-B5ch; 24 K-K2! BxKP; 25 BxB, RxB; 26 RxP!=.

22 . . . .   K-B2
23 K-K2   P-Kt4!

Taking advantage of White's weak 22nd move. The threat is . . . P-KKt5.

24 P-Kt4

But now the RP is again weak.

24 . . . .   P-R4!
25 P-R3   B-Kt
26 B-Kt2   Kt-Kt3
27 Kt-B5   B-K
28 Kt-Kt3

Not 28 B-R3? Kt-B5!

28 . . . .   Kt-B5

Threatening to win the QBP.

29 B-B

White cannot avoid the crippling of his K side Ps, for after 29 B-R, Kt-R6; 30 QR-QB, PxP; 31 BPxP, B-B5; 32 Kt-Q2, B-B3 his position would be untenable.

29 . . . .   PxP
30 BPxP   B-K4!

The P is attacked for the first time; it cannot be defended di-

rectly, for if 31 B-Q2 KtxB and
White is lost.

31 Kt-Q4

Position after White's 31st move

| 31 . . . . | BxKt! |
| 32 PxB | Kt-R6 |

Obtaining two passed Ps; the Bs
of opposite color have no signifi-
cance.

33 BxKt	RxBch
34 K-Q3	RxP
35 B-Q6	P-Kt5
36 QR-QB	B-Kt4ch
37 K-K3	K-Kt3

If 37 . . . RxPch; 38 RxR, R-
R6ch; 39 K any, RxR; 40 R-B7
ch, K-Kt3; 41 B-B8, R-R2; 42 R
xR, KxR the game is won for
Black, but it is a bit difficult.
White's RP will not run away.

38 R-B5	R-R6ch
39 K-B2	B-Q6
40 R-K	RxP
41 R-B7	R-QR7ch
42 K-Kt	R-KR5
43 P-K5	RxPch
44 K-R	B-K5ch
Resigns	

Spielmannn says of this game:
"Although Burn did not play this
game as well as he might have,
Lasker's performance was consistently splendid. Probably no other
master would have pressed home
the slight opening advantage so
brilliantly and methodically."

GAME No. 42

Paris 1900

Queen's Gambit

White	Black
Dr. E. Lasker	**G. Maroczy**
1 P-Q4	P-Q4
2 P-QB4	P-K3
3 Kt-QB3	Kt-KB3
4 Kt-B3	PxP
5 P-K3	

If 5 P-K4, B-Kt5! gives Black
a good game.

5	P-B4
6 BxP	P-QR3
7 P-QR4	

Creating a hole at QKt4, but
cramping Black's position.

| 7 . . . | Kt-B3 |
| 8 O-O | PxP |

Simpler is 8 . . . B-K2; 9 Q-
K2, PxP; 10 R-Q, P-K4; 11 PxP,
PxP; 12 KtxP, KtxKt; 13 Q-K5,
Q-Q3!=.

9 PxP	B-K2
10 B-K3	O-O
11 Q-K2	Q-R4

Steinitz's maneuver.

12 KR-Q	R-Q
13 QR-B	Kt-QKt5
14 Kt-K5	Kt(B3)-Q4?

Black's next few moves are incomprehensible. 14 . . . B-Q2 followed by . . . B-K would have
equalized.

| 15 B-Kt3 | R-B? |

. . . B-Q2 was still the move,
for the possible reply 16 Kt-B4,

Q-B2; 17 KtxKt, KtxKt leads to nothing.

16 Kt-K4!

Now White is able to avoid exchanges and thus build up a promising attack.

| 16 . . . . | Q-Q |
| 17 P-B4 | P-QKt3 |

Inferior to . . . B-Q2-QB3.

18 B-Q2	B-Kt2
19 Kt-Kt3	R-B
20 P-B5	

Undermining the position of the blockader on Black's Q4.

20 . . . .   RxR

Not good because it relinquishes control of the QB file; but Black has no really good moves.

21 RxR   PxP

If 21 . . . B-Kt4; 22 BxKt (Kt4), BxR; 23 BxR, QxB; 24 Kt-Q3, Kt-B5; 25 KtxKt, BxKt; 26 PxP with a winning game.

22 KtxP(B5)

Position after White's 22nd move

22 . . . .   B-KB3

A mistake in a bad position. The Tournament Book recommends 22 . . . B-B; 23 BxKt (Kt4), BxB; 24 Kt-B6, Q-Kt4 with a defensible

position. But Lasker would have refuted 22 . . . B-B with 23 Ktx BP!! (see the note to White's 20th move), which leads to some charming positions:

I   23 . . . KxKt; 24 RxB! Q-Q2 (forced; if 24 . . . QxR; 25 QxBch, K-Kt3; 26 Kt-R4ch, K-R4; 27 Q-Kt5 mate); 25 Q-R5ch and wins.

II   23 . . . RxKt; 24 QxB!!

a) 24 . . . RxQ; 25 RxB! Qx R; 26 KtxRch etc.

b) 24 . . . QxQ; 25 KtxQch, KtxKt(25 . . . RxKt; 26 RxBch, K-B2; 27 BxKt(Kt4) etc.); 26 BxKt and Black's position is hopeless.

c) 24 . . . KtxQ; 25 KtxKtch, QxKt (or 25 . . . K-R; 26 RxB, or 25 . . . K-B; 26 RxB, KxKt; 27 BxKtch); 26 RxBch, Q-B; 27 BxRch, KxB; 28 RxQch, KxR; 29 BxKtch and Black can resign.

23 BxKt(Kt4)	KtxB
24 KtxBP!	RxKt
25 Q-K6	K-R

There is no defense: if 25 . . . Q-KB; 26 R-B7 wins; or if 25 . . . B-Q4; 26 BxB, KtxB; 27 R-B8; while if 25 . . . Kt-Q4; 26 Kt-Q6, Q-K2; 27 BxKt! BxPch; 28 K-R winning easily.

26 QxR	BxPch
27 K-R	Kt-Q6
28 R-B	BxPch

Not bad, because the position is beyond good and evil!

| 29 KxB | Q-Kt4ch |
| 30 K-R3 | Resigns |

An elegant game. It is, incidentally, one of those rare encounters where Lasker wins by a direct attack on his adversary's K.

GAME No. 43

Paris 1900
Dutch Defense

White	Black
Dr. E. Lasker	**H. N. Pillsbury**

1 P-Q4	P-KB4
2 P-K4	PxP
3 Kt-QB3	Kt-KB3
4 B-KKt5	P-B3

Perhaps 4 . . . P-QKt3 is preferable.

5 P-B3

The only continuation which enables White to maintain the initiative. If 5 BxKt, KPxB; 6 KtxP, P-Q4=.

5 . . . . PxP

. . . P-K6 is no better, since it does not lessen the force of White's attack.

6 KtxP P-K3

Pillsbury's opening play is inconsistent, so that he soon obtains an inferior game. 6 . . . P-KKt3 was in order.

7 B-Q3	B-K2
8 Kt-K5!	

An excellent move which at least regains the P sacrificed. The tempting reply 8 . . . P-Q3 is refuted by 9 BxKt! BxB; 10 Q-R5ch, P-Kt3; 11 BxPch, K-K2! 12 B-K 4!! PxKt; 13 PxP, B-Kt2; 14 R-Q regaining the piece with the superior game.

8 . . . . O-O

Or 8 . . . Q-B2; 9 BxKt, BxB; 10 Q-R5ch, P-Kt3; 11 BxPch! etc.

Position after Black's 8th move

9 BxKt! RxB

There is nothing better:

I 9 . . . BxB; 10 Q-R5, P-KR3; 11 Q-Kt6, BxKt; 12 PxB with a winning attack, for example 12 . . . Q-Kt4; 13 Q-R7ch, K-B2; 14 O-O ch, K-K2; 15 RxR, KxR; 16 R-Bch, K-K2; 17 Q-R8 and mate can be staved off only with problem moves, or 12 . . . R-B2; 13 Q-R7ch, K-B; 14 B-Kt6 and the R cannot move; or 12 . . . R-B5; 13 Kt-K2, R-B2; 14 Q-R7ch as above.

II 9 . . . PxB; 10 Q-Kt4ch, K-R; 11 Kt-Kt6ch! PxKt; 12 BxP, P-B4 forced; 13 Q-R5ch, K-Kt2; 14 Q-R7ch, K-B3; 15 Kt-K4ch! P xKt; 16 O-Och, K-Kt4; 17 Q-R5 mate.

10 Q-R5 P-KKt3

Superior to 10 . . . P-KR3; 11 Kt-Kt4, R-B5; 12 KtxPch! and wins.

11 KtxKtP!

The point of the combination begun on White's 8th move. If in reply 11 . . . PxKt; 12 BxP, Rx B forced; 13 QxRch, K-R; 14 O-O (threatening R-B7), Q-Kt; 15 Q-R5ch winning.

11	. . . .	Q-K
12	KtxBch	QxKt
13	O-O-O	

13 Kt-K4, R-Kt3; 14 Kt-Kt3, R-B3 is less convincing than the text.

| 13 | . . . . | P-Q4 |
| 14 | QR-K | |

Good; but more forceful was 14 KR-B, Kt-Q2; 15 R-B3.

14	. . . .	Kt-Q2
15	R-K3	R-B2
16	R-Kt3ch	K-R

Not 16 . . . R-Kt2?? 17 QxPch.

| 17 | B-Kt6 | R-Kt2 |

Or 17 . . . R-B3; 18 Kt-Q, Kt-B; 19 Q-R4!(threatening R-B) with advantage, for if 19 . . . R-B2; 20 BxR!!

18	R-B	Kt-B3
19	Q-R4	Kt-Kt
20	QxQ	RxQ
21	B-Q3	B-Q2

Pillsbury has defended himself very well; apparently he will now have time to consolidate his position and thereby obtain equality.

22 Kt-Kt!

Beginning a profound maneuver. Black's weak K side and backward KP are sufficiently troublesome to give White the necessary time to bring his Kt to an effective post.

| 22 | . . . . | QR-K |

If 22 . . . R-Kt2; 23 Kt-Q2, RxR; 24 PxR, K-Kt2; 25 Kt-B3, Kt-B3; 26 Kt-K5, B-K; 27 P-KKt4, P-KR3; 28 K-Q2±. 22 . . . P-K4 was not feasible because of 23 PxP, RxP; 24 R-B7, R-K2; 25 R xKtch! etc.

| 23 | Kt-Q2 | P-K4 |

Else Kt-B3-K5 will leave Black's KP permanently backward.

24	PxP	RxP
25	Kt-B3	R-K6
26	Kt-Kt5!	RxR
27	PxR	P-KR3

Not 27 . . . R-K2; 28 BxP! R xB; 29 KtxR, KxKt; 30 R-B7ch.

| 28 | Kt-B7ch | K-Kt2 |
| 29 | Kt-Q6 | |

Threatening both KtxP and R-B7ch.

| 29 | . . . . | R-K2 |
| 30 | KtxP | |

Although White has won a P, the win is by no means easy, because of his doubled P.

| 30 | . . . . | Kt-B3 |
| 31 | Kt-B5 | B-Kt5 |

If 31 . . . Kt-R4; 32 KtxB, R xKt; 33 P-KKt4, Kt-B3; 34 B-B5, R-KB2; 35 R-B3±.

| 32 | R-B4 | B-B |
| 33 | R-QR4 | Kt-Kt5 |

If now 33 . . . Kt-R4; 34 P-KKt4, Kt-B3; 35 B-B5 etc.

| 34 | B-R6 | B-B4 |

If 34 . . . BxB? 35 RxKtch wins a piece.

35	R-KB4	Kt-K6
36	P-B3	K-Kt3
37	R-B2	B-K5
38	P-Kt3	

38 KtxB, PxKt would give Black a dangerous passed P. The text enables White, at the cost of a P, to advance his K on the Q side.

| 38 | . . . . | BxP |
| 39 | B-Q3ch | K-Kt4? |

Up to this point Pillsbury's defense has been exemplary, but here

he goes astray. 39 . . . B-K5!
would have equalized:

I 40 BxBch, PxB; 41 R-K2,
Kt-Q4; 42 K-Q2 (or 42 RxP, Rx
R; 43 KtxR, K-B4; 44 Kt-Q6ch,
K-Kt5; 45 P-B4, Kt-K2; 46 Kt-
K4, K-B6 etc.), Kt-B3 and Black
at least draws.

II 40 KtxB, PxKt; 41 B-Kt,
Kt-Q4! 42 P-B4(or 42 K-Kt2, K-
Kt4), Kt-B6 and again Black has
no serious difficulties.

His previous strenuous exer-
tions or time-pressure may account
for this lapse.

40 R-B8	K-Kt5
41 R-Kt8ch	K-B6
42 R-Kt6	Kt-Kt5
43 B-B5	P-KR4
44 R-Kt5	R-K8ch

. . . KxP would have been
slightly stronger, but White would
still have won because of the weak
Q side Ps.

45 K-Kt2	R-KR8
46 B-Kt6	KxP
47 BxP	B-B6
48 BxKt	BxB
49 R-Kt6	R-R7ch
50 K-R3	R-QB7
51 Kt-Q3!	

Avoiding the trap 51 RxP, Rx
P! 52 Kt-K4ch, PxKt; 53 RxRch,
K-B7; 54 R-B7, P-K6; 55 RxP,
P-K7; 56 R-K7, P-K8=Q; 57 R
xQ, KxR and the game is drawn.

51	K-R5

Not 51 . . . RxP; 52 Kt-K5,
K-B5; 53 KtxB, R-Kt6; 54 Kt-K5!
and wins.

52 Kt-K5

Simpler than 52 RxP, P-Q5!
and Black has a passed P.

52	B-B4
53 RxP	K-Kt6
54 R-B5	R-Q7
55 Kt-B6	K-B5
56 Kt-Kt4	

KtxP was also good.

56	P-Q5
57 PxP	RxP
58 R-R5	R-Q2
59 Kt-B6	

A slight inaccuracy which how-
ever does not affect the ultimate
outcome. 59 Kt-Q5ch would have
won a bit more quickly, for if 59
. . . K-Kt4(59 . . . K-K5 or 59
. . . K-Kt5 or 59 . . . K-B6; 60
Kt-B6); 60 Kt-K3, R-KB2; 61
KtxB, RxKt; 62 RxRch, KxR; 63
K-Kt4 etc. winning easily.

59	B-K5
60 KtxP	R-Q7

There followed: 61 Kt-Kt5, R-
Q4; 62 K-Kt4, B-Q6; 63 Kt-B7,
RxR; 64 KxR, K-K4; 65 K-Kt4,
K-Q3; 66 Kt-Kt5ch, K-B3; 67 P-
R4, K-Kt3; 68 Kt-R3, B-K7; 69
Kt-B4ch, K-R3; 70 K-B3, B-Q8;
71 Kt-Kt2, B-R4; 72 P-Kt4, B-K;
73 K-Kt3, B-B3; 74 K-B4, B-Q2;
75 K-B5, B-Kt5; 76 Kt-B4, B-Q8;
77 P-Kt5ch, K-R2; 78 P-R5, B-
B6; 79 Kt-K5, B-Kt2; 80 Kt-B6
ch, K-R; 81 K-Kt6, B-R3! 82 Kt-
Kt4, B-Kt2; 83 Kt-R6, B-B6; 84
Kt-B7ch, K-Kt; 85 P-R6 and
Black resigned.

GAME No. 44

Cambridge Springs 1904
Queen's Gambit Declined

White	Black
Dr. E. Lasker	**E. Delmar**

1 P-Q4	P-Q4
2 P-QB4	P-K3
3 Kt-QB3	Kt-KB3
4 B-Kt5	QKt-Q2
5 P-K3	B-K2
6 Kt-B3	P-KR3
7 B-R4	P-B3
8 Q-B2	PxP

It is better to spare a tempo by deferring this capture until White has moved the KB.

9 BxP   Kt-Kt3

An artificial maneuver which contributes very little to the problem of how Black is to free his game.

10 B-K2

After the more natural B-Q3, Black could reply 10 . . . KKt-Q 4, threatening . . . Kt-Kt5 and thus forcing an exchange of Bs.

10	KKt-Q4
11 B-Kt3	KtxKt
12 PxKt	O-O
13 O-O	B-Q2

A colorless move, but Black has no really good plan at his disposal.

14 P-QR4!	Kt-Q4
15 KR-Kt	

With his last two moves, White has built up a formidable position on the Queen's wing.

15 . . . .   B-B?

. . . P-QKt3 was essential to prevent Lasker's next move.

16 P-R5!

Intensifying the pressure on the open file; White intends P-B4 without having to fear . . . Kt-Kt5 followed by . . . P-QR4.

16 . . . .   B-Q3
17 P-B4!

Lasker is quite willing to exchange Bs, as he foresees that the ensuing weakness of the black squares will make possible the subsequent tour of White's Kt to Q6.

17 . . . .   Kt-K2

Not 17 . . . BxB; 18 PxKt, B-Q3; 19 PxBP, Q-B2; 20 PxP!

18 P-B5	BxB
19 RPxB	P-R3

Allowing White an important point of invasion at QKt6.

20 Kt-K5	Q-B2
21 Q-Kt2!	

In order to prevent Black from bringing out his B; furthermore . . . R-Kt is impossible because of BxP.

21	R-Q
22 Kt-B4	R-Kt
23 Kt-Q6	

This powerfully posted Kt paralyzes Black's attempts at counterplay.

23 . . . .   Kt-B4

A desperate but superficial resource; Black's Q side Ps were untenable in any event.

24 KtxKt	PxKt
25 BxP	P-B5

Threatening to win the exchange by . . . B-B4.

26 Q-Kt6

This move, as powerful as it is simple, leaves no doubt about the result.

26	QxQ
27 RxQ	PxKtP
28 PxP	R-K
29 K-B2	R-K3
30 B-B4!	R-B3ch
31 K-Kt	R-R

White threatened 32 P-R6, R-R; 33 QR-Kt, PxP; 34 R-Kt8 and wins.

| 32 P-K4 | R-Kt3 |

Position after Black's 32nd move

Lasker now forces the win with a few energetic strokes.

33 P-R6!	PxP
34 QR-Kt	B-K3
35 P-Q5	PxP
36 PxP	B-B4
37 R-Kt8ch	K-R2

37 . . . RxR; 38 RxRch, K-R2; 39 P-Q6, B-Q2; 40 B-Q3, P-B4; 41 R-Q8 is equally hopeless.

38 RxR	BxR
39 P-Q6	B-B4
40 B-Q3	Resigns

An elegant conclusion to a well-played game.

GAME No. 45

Cambridge Springs 1904
Sicilian Defense

| White | Black |
| **Dr. E. Lasker** | **W. E. Napier** |

1 P-K4	P-QB4
2 Kt-QB3	Kt-QB3
3 Kt-B3	P-KKt3
4 P-Q4	PxP
5 KtxP	B-Kt2
6 B-K3	P-Q3
7 P-KR3	Kt-B3
8 P-KKt4	

Divers subtle motivations have been imputed to Lasker's last two moves; the conscientious analyst can say with certainty only that they are objectively bad, since they are made with a view to an attack which is premature and can therefore be repulsed.

| 8 . . . . | O-O |

Seemingly a case of "castling into it"; but Napier rightly realizes that he must meet the wing advance with a counter-thrust in the center.

9 P-Kt5	Kt-K
10 P-KR4	Kt-B2
11 P-B4	P-K4!
12 KKt-K2	P-Q4! ?

Beginning a whole series of glorious combinations, but the simple move 12 . . . B-Kt5 (suggested by Dr. Kaufmann) would have given him a fine game without any risk whatever.

13 KPxP

On 13 KtxP Black obtains an excellent game with 13 . . . PxP; 14 KtxKt, (14 B-B5, R-K; or 14 BxBP, KtxKt; 15 PxKt, Kt-Kt5 is even better for Black), QxKt; 15

BxBP, Q-K2; 16 B-Kt2, Q-Kt5ch
etc. (Marco).

13 . . . .   Kt-Q5!

Marco points out that 14 BxKt,
PxB; 15 KtxP, KtxP would now
clearly be in Black's favor:

I   16 KtxKt, QxKt; 17 Kt-B3,
QxQch (the simplest); 18 RxQ,
BxP.

II 16 KKt-K2, Kt-K6; 17 Qx
Q, RxQ; 18 R-B, B-B4.

14 KtxKt!   KtxP!

And now if 15 KtxKt? PxKt! 16
BxP, QxKt; 17 BxB, QxR; 18 BxR,
QxPch∓ (Marco).

15 Kt-B5!!

A beautiful parry, which seems
to win a piece.

15 . . . .   KtxKt!

An equally fine reply, which
Napier must have foreseen when
he advanced the QP.

16 QxQ   RxQ
17 Kt-K7ch!

Napier deserves great credit for
having calculated that he can still
maintain the balance of power (in
material!). For if 17 KtxB, Kt-Q4;
18 B-Q2, PxP ∓; or 17 PxKt,
BxKt∓.

17 . . . .   K-R!

Consistently playing the best
moves: if 17 . . . K-B? 18B-B5,
Kt-K5; 19 B-QR3, Kt-Q3; 20 Kt
xB, QRxKt; 21 O-O-O, K-K2; 22
B-Kt2 and wins.

Marco points out that we can
appreciate the depth of Napier's
play when we note that White is
now seemingly without a good
continuation:

I   18 KtxB, Kt-Q4! (or 18
. . . PxP; 19 B-Q2, Kt-K5!)∓.

II   18 PxKt, PxP; 19 B-Q4, B
xB; 20 PxB, R-K and Black is a
P ahead with the superior position.

But the ever resourceful Lasker
has a way out!

Position after Black's 17th move

18 P-R5!!

Giving the game a wholly new
turn! Black is now threatened with
a crushing attack on his K, for
example 19 RPxP, BPxP; 20 Ktx
Pch, K-Kt; 21 B-B4ch, Kt-Q4; 22
BxKtch, RxB; 23 Kt-K7ch etc.

18 . . . .   R-K!
19 B-B5!   KtPxP!

Says Marco: "Is it not queer
that Napier avoids 19 . . . KPxP,
which would remove the attack on
his KtP, protect the Kt, and increase the scope of his KR and
KB? This question deserves careful
study (after 19 . . . KPxP):

I   20 PxKt, BxPch; 21 K-B2,
BxR; 22 B-B4, B-Kt2; 23 KtxPch,
BPxKt; 24 PxP, P-KR3; 25 Rx
Pch! BxR; 26 PxB, R-Q; 27 B-
K7 and wins.

II 20 PxKt, BxPch; 21 K-B2,
BxR; 22 B-B4, B-B6; 23 BxBP,

RxKt best; 24 PxP!! RxB; 25 Px R, B-Kt2 (25 . . . B-B4; 26 P-B8 = Qch yields White a winning end-game); 26 P-Kt6, P-KR3; 27 RxPch; BxR; 28 B-Q4ch, B-Kt2; 29 P-B8=Q mate.

III Perhaps Black can avoid these unfortunate variations by a timely sacrifice of the exchange?! Let us see: 20 PxKt, RxKtch!! 21 BxR, BxPch; 22 K-B2, BxR; 23 B-B4, B-Q5ch; 24 K-B3, B-KB4! and the game slowly begins to in-cline in Black's favor. True; but White has a much better line of play after 19 . . . KPxP.

IV 20 PxP! PxP; 21 B-B4!! P-Kt4!! best; 22 B-B7, B-Kt2; 23 R-R2, Kt-Q4; 24 BxR, RxB; 25 O-O-O! (better than R-K2), Ktx Kt; 26 BxKt (if white is too stingy to give up the QKtP, he can play R-Q7), BxPch! 27 KxB, RxB. The two Ps are hardly compensation for the exchange: 28 KR-Q2, K-Kt2; 29 R-Q7, K-B2; 30 K-B3, P-B6; 31 RxRch, KxR; 32 K-Q4. Black's BP is quite harmless, and White's R is free to pick up some Ps. Black has no satisfactory de-fense, and thus 19 . . . KPxP is shown to be hopeless."

20 B-B4!!

20 PxKt, B-B; 21 B-Kt5! Rx Kt; 22 BxR, BxB would be quite satisfactory for Black, as his strong Bs compensate for his exchange minus.

20 . . . .   PxP!!

A stroke of genius which gives a new lease of life to the attack. Did Black have anything better? We will answer this question with the aid of the indispensable Marco,

whose analysis to this game is in itself a work of art:

I 20 . . . B-B; 21 BxBP, Bx Kt; 22 BxR, BxB; 23 PxKt, B-K Kt5; 24 BxP and Black has noth-ing to show for his being the ex-change down.

II 20 . . . B-K3; 21 BxB, P xB; 22 PxKt, B-B! 23 B-Q6! Px P (if 23 . . . BxKt; 24 BxPch, K-Kt; 25 RxP±); 24 RxP, Bx Kt; 25 B-K5ch, K-Kt; 26 O-O-O, B-B! 27 B-B6! and Black's position is extremely uncomfortable; his only chance would be to give up his KRP by 27 . . . K-B2 with a view to utilizing his KP and BP.

21 BxBP!

From this point on, Lasker's moves are not spectacular, but they are exceedingly well timed and forceful. Yet according to Napier himself, Lasker had only three minutes for this and his next nine moves!

21 . . . .   Kt-K5!!

A magnificent attempt to force the game. One of the many piquant features of this superb struggle is the unconcern with which the players have allowed this Kt to re-main *en prise*.

22 BxR   BxP
23 QR-Kt   B-B6ch
24 K-B   B-KKt5!

The game has reached its high point. Black is a R down, but he threatens . . . RxB or . . . KtxB or . . . Kt-Kt6ch or . . . Kt-Q7 ch. How can White defend him-self against this bewildering array of threats?

25 KBxP!

An amazing reply, but a most

efficacious one: Lasker returns the R, in order to win some Ps!

| 25 . . . . | BxB |

If 25 . . . Kt-Kt6ch; 26 K-B2, BxB (26 . . . KtxB? 27 R-R4!); 27 RxB! transposes into the text continuation.

26 RxB!	Kt-Kt6ch
27 K-Kt2	KtxR
28 RxP	P-R4
29 R-Kt3!	B-Kt2
30 R-KR3	Kt-Kt6
31 K-B3!	R-R3

31 . . . B-K4? 32 Kt-Kt6ch.

32 KxP	Kt-K7ch
33 K-B5	Kt-B6
34 P-R3	Kt-R5
35 B-K3	Resigns

For P-Kt6 will win easily.

Surely it is no exaggeration to say that this game is one of the most beautiful, most profound, most exciting and most difficult in the whole literature of chess!

GAME No. 46

Cambridge Springs 1904

Ruy Lopez

White	Black
A. W. Fox	**Dr. E. Lasker**
1 P-K4	P-K4
2 Kt-KB3	Kt-QB3
3 B-Kt5	P-QR3
4 BxKt	KtPxB

It is interesting to see that Lasker avoids the exchange of Qs with the black pieces. The text move is played much more rarely than . . . QPxP, but it puts the players on their own resources, which was doubtless Lasker's object.

| 5 P-Q4 | PxP |

| 6 QxP | P-Q3 |

After this Black has difficulty in completing his development.

7 O-O	Kt-K2
8 Kt-B3	Kt-Kt3
9 R-K	

Tarrasch rightly points out that White does not understand how to make use of his superior position. He should endeavor to make way for the advance of his KBP.

| 9 . . . . | P-B3 |

Black has a cramped but solid position. The text prepares for . . . B-K2 and stops P-K5 for good.

| 10 Kt-K2 | |

A time-wasting maneuver which forces Black to improve his position. The correct line of play was 10 Q-B4! P-QB4 (if 10 . . . B-Q2; 11 Kt-Q4, Kt-K4; 12 Q-K2 ±); 11 B-K3 followed by QR-Q ±.

10	B-K3
11 Kt-Kt3	P-QB4
12 Q-B3	B-K2

White still has some advantage left; his pieces are posted more aggressively, while Black's KB is stalemated and his Q side Ps may become weak. A good continuation in accordance with the nature of the position would have been 13 B-K3, O-O; 14 QR-Q, Q-Kt; 15 Kt-B5 etc.

| 13 Kt-B5 | O-O |

(See diagram on next page)

14 Kt-Kt5?	BxKt
15 PxB	PxKt
16 PxKt	PxP

The result of White's "combination" is that he has given his op-

Position after Black's 13th move

ponent another open file and a beautiful diagonal for his B—and White must compromise his K side in order to regain the P.

17 Q-Q3	R-B4
18 P-KKt4	R-B2
19 QxKtP	B-B3!

Badly hampering White's development.

20 P-QB3	R-Kt!
21 R-K3	Q-Q2!
22 Q-R5	R-K2
23 RxR	

And not 23 R-R3 because of . . . R-K8ch; 24 K-Kt2, Q-B3ch; 25 P-B3, Q-Kt4 and White can resign.

| 23 . . . . | QxR |
| 24 B-Q2 | |

Forced, else . . . Q-K8ch, followed by . . . R-K, will be deadly.

| 24 . . . . | RxP |
| 25 R-K | |

Regains the P. All this is very ingenious, but far less important than the prosaic fact that White's Pawn position is ruined.

| 25 . . . . | B-K4 |
| 26 BxP | Q-B |

If now 27 P-KB4, Q-R! wins.

27 B-R4	Q-B2!
28 QxQch	KxQ
29 R-K3	R-B7!

Better than . . . RxRP, as Black now obtains two passed Ps.

| 30 B-Q8 | BxP |
| 31 R-K7ch | |

Or 31 BxP, B-K4; 32 R-Q3, P-B5; 33 R-Q, K-K3 etc.

31	K-B
32 RxBP	B-K4
33 P-Kt5?	K-K
34 B-K7	P-Q4!
35 RxP?	

A blunder, but after R-Kt7 or R-R7 Black would win without any difficulty.

| 35 . . . . | R-Q7! |

There followed: 36 R-R5, KxB; 37 K-Kt2, K-K3; 38 RxPch, K-B 4; 39 P-KR4, B-Q5; 40 R-R8, K-Kt5; 41 R-KB8, RxP; 42 R-B7, RxPch; 43 RxR, BxR; 44 KxB, KxP; 45 K-K3, KxP; White resigns.

GAME No. 47

Cambridge Springs 1904
Ruy Lopez

| White | Black |
| **Dr. E. Lasker** | **M. Tchigorin** |

1 P-K4	P-K4
2 Kt-KB3	Kt-QB3
3 B-Kt5	P-QR3
4 BxKt	QPxB
5 P-Q3	B-Q3

More usual is . . . B-QB4 or . . . P-B3!

| 6 B-K3 | Kt-K2 |
| 7 P-Q4 | B-Kt5 |

A strangely inconsistent move.

The correct continuation (and one which seems the logical conse-quence of Black's last two moves), was . . . P-B3. In this way Black could hold the center with about even chances.

    8 QKt-Q2   Kt-Kt3
    9 P-KR3   BxKt

Freeing White's game appre-ciably. Tarrasch suggests . . . B-K3 or . . . B-Q2 as better moves.

    10 KtxB   Q-K2
    11 Q-Q3   O-O

One would expect castling on the other wing at this point, after which Black would have distinct counter-chances in the center, in addition to saving a tempo in de-veloping the Rs.

    12 O-O-O   KR-K
    13 KR-K   PxP

Why not . . . QR-Q first? The text gives White's B a powerful diagonal, leading to a strong attack after Tchigorin's inaccurate play in the sequel.

    14 BxP   B-B5ch

A pointless continuation unless Black intends to exchange Rs on the Q file. Better would have been . . . Kt-K4.

    15 K-Kt   P-QB4
    16 B-B3   QR-Q
    17 Q-K2   P-QKt4

Black changes his mind from move to move. Here he might have exchanged all the Rs, else his 16th move is meaningless.

    18 P-KKt3   B-Q3
    19 P-KR4   P-KB3

Somewhat mysterious. Tarrasch rightly recommends 19 . . . Kt-K4 in order to exchange at least one pair of minor pieces, thus avoiding the evils attendant upon the text.

    20 P-R5   Kt-B
    21 Kt-R4

"The Kt now takes up a dom-inating position; the absence of Black's QB becomes painfully no-ticeable." (Tarrasch).

    21 .. . . .   P-Kt3

The remedy is worse than the disease.

    22 PxP   PxP
    23 P-B4   Q-B2

In order to forestall P-K5, but . . . Q-Kt2 would have been bet-ter.

    24 Q-Kt4   P-Kt5

A desperate move, but too late.

Position after Black's 24th move

    25 Kt-B5!   Q-B5

At first sight . . . Q-K3 seems more plausible, but Tarrasch gives the following refutation: 25 . . . Q-K3; 26 Kt-R6ch, K-Kt2; 27 P-B5, Q-B; 28 BxPch! KxB; 29 Q-R4ch, K-Kt2; 30 P-B6ch, K-R; 31 P-B7, R-K3; 32 Kt-B5ch, Kt-R2; 33QxKtch! KxQ; 34 R-R mate.

    26 BxBP   R-Q2
    27 Kt-R6ch   K-R2
    28 P-K5   Q-K3

29 Q-R4

Another winning continuation would be 29 QxQ, RxQ; 30 R-R etc.

| 29 . . . . | P-Kt4 |
| 30 QxP | Resigns |

GAME No. 48

Cambridge Springs 1904

Petroff Defense

White	Black
Dr. E. Lasker	**R. Teichmann**
1 P-K4	P-K4
2 Kt-KB3	Kt-KB3
3 KtxP	P-Q3
4 Kt-KB3	KtxP
5 Q-K2	

This move, introduced by Morphy in a well-known game against Lowenthal, was revived by Lasker after a very distressing experience with this defense against Pillsbury (St. Petersburg 1895-6).

5	Q-K2
6 P-Q3	Kt-KB3
7 B-Kt5!	

Morphy's move, which gives White some advantage despite the symmetrical nature of the position.

| 7 . . . | QxQch |

Doubtless playing for a draw. For 7 . . . B-K3 see Game No. 75. 7 . . . B-Kt5; 8 BxKt, BxKt? 9 Q xQch would cost Black a piece.

| 8 BxQ | B-K2 |
| 9 Kt-B3 | |

White is a tempo ahead in a symmetrical position. It is interesting to see how Lasker (with the help of his opponent, to be sure) increases his advantage from move to move. Black should now have played 9 . . . P-B3 and if 10 P-

Q4, B-K3; 11 O-O-O, QKt-Q2 with nothing to fear and an early draw in prospect.

| 9 . . . . | B-Q2 |

In order to prevent Kt-Kt5 (better . . . P-B3). Tarrasch now calls attention to the superiority of White's QB over that of his opponent: a new advantage for White.

| 10 O-O-O | Kt-B3 |
| 11 KR-K | O-O? |

A weak move. Castling on the other wing was clearly indicated, although White would still have the better game after 12 P-Q4.

| 12 P-Q4 | |

Threatening the further advance of this P, which would put the hostile Kt out of play for quite a while.

| 12 . . . . | Kt-KKt5 |

This allows White to obtain a winning position, but it is no longer possible to suggest a wholly adequate move. 12 . . . P-Q4 would of course lose a P, or if 12 . . . KR-K; 13 P-Q5, Kt-K4; 14 KtxKt, PxKt; 15 B-Kt5±.

| 13 BxB | KtxB |
| 14 B-Kt5! | |

A powerful continuation which turns the game distinctly in White's favor.

| 14 . . . . | BxB |

Or 14 . . . QKt-B3; 15 P-Q5, Kt-Kt; 16 P-KR3, Kt-KB3; 17 P-KKt4±.

15 RxKt	B-R3
16 RxQBP	KtxBP
17 R-K	KR-K
18 QR-K7	RxR
19 RxR	

It is certainly surprising to note that by perfectly simple moves in a more or less innocuous variation, Lasker has obtained a won game. The position of his R is qualitatively superior, he has a "steady source of income" from Black's weak Ps, while in addition Black's pieces are all placed rather unfortunately—this being due in large measure to his blunder on the 11th move.

19 . . . .   R-Q

In order to parry the threat of R-Q7.

Position after Black's 19th move

20 Kt-KKt5   Kt-Kt5

Black had a difficult problem before him. He could not very well play 20 . . . P-B3 because of 21 Kt-K6. And 20 . . . R-KB is easily refuted by 21 KKt-K4, Ktx Kt; 22 KtxKt, P-Q4; 23 Kt-B3 or Kt-B5 etc.

21 P-KR3

Lasker plays very carefully, but 21 KtxBP (better than 21 RxBP, P-R3; 22R-B4, Kt-K6 and Black has counter-play), R-KB; 22 Ktx P would have won more quickly after . . . R-B8ch; 23 K-Q2, R-

B7ch; 24 Kt-K2 and the threat of P-QKt4 renders Black's game hopeless (Tarrasch). The text is also quite good.

21 . . . .   Kt-B3

Black could also defend the BP directly by 21 . . . Kt-R3, but after 22 P-KKt4 followed by P-Kt4 his game is manifestly hopeless.

22 P-QKt4

Not 22 RxBP? because of . . . P-KR3, nor 22 KtxBP? K-B; 23 R-B7, Kt-K etc. (Tarrasch).

22 . . . .   B-B8
23 RxKtP   R-R

Forced, else White wins easily by obtaining two passed Ps.

24 P-Kt3   B-Kt7
25 R-K7   R-QB

Or 25 . . . P-KR3; 26 R-K2!

26 Kt-Kt5   Kt-Q4
27 R-K2!

This settles matters, allowing White to win the QP for his own QKtP.

27 . . . .   B-B8
28 KtxQP   BxR
29 KtxR   KtxP
30 P-R3   Kt-Q4
31 Kt-Q6

31 KtxQRP was also possible, and if 31 . . . Kt-K2; 32 P-QR4 followed by Kt-Kt5.

31 . . . .   P-B3
32 Kt-K6   B-B8
33 P-KR4   B-R6
34 Kt-KB4   KtxKt
35 PxKt   K-B
36 K-Q2   K-K2
37 Kt-K4   K-K3
38 P-B4   Resigns

GAME No. 49

Match 1907

Ruy Lopez

White	Black
F. J. Marshall	**Dr. E. Lasker**

1 P-K4	P-K4
2 Kt-KB3	Kt-QB3
3 B-Kt5	Kt-B3
4 P-Q4	

A weak variation. For the stronger 4 O-O see Game No. 24.

4	PxP
5 O-O	B-K2
6 P-K5	Kt-K5
7 KtxP	O-O
8 Kt-B5	P-Q4
9 BxKt	

9 KtxBch, KtxKt; 10 P-KB3, Kt-B4; 11 P-QKt4, Kt-K3; 12 P-KB4 (Zukertort-Tchigorin, Berlin 1881), is far more promising.

9	PxB
10 KtxBch	QxKt
11 R-K	

Forced: if 11 P-KB4, Q-B4ch; or 11 B-B4, P-KKt4! In both cases Black gains some material.

| 11 . . . . | Q-R5 |

Beginning a brilliant but not wholly sound attack; whereas the simple . . . P-B3 would have sufficed to maintain Black's advantage. If then 12 P-KB3, Kt-Kt4 (but not 12 . . . Kt-B4; 13 P-QKt3, PxP; 14 B-R3±); 13 BxKt, PxB; White's passed P is weak, while the open KB file will enable Black to build up a strong attack.

| 12 B-K3 | P-B3 |

Intending the sacrifice which follows. But 12 . . . P-KB4 and if

13 P-KB3, P-B5! was superior (Tarrasch).

| 13 P-KB3 | PxP!? |

Position after Black's 13th move

| 14 PxKt | P-Q5 |

It is true that an attempt to save the B would lose at once:

I   15 B-Q2, B-Kt5! 16 Q-B (or 16 P-KKt3, Q-R6; 17 R-K2, R-B7!! 18 KxR, QxRPch and mate in three), R-B7! 17 B-Kt5 (or 17 R-B, QR-KB), RxPch! 18 KxR, B-R6ch; 19 K-R, Q-B7 and mate in two.

II   15 B-B, Q-B7ch; 16 K-R, B-Kt5! and wins. But White could simply have played 15 Q-K2! (Tarrasch), PxB (necessary; if 15 . . . B-Kt5 or . . . B-R3; 16 B-B2 wins); 16 QxP; Black's attack is no longer serious, and White's more solid Pawn position should decide the game in his favor.

| 15 P-KKt3 | Q-B3? |

15 . . . Q-R6 would have won at once, as the following analysis by Tarrasch proves: 16 BxP (if 16 B-Q2 or B-B, R-B7! 17 KxR, QxRPch; 18 K-B3, P-KR4 and mate next move), B-Kt5; 17 Q-Q2, PxB;

I 18 QxP, QR-Q; 19 Q-B5 (if
19 Q-B4ch, K-R; 20 Kt-B3, R-B
7! 21 KxR, QxRPch; 22 K-K3, Qx
P mate), R-B6; 20 Kt-B3, RxPch;
21 PxR, QxPch; 22 K-B, R-Q7
and mate is unavoidable.

II 18 Q-Kt2, Q-R4; 19 Kt-Q2,
R-B2 and White is helpless against
the doubling of the Rs followed
by R-B7 (if 20 R-KB, B-R6).

16 BxP?

Here White had the choice of
three superior continuations:

I 16 B-Q2, Q-B7ch; 17 K-R,
B-R6; 18 R-Kt, P-KR4 (threaten-
ing . . . B-Kt5-B6ch. 18 . . . B-
B8 could be answered by 19 B-K);
19 Kt-R3! (19 QxP? QxRch), B-
Kt5; 20 R-KB! BxQ; 21 RxQ, Rx
R; 22 RxB, R-K7; 23 B-R5 with
a draw as the probable result.

II 16 R-B! QxRch; 17 QxQ,
RxQch; 18 KxR, B-R3ch (18 . . .
PxB? 19 K-K2±); 19 K-B2, R-B
ch; 20 B-B4, PxB; 21 Kt-Q2! with
excellent drawing chances in view
of Black's ragged Ps (these two
variations are analysis by Tarrasch).

III 16 Q-K2, PxB; 17 QxP, B-
R6; 18 Kt-B3 and White's game is
still tenable.

16	PxB
17 R-B	QxRch
18 QxQ	RxQch
19 KxR	

The ending is approximately
even: with . . . B-R3ch Black can
get all his pieces into play quickly,
while White has the superior Pawn
position. Once White's Kt reaches
QKt3, Black's Ps will be seriously
weak.

| 19 . . . . | R-Kt! |

Beginning one of the most remarkable end-game combinations
in the history of chess! "Never miss
a check" is not one of Lasker's
favorite maxims. By postponing the
development of the B he is able to
force a weakening in White's Pawn
structure; a conception worthy of a
great master.

20 P-Kt3

Thus the Kt has been deprived
of its best square.

| 20 . . . . | R-Kt4!! |

The mobility of the R attains its
maximum on this rank, where it
can be played to either side
quickly.

21 P-B4

A bad move, but there are no
good ones: if 21 Kt-R3, R-QR4;
22 Kt-B4, B-R3; 23 K-K2, BxKt
ch; 24 PxB, K-B2 and now it is
White's Ps that are hopelessly
weak; or 21 Kt-Q2, R-QB4; 22 R-
B, B-R3ch; 23 K-K, R-B6 and
White's position is badly cramped

| 21 . . . . | R-KR4 |
| 22 K-Kt | P-B4 |

The weak QP has thus been
transformed into a powerful pro-
tected passed P.

| 23 Kt-Q2 | K-B2 |
| 24 R-Bch? | |

"Never miss a check." But here
the check is worse than useless: it
is directly harmful because it
weakens the Q side. 24 P-QR3 was
White's best chance.

24	K-K2
25 P-QR3	R-R3!
26 P-KR4	

Not 26 P-QKt4, R-R3. The

text is intended to free White's K, but it only creates an additional weakness.

26	R-R3
27 R-R	B-Kt5
28 K-B2	K-K3
29 P-R4	

29 Kt-B3, BxKt; 30 KxB, K-K4 was just as bad.

29	K-K4
30 K-Kt2	R-KB3!
31 R-K	P-Q6

The "lust to expand" of the passed P!

32 R-KB	K-Q5
33 RxR	PxR
34 K-B2	P-B3

Forcing the win of the KP, since White will soon be in *Zugzwang*. Marshall might have spared himself the rest. There followed: 35 P-QR5, P-QR3; 36 Kt-B, KxP; 37 K-K, B-K7; 38 Kt-Q2ch, K-K6; 39 Kt-Kt, P-B4; 40 Kt-Q2, P-R4; 41 Kt-Kt, K-B6; 42 Kt-B3, KxP; 43 Kt-R4, P-B5; 44 KtxP, P-B6; 45 Kt-K4ch, K-B5; 46 Kt-Q6, P-B4; 47 P-Kt4, PxP; 48 P-B5, P-Kt6; 49 Kt-B4, K-Kt6; 50 Kt-K3, P-Kt7 and White resigned.

GAME No. 50

Philadelphia 1907
Giuoco Piano

White	Black
M. Morgan	**Dr. E. Lasker**
S. L. Stadelman	

1 P-K4	P-K4
2 Kt-KB3	Kt-QB3
3 B-B4	B-B4
4 P-B3	Kt-B3
5 P-Q3	

A tame variation which leads to no advantage for White. More energetic is either P-Q4 or O-O.

| 5 . . . . | P-Q3 |
| 6 P-QKt4 | |

It has long been known that this advance results in a weakening of White's Q side Ps.

6	B-Kt3
7 P-QR4	P-QR3
8 O-O	Kt-K2
9 B-K3	P-B3
10 Q-K	

A portentous if somewhat incomprehensible move.

10	Kt-Kt3
11 QKt-Q2	O-O
12 B-R2	B-B2

. . . P-Q4 can no longer be prevented.

13 P-R5

Fixing the Q side Ps is of little value here: the issue will be decided on the other wing.

| 13 . . . | P-Q4 |
| 14 R-Q | R-K |

Now White's position is bad: the Allies play purposelessly, while Lasker, on the other hand, steadily strengthens his position.

15 B-Kt5	B-K3
16 Kt-R4	Kt-B5
17 B-Kt	B-Kt5!
18 P-B3	

After 18 KKt-B3 (or 18 QKt-B3) White can do nothing but squirm ungracefully.

18	B-Q2
19 K-R	P-R3
20 BxKt(B6)	

Or 20 BxKt(B4), PxB; 21 Q-B2, P-KKt4; 22 Kt-B5, BxKt; 23 PxB, R-K6∓.

| 20 . . . . | QxB |
| 21 P-Kt4 | |

Black was already threatening to win a P by . . . P-KKt4; but P-Kt3 was certainly better than the text.

| 21 . . . . | QR-Q |
| 22 P-B4 | |

The Allies impatiently force a clarification in the center, but R-Kt was more prudent.

| 22 . . . . | PxBP |
| 23 KtxP | |

Leaving a backward QP, but 23 PxP, B-K3 was even worse.

23	B-K3
24 Kt-K3	B-Kt6
25 R-Q2	P-B4!
26 Kt(R4)-Kt2	PxP
27 R-Kt2	KtxP!

More forceful than 27 . . . B-K3; 28 QxP.

| 28 BxKt | RxB |
| 29 QxP | Q-K3! |

Seemingly White has a forced draw by 30 KR-QKt, B-R7; 31 R-R, B-Kt6; 32 KR-QKt, B-R7; 33 R-R etc.

| 30 KR-QKt | R-QB!! |

Beginning a magnificent combination.

(See diagram next column)

31 Kt-B5

If 31 RxB, B-Q3; 32 RxR (best: if 32 QxP, RxR; 33 QxR, R-B8ch; 34 Kt-K, RxKtch; 35 K-Kt2, RxR; 36 QxR, B-B2∓), BxQ; 33 RxB, R-B8ch; 34 Kt-Q (but not 34 R-Q, RxRch; 35 KtxR, Q-Q3; 36 R-Kt, Q-Q6 and wins), Q-R7; 35 Kt-K3, Q-K7; 36 R(Kt4)-Kt3, R-

Position after Black's 30th move

R8; 37 R-R3 best, RxR; 38 RxR, QxPch; 39 K-Kt, QxP. In this position, which Lasker was aiming for, White has a R and two Kts for Q and three Ps, but he cannot ward off loss: his pieces are tied to the defense, and Black can advance his K side Ps with deadly effect.

| 31 . . . . | R(B)-Q! |
| 32 Kt-K | |

If now 32 RxB, RxR; 33 QxR (or 33 RxR, R-Q8ch; 34 Kt-K, Rx Ktch), QxQ; 34 RxQ, R-Q8ch; 35 Kt-K, RxKtch; 36 K-Kt2, BxP; 37 RxP, B-B6∓.

| 32 . . . . | B-Q8!! |

It is clear that Lasker must have had this continuation in mind when he made his 27th move, for any other move would lose a piece outright.

33 KtxR

That Black should obtain a winning attack was not easy to foresee: yet White has little choice, for if 33 Kt-K7ch, K-R2; 34 Kt-Q5, B-Q3; 35 Q-Kt6, R-Q2!! 36 KtxR, BxPch;

I 37 R-Kt2, BxRch; 38 KxB, QxPch; 39 K-B, QxP; 40 Q-Kt3

(if 40 Kt(Q5)-Kt4, BxKt and the B cannot be recaptured), B-B! 41 Kt(Q5)-Kt4, BxKt; 42 KtxB, R-Q7 and mate is unavoidable.

II 37 K-Kt, QxPch; 38 K-B, BxP; 39 Kt(Q5)-Kt4, KBxKt; 40 KtxB, BxR; 41 RxB, Q-B4ch and White loses his R. A very beautiful combination!

33	BxPch
34 K-Kt	RxKt
35 R-QB?	

As so often in difficult positions, a blunder occurs. 35 QxP was relatively best, although after . . . BxRP; 36 P-R3, Q-B5 Black maintains his powerful attack.

| 35 . . . . | BxKtP!! |
| 36 RxB | |

36 Kt-K7ch would also be inadequate: 36 . . . K-R2; 37 RxB, R-Q8ch; 38 K-B2 (or 38 K-Kt2, B-R6ch followed by . . . Q-Kt5), Q-B3ch and wins.

36	BxKt
37 PxB	R-Q8ch
38 K-Kt2	

If instead 38 K-B2, QxPch leading to a quick mate.

| 38 . . . . | Q-Q4ch |
| 39 K-B2 | |

If 39 K-Kt3, R-Kt8ch etc.

| 39 . . . . | Q-R8 |
| 40 QxP | |

Allowing mate. But there was no defense:

I 40 R-B8ch, K-R2; 41 Q-Kt3, QxPch; 42 K-B3, R-B8ch; 43 K-K3, R-K8ch; 44 K-Q3, Q-Kt6ch; 45 K-B2, Q-B7ch; 46 K-B3, R-K6 ch; 41 K-Kt4, RxQch; 48 KxR, QxP and in view of Black's array

of Ps, the end is only a question of time.

II 40 R-K2, QxPch; 41 K-B3, Q-R6ch; 42 K-K4, Q-Q6ch and mate in five.

40 . . . .   Q-B8ch

Black now announced mate in five: 41 K-K3, R-Q6ch; 42 K-K4, Q-B6ch; 43 KxP, Q-K6ch; 44 Q-K4, P-B3ch; 45 K-K6, QxQ mate.

This unusually difficult game shows Lasker at his best.

GAME No. 51

Match 1908

Ruy Lopez

| White | Black |
| **Dr. E. Lasker** | **Dr. S. Tarrasch** |

1 P-K4	P-K4
2 Kt-KB3	Kt-QB3
3 B-Kt5	P-QR3
4 BxKt	

Lasker is the only great master who has consistently and successfully played this variation.

4	QPxB
5 P-Q4	PxP
6 QxP	QxQ
7 KtxQ	P-QB4

This weakens Black's Q side Ps. Best is 7 . . . B-Q2; 8 Kt-QB3, P-B3; 9 B-B4, O-O-O; 10 O-O-O, Kt-K2; 11 Kt-Kt3, Kt-Kt3 with at least an even game for Black (Bernstein-Alekhine, Berne 1932).

| 8 Kt-K2 | B-Q2 |
| 9 P-QKt3 | |

An indifferent idea. 9 B-B4 followed by Kt-Q2, with pressure on Black's Q side Ps, seems better.

9 . . . .   B-B3

9 . . . O-O-O followed by . . . Kt-K2-Kt3 was superior. Once Black has played . . . P-KB3, White's B will have little scope.

10 P-KB3   B-K2

The idea of exchanging Bs is illogical, since Black's only compensation for his weak Q side is his two Bs.

11 B-Kt2   B-B3
12 BxB   KtxB

A further disadvantage: the Kt is unsatisfactorily placed at KB3, where it blocks the KBP.

13 Kt-Q2   O-O-O
14 O-O-O   R-Q2
15 Kt-KB4   R-K
16 Kt-B4   P-QKt3
17 P-QR4   P-QR4

A purposeless advance. . . . K-Kt2 followed by . . . P-QKt4 would have given Black counter-play.

18 RxR   KtxR
19 R-Q   Kt-K4

The ending is in White's favor because of the relative immobility of Black's B. Black can hardly do more than mark time.

20 KtxKt   RxKt
21 P-B4!

Preventing . . . P-B5.

21 . . . .   R-K

If instead 21 . . . P-B4; 22 Kt-Q3, R-K; 23 PxP, R-B; 24 Kt-K5! and White can maintain the P.

22 Kt-R5   R-Kt

. . . P-Kt3 would only further reduce the mobility of his B.

23 R-Q3   P-B3
24 K-Q2   B-K
25 Kt-Kt3   B-Q2

26 K-K3   R-K
27 Kt-R5   R-K2
28 P-KKt4   P-B3

Black's unwieldy Q side still hinders him from forming any satisfactory plan. Hoffer suggests playing the K to the K side, but this would only weaken the Ps still more!

29 P-R4   K-B2
30 P-Kt5   P-B4
31 Kt-Kt3   PxP

31 . . . P-Kt3; 32 K-B4 would have been inferior for Black.

32 KtxP   B-B4
33 P-R5   R-Q2

Securing control of the Q file, for if 34 RxRch, KxR; 35 K-B4, K-K3 etc. and White cannot win.

34 R-B3   R-Q8
35 K-B4

Position after White's 35th move

35 . . . .   B-Q2?

Better was 35 . . . BxKt; 36 Px B, K-Q3; (but not 36 . . .R-KR8; 37 K-Kt4, R-Kt8ch; 38 K-B5, R-KR8; 39 P-K5! RxP; 40 R-Q3, P-R3; 41 P-K6! RxPch; 42 K-B4, R-Kt8; 43 R-Q7ch, K-B; 44 K-K5 and White should win); with a draw as the probable outcome. After the text Lasker forces the win very neatly.

36	R-K3	R-KR8
37	Kt-Kt3	R-R5ch
38	K-K5	R-R6
39	P-B4	K-Q
40	P-B5	R-R5

Or 40 . . . K-K2; 41 P-B6ch, PxP; 42 PxPch, K-B2; 43 K-Q6 and White will win all the Q side Ps, since if 43 . . . B-K; 44 R-K7ch, K-B (44 . . . KxP; 45 Kt-K4ch); 45 Kt-B5 wins quickly for White.

41	P-B6	PxPch
42	KxP	B-K
43	Kt-B5!	

Pretty and decisive.

43 . . . .   R-B5

. . . RxP is refuted by 44 Rx Bch!

44	P-Kt6	PxP
45	PxP	R-Kt5
46	RxBch!	

The quickest; but 46 R-Kt3 would also have won.

| 46 | . . . . | KxR |
| 47 | P-Kt7 | K-Q2 |

Or 47 . . . R-Kt8; 48 Kt-R6 and wins.

48 Kt-R4

Care was still required, for 48 Kt-R6, RxP! 49 KxR, K-K3 would have given Black excellent drawing chances.

48	. . . .	RxP
49	KxR	K-K3
50	Kt-B3	K-B4
51	K-B7	K-K5
52	K-K6	K-Q6
53	K-Q6	K-B6

Or 53 . . . P-Kt4; 54 BPxP, PxP; 55 KxP, P-Kt5; 56 Kt-Q4 and wins.

| 54 | KxP | KxP |
| 55 | K-Kt5 | Resigns |

A simple, but pleasing game.

GAME No. 52

Match 1908

Ruy Lopez

White	Black
Dr. E. Lasker	**Dr. S. Tarrasch**
1 P-K4	P-K4
2 Kt-KB3	Kt-QB3
3 B-Kt5	P-QR3
4 B-R4	Kt-B3
5 O-O	B-K2

The strange circumstance that Tarrasch does not play his favorite defense 5 . . . KtxP here is accounted for by the fact that it was not considered wholly sound at this time (it was rehabilitated two years later by Schlechter in his match with Lasker).

6 R-K	P-QKt4
7 B-Kt3	P-Q3
8 P-B3	Kt-QR4
9 B-B2	P-B4
10 P-Q4	Q-B2
11 QKt-Q2	Kt-B3
12 P-KR3	O-O
13 Kt-B	BPxP
14 PxP	KtxQP
15 KtxKt	PxKt
16 B-Kt5	

In a previous game of the match Lasker played 16 Kt-Kt3, but after 16 . . . Kt-Q2; 17 B-Kt3, Q-Kt3; 18 Kt-B5, B-B3; 19 B-KB4, Kt-K4 Tarrasch retained the P with advantage. In Tarrasch's opinion the text refutes the variation.

16 . . . .   P-R3?

Tarrasch states that 16 . . . Kt-Q4; 17 BxB, KtxB is better than the text. He goes on to say, "White then attacks the QP with Q, R and Kt, while Black can only defend it twice. When it is captured, the weak isolated P at Q3 will be under attack." This view is however incorrect: after 16 . . . Kt-Q4; 17 BxB, KtxB; 18 Kt-Kt3, B-K3 White will find it difficult to regain the P with advantage, say 19 Kt-K2, Kt-B3; 20 R-QB, Q-Kt3; 21 Q-Q2 (if 21 Q-Q3, Kt-Kt5∓), P-Q4; 22 PxP, BxQP; 23 QR-Q, QR-Q and the QP is immune from capture. 16 . . . Kt-Q4 was therefore the right move.

17 B-KR4   Q-Kt3
18 Q-Q3   P-Kt4?

Weakens the K side too much. The threat of 19 P-K5, PxP; 20 BxKt, BxB; 21 Q-R7 mate could have been met very simply by 18 . . . R-K, although White would still maintain the better game with 19 QR-Q.

19 B-KKt3   B-K3
20 QR-Q

(See diagram next column)

20 . . . .   KR-B?

In spite of the apparent danger, the QRP could and should have captured:

I 20 . . . BxQRP; 21 P-Kt3, KR-B;

(a) 22 R-R, R-B6; 23 Q-Q, P-Q6; 24 RxB, PxB; 25 RxBP, Rx R (safer than 25 . . . RxP; 26 Kt-K3); 26 QxR, Kt-R4!∓.

(b) 22 P-K5, PxP; 23 BxP, R-B6; 24 Q-B5, R-Q! 25 BxKt, Qx

Position after White's 20th move

B; 26 RxB! QxQ! 27 BxQ, BxP; 28 R-R, P-Q6 with at least a draw.

II 20 . . . BxQRP; 21 P-K5, B-B5; 22 Q-B5, B-K3; 23 Q-B3, PxP; 24 BxP, B-Q4! 25 Q-Q3, B-B5; 26 Q-B5, B-K3 and White must allow the perpetual check to his Q; for if 27 Q-Q3, B-B5; 28 Q-Q2, KR-Q; 29 BxP (or 29 P-QKt3, P-Q6!), B-B4∓.

21 B-Kt

White's game is now decidedly superior. He regains his P or else works up a powerful attack.

21 . . . .   Kt-Q2
22 P-K5

If 22 QxQP, QxQ; 23 RxQ, Kt-K4 with some chances.

22 . . . .   Kt-B
23 Q-KB3

Capturing the P would free Black's game too much: 23 QxQP, QxQ; 24 RxQ, PxP; 25 BxP, R-Q∓.

23 . . . .   P-Q4

There is nothing better, for example 23 . . . K-Kt2; 24 Q-R5, Kt-Kt3? 25 PxP, BxQP; 26 RxB! The text at any rate closes the diagonal of White's QB.

| 24 | Q-R5 | K-Kt2 |
| 25 | P-B4 | P-B4? |

Another disastrous weakening
of the K side. Tarrasch recommends
25 . . . Kt-Kt3! 26 P-B5, P-Q6
dis ch; 27 B-B2, B-QB4; 28 Kt-
K3, Kt-B5; 29 Q-Kt4, P-Q5; 30
Kt-B, B-Q4 and Black has counter-play. But White has a better
continuation in 28 P-B6ch! K-R2;
29 Kt-K3±. Black's best line
would have been 25 . . . P-Q6
dis ch; 26 B-B2 (or 26 K-R, Kt-
Kt3 with a difficult game), B-QB4;
27 BxB, QxBch; 28 K-R, PxP;
29 BxP.

26	PxP e.p. ch	BxP
27	PxP	PxP
28	B-K5!	P-Q6 dis ch
29	K-R	Kt-Kt3
30	QxP!	B-B2
31	Kt-Kt3	

BxP is also good; the text is
simpler because it prevents 31 . .
BxB; 32 RxB, Q-KB3.

31	. . . .	BxB
32	RxB	R-R
33	BxP	R-QR2
34	QR-K	

Threatening R-K6.

34	. . . .	K-B
35	BxKt	QxB
36	Q-K3	R-B2
37	Kt-B5	

Threatening 37 Q-R3ch, K-Kt;
38 Kt-K7ch.

| 37 | . . . . | Q-QB3 |
| 38 | Q-Kt5 | Resigns |

GAME No. 53

Match 1908

French Defense

| White | Black |
| **Dr. E. Lasker** | **Dr. S. Tarrasch** |

1	P-K4	P-K3
2	P-Q4	P-Q4
3	Kt-QB3	Kt-KB3
4	B-Kt5	B-Kt5
5	PxP	QxP

After his catastrophic defeat in
the fifth game of the match (see
Game No. 52), Tarrasch regularly
answered 1 P-K4 with the French
Defense. In his Book of the Match,
he expresses the opinion that his
last move yields White an advantage after the subsequent break-up
of Black's K side Ps.

6 Kt-B3

If 6 BxKt, PxB; 7 Q-Q2, Q-
Q R 4 (Capablanca - Bogoljubow,
New York 1934) with an excellent
game for Black.

| 6 | . . . . | P-B4 |

Simpler would have been:

I 6 . . . QKt-Q2; 7 B-Q3, P-
B4; 8 O-O, BxKt; 9 PxB, P-B5
(Alapin).

II 6 . . . Kt-K5; 7 B-Q2, BxKt;
8 PxB, KtxB.

7	BxKt	PxB
8	Q-Q2	BxKt
9	QxB	Kt-Q2
10	R-Q	

Not the strongest. Tarrasch sug-
gests the interesting possibility 10
O-O-O (threatening B-B4), QxR
P (or 10 . . . PxP; 11 KtxP, Qx
RP; 12 B-B4, Q-R8ch; 13 K-Q2,
Q-R5; 14 B-Kt5 winning the Q);
11 PxP, Q-R8ch; 12 K-Q2, Q-R5;

13 Kt-Q4±.

10 . . . .   KR-Kt

In order to hinder the development of White's B.

11 PxP   QxBP

Schlechter recommends 11 . . .
Q-K5ch; 12 B-K2 (12 K-Q2, Q-
B5ch), RxP etc.

12 Q-Q2   Q-Kt3

This move has been strongly
criticised but it is not bad if followed up properly.

13 P-B3

Position after White's 13th move

13 . . . .   P-QR3?

Waste of time. The correct move
was 13 . . . Kt-B4;

I   14 P-KKt3, P-K4; 15 B-Kt2
(15 Q-B2, B-Kt5; 16 QxP? K-K2
∓), B-Kt5.

II   14 B-Kt5ch, K-K2! 15 O-O,
P-K4 with a view to . . . B-R6
or . . . B-Kt5 followed by . . .
Kt-K3, or simply . . . B-K3.

III   14 P-QKt4, Kt-K5; 15 Q-
B2, P-B4; 16 Kt-K5 (16 P-KKt3,
B-Q2; 17 B-Kt2, O-O-O!), Q-B2;
17 B-Kt5ch, K-K2∓.

IV   14 Q-Q6, QxQ; 15 RxQ,
K-K2; 16 R-Q2, B-Q2; 17 P-KKt

3, B-B3; 18 B-Kt2∓.

14 Q-B2   P-B4

After . . . Kt-B White could
continue Kt-Q2 and the Kt will
arrive at Q6, whereas after the text
Kt-Q2 can be answered with . . .
Kt-K4 (Tarrasch).

15 P-KKt3   Kt-B4

Now this comes too late, as
Lasker very convincingly demonstrates.

16 B-Kt2   Q-B2

Tarrasch points out that 16 . . .
B-Q2 would be answered by 17
Kt-K5, whereupon 17 . . . O-O-
O is impossible because of 18 KtxP.

17 Q-K2

In order to play Kt-K5 after
. . . B-Q2, which was Black's
best line of play.

17 . . . .   P-QKt4?

As just pointed out, Black
should have played 17 . . . B-Q2;
18 Kt-K5, O-O-O; 19 KtxB (on
19 KtxP Tarrasch would have obtained a powerful counter-attack
by . . . B-Kt4; 20 P-QB4, RxR
ch; 21 QxR, B-R5; 22 Kt-Q6ch,
K-Kt; 23 P-Kt3, R-Q etc.), RxKt;
20 O-O∓.

Black's last move creates a new
weakness on the Q side and it is
not surprising that it collapses in
a few moves under Lasker's energetic onslaught.

18 O-O   B-Kt2

Another weakness of this move
(as compared to . . . B-Q2) is
that Black is now unable to get
his K into safety.

19 P-B4!   P-Kt5

Enabling the White Q to get to

KR6 with tempo, but after 19 . . .
PxP; 20 QxP Black's K is danger-
ously exposed, for example 20 . . .
Q-K2; 21 KR-K, B-K5; 22 Kt-Q4,
BxB; 23 KxB and wins, or 21 . . .
R-QB; 22 Kt-K5, BxB; 23 KxB,
Q-Kt2ch; 24 K-Kt, P-QR4; 25 R-
Q6, K-B; 26 Q-KR4, Q-K2; 27
Q-R6ch, R-Kt2; 28 KR-Q, K-Kt;
29 Kt-B6 and wins.

20 Q-Q2!

Simultaneously threatening both
wings.

| 20 . . . | R-Kt |
| 21 Q-R6 | BxKt |

In order to bring the Q to the
protection of the K side; but now
White attacks the vulnerable points
on the other wing.

| 22 BxB | Q-K4 |

Protecting the RP by a transparent trap.

| 23 KR-K | QxP |

On 23 . . . Q-Kt2 the same
reply would be equally crushing.

| 24 Q-B4 | R-QB |
| 25 Q-Q6 | P-B3 |

There is nothing better against
the fearful threat of B-B6ch.

26 B-R5ch	R-Kt3
27 BxRch	PxB
28 RxPch	Resigns

White mates in five moves at
most.

GAME No. 54

St. Petersburg 1909
Ruy Lopez

White	Black
Dr. E. Lasker	**L. Forgacs**
1 P-K4	P-K4
2 Kt-KB3	Kt-QB3
3 B-Kt5	P-Q3
4 P-Q4	B-Q2
5 Kt-B3	Kt-B3
6 PxP	PxP

White's 6th move releases the
pressure on Black's center, but it
is typical of Lasker's style that he
does not usually play the so-called
"best" moves in the opening.

7 B-Kt5	B-QKt5
8 O-O	BxKt
9 PxB	P-KR3
10 B-KR4	Q-K2

Black has freed his game and
appears to have a satisfactory position.

11 Q-Q3	P-R3
12 B-R4	R-Q
13 Q-K3	P-KKt4
14 B-KKt3	P-Kt4?

This causes a weakness on Black's
QB4 which is subsequently exploited by Lasker with great virtu-
osity.

| 15 B-Kt3 | Kt-KR4 |
| 16 Kt-K! | |

An excellent move: the Kt is to
be brought to Q3 to exert pressure
on QB5.

| 16 . . . . | Kt-R4 |
| 17 Kt-Q3 | |

Preventing . . . P-QB4.

| 17 . . . | Kt-KB5 |
| 18 P-B3! | |

Very finely played! Dr Euwe points out that in the present in-stance a B posted at QB5 is more effective than a Kt—the reason for this being that a Kt on QB5 would attack white squares, which, how-ever, can be protected by Black's remaining B.

The B posted on QB5, on the other hand, attacks black squares, thus accentuating the weakness arising from the absence of Black's KB.

18 . . . .   KR-Kt

Black considers his Kt at KB5 well posted for a counter-attack and does not therefore play 18 . . . KtxKt; 19 PxKt, P-QB4, which would release the pressure on his weak QB4, but would at the same time undouble White's Ps and allow him the advantage of two Bs. Removing the KB would open the R file. All in all Forgàcs has only a choice of evils and hence he decides to stake the game on his chances of attack.

19 KR-Q   R-Kt3

Perhaps to defend the QRP should he decide to play . . . Ktx B. The variation 19 . . . KtxKt; 20 PxKt, P-KKt5 would be met by 21 P-KB4.

20 B-B2   B-B
21 Q-K

Now the threat of B-B5 becomes acute.

21 . . . .   KtxKt

If 21 . . . Kt-Kt2 (in order to prevent B-B5); 22 P-QR4±.

22 PxKt   KtxB

Black hopes to remain with Bs of opposite color and resulting

drawing chances. The alternative 22 . . . P-QB4 is unfavorable be-cause of 23 P-Q4, opening up the game to White's advantage.

23 PxKt   P-QB4

White was threatening P-QKt4 followed by B-B5.

24 P-QKt4!   PxP
25 PxP   P-Kt5

An attempt at counter-attack.

26 B-B5

White has finally attained his object. Note how powerful his position becomes after this move.

Position after White's 26th move

26 . . . .   Q-Kt4
27 PxP   QxP
28 R-R2!   B-K3
29 R-KB2   B-B5
30 Q-B   B-Kt6
31 R-R

Threatening 32 R-B5.

31 . . . .   Q-Q2
32 R-B3   Q-B3
33 Q-B2   R-Q2

There is nothing to be done. If 33 . . . B-K3; 34 R-KB followed by R-B6, or 34 R-B6 at once with decisive advantage.

34 Q-Kt2!

The full strength of this move may have been overlooked by Black, but his position was very difficult in any event.

| 34 . . . . | Q-K3 |
| 35 P-Q4 | PxP |

If 35 . . . B-B5; 36 P-Q5, Q-Kt5; 37 QxPch, K-Q; 38 Q-Kt8 mate.

36 QxB	QxP
37 Q-Q3	Q-Q4
38 QxR!	Resigns

GAME No. 55

St.Petersburg 1909
Ruy Lopez

White	Black
Dr. E. Lasker	**G. Salwe**
1 P-K4	P-K4
2 Kt-KB3	Kt-QB3
3 B-Kt5	P-Q3
4 P-Q4	B-Q2

The Steinitz Defense was played a great deal in this tournament.

| 5 Kt-B3 | Kt-B3 |
| 6 O-O | |

A more aggressive continuation would be 6 BxKt, BxB; 7 Q-Q3 followed by P-QKt3 and B-Kt2 or else by B-Kt5 and O-O-O.

| 6 . . . . | B-K2 |
| 7 B-Kt5 | PxP |

After 7 . . . O-O Black would get into difficulties. Lasker gives the following analysis after 7 . . . O-O; 8 BxQKt, BxB; 9 PxP:

I 9 . . . KtxP; 10 KtxKt, Bx Kt; 11 BxB, QxB (11 . . . BxKt; 12 BxQ, BxQ; 13 BxP winning a P); 12 PxP, QxP; 13 QxQ, PxQ; 14 Kt-Q4±.

II 9 . . . PxP; 10 KtxP, BxP (10 . . . KtxP? 11 KtxB, PxKt; 12 QxQ, BxQ; 13 KtxKt); 11 Qx Q, BxQ; 12 KtxP, BxBP; 13 KtxB, QRxKt; 14 KR-B, B-Q6; 15 Kt-R4±.

8 KtxP	O-O
9 KBxKt	PxB
10 Q-Q3	R-K
11 QR-K	

White has secured a splendid development and it is not easy for his opponent to free himself.

| 11 . . . . | P-B4 |

The customary maneuver of 11 . . . P-KR3; 12 B-R4, Kt-R2 would be pointless here as White would play 12 B-B!

12 Kt-Kt3	Kt-Kt5
13 BxB	RxB
14 P-B4	

After this, Black's Kt is necessarily out of play for a long time.

14	R-Kt
15 P-KR3	Kt-R3
16 P-B5!?	

Subsequently Lasker came to the conclusion that P-KKt4 would have been stronger. He chose the text because it allows him to play R-B4-R4 as well as Q-Kt3.

| 16 . . . . | P-KB3 |

Black's game is fearfully cramped and his pieces have little scope. As a result of Lasker's last move (which could have been played only by a tyro or by a great master!), Black can exert pressure on the KP, and in addition he has the square K4 at his disposal. The skilful way in which Lasker overcomes the difficulties inherent in this type of position should be

compared to the play in the celebrated game with Capablanca
(Game No. 74).

17 Kt-Q5	R-K
18 P-B4	Kt-B2
19 Q-QB3	

In order to bring the Kt at Kt3
to a more effective post.

| 19 . . . . | R-K4 |
| 20 Kt-Q2 | P-B3 |

With this move Salwe only adds
to his repertoire of weaknesses!—
but he must seek freedom for his
pieces at all costs.

21 Kt-B4	Q-Kt3
22 P-QKt3	QR-K
23 Q-Kt3	K-R
24 Kt-R5	R-KKt
25 R-B4	Q-Q
26 Kt-B3	

An "experiment": if 26 . . . R
(K4)-K; 27 R-Kt4 wins.

| 26 . . . . | R-K2 |
| 27 R-R4 | |

After 27 R-Kt4, Black would
now defend himself adequately
with . . . Q-KB.

| 27 . . . . | Q-K |

(See diagram next column)

An interesting and difficult position, on which Nimzowitsch comments, "Black's cramped K side
and his QP are critical weaknesses;
White is however hampered in
exploiting them by the weakness
of his KP. The result is that the
forces directed against the QP are
not very elastic. The P can be attacked only by a R on the file and
by the Q on the diagonal. The
maneuvering possibilities on the K
side are somewhat more varied;

Position after Black's 27th move

the position of the Q and R on
the KKt and KR files can always
be interchanged. To make effective
use of these slight means is indeed
the sign of a great master."

28 Q-B2!

Lasker sees that he cannot make
any further progress with direct
attacks (if for example 28 Kt-B4,
Kt-R3), and hence he attacks both
of Black's weaknesses contrapunt-
ally until there is no longer any
adequate defense.

| 28 . . . . | R-B |
| 29 Q-Q2! | |

Attacking the QP, which makes
. . . Kt-R3 impossible (Nimzowitsch).

| 29 . . . . | Q-Kt |

As a result of Lasker's last
moves, Black's attack on the KP
has been weakened, so that R-Q
will now be possible.

| 30 K-R | R(B)-K |
| 31 R-Kt4! | |

Black's R must be drawn away
away from the K file in order to
free White's QR.

| 31 . . . . | R-Kt |

If 31 . . . Kt-R3; 32 KtxBP±.

| 32 R-Q | Q-Kt5 |

It would have been wiser to return . . . Q-K; Black relies too
much on the unsupported invasion
of the Q.

33 Q-KB2!   Q-B6
34 Q-R4

Suddenly returning to the attack.

34 . . . .   Kt-R3
35 R-B4   Kt-B2
36 K-R2   R(Kt)-K
37 Q-Kt3   R-KKt

If now 38 R-Kt4, Kt-R3; 39 R-
R4, P-Q4! 40 BPxP, PxP; 41 RxP,
B-B3 (Lasker).

38 R-R4!

Now 38 . . . P-Q4 is inadequate because of 39 BPxP, PxP;
40 Kt-B4!

38 . . . .   P-Kt4

Creating an unavoidable but decisive weakness; but White threatened Kt-B4, rendering the QP untenable.

39 PxP e.p.   RxKtP
40 Q-B2   P-B4

Else White fixes the P on B3
and finally captures it.

41 Kt-B4   R-B3
42 Kt-K2   Q-Kt7?
43 R-Q2   Q-R8
44 Kt-Kt3

Threatening 45 PxP, BxP; 46
KtxB, RxKt; 47 RxPch!

44 . . . .   K-Kt
45 PxP   BxP
46 Kt-Q4!

A pretty move which forces the
game. There followed: 46 . . . P
xKt; 47 KtxB, K-B; 48 QxP, QxQ;
49 KtxQ, Kt-K4; 50 R-R5, R
(K2)-KB2; 51 P-B5! PxP; 52 Rx
Kt, PxKt; 53 RxP, R-B7; 54 R-Q

8ch, K-Kt2; 55 R-QR5, R-B7; 56
P-R3! P-B4; 57 R-QB8, R-Kt7;
58 R-Kt5, R(B2)-B7; 59 R-Kt7
ch, K-Kt3; 60 R-B6ch, R-B3; 61
RxBP, R-R3; 62 P-QR4! R-KB3;
63 R-B3, P-QR3; 64 R-Kt3ch, K-
R3; 65 R(Kt3)-Kt7, resigns.

GAME No. 56

St. Petersburg 1909
English Opening

White   Black
Dr. S. Tarta-
kower   **Dr. E. Lasker**

1 P-QB4   P-K4
2 Kt-QB3   Kt-KB3
3 P-KKt3   B-K2

At this time Tartakower was a
youngster, always on the lookout
for interesting complications and
spirited, enterprising play. Lasker,
foreseeing that his youthful opponent would play for a win, purposely adopted a conservative development.

4 B-Kt2   O-O
5 Kt-B3   P-Q3
6 O-O   QKt-Q2
7 P-Q3

7 P-Q4 would have been
stronger; Black would doubtless
have transposed into the Hanham
Variation with . . . P-B3 and
. . . Q-B2. The text aims at an
attack on Black's center from the
other flank, as White's next move
shows.

7 . . . .   P-B3
8 Kt-K

Preventing . . . P-Q4 and preparing P-B4.

8 . . . .   Kt-Kt3

9 P-K4	P-Q4
10 BPxP	PxP
11 PxP	

On 11P-B4! Lasker gives ...
KPxP; 12 P-K5, Kt-Kt5; 13 PxP,
P-Q5; 14 Kt-K4, Kt-Q4; 15 Kt-
QB2, P-B3; 16 P-KR3, Kt(Kt5)-
K6; 17 KtxKt, PxKt; 18 Q-Kt3,
K-R; 19 Kt-Kt3, B-QB4, but Tar-
takower continues this variation 20
Kt-K2, Kt-B2; 21 P-Q4! BxP; 22
KtxB, QxKt; 23 BxKP±.

11	KKtxP
12 KtxKt	KtxKt
13 P-Q4	

Ridding himself of the weak QP
and considerably increasing his
command of the board.

13	PxP
14 QxP	B-K3

Now the position seems perfectly
even (almost a shade in White's
favor, except for his neglected
development).

15 Kt-B2	B-B3

Stronger than 15 . . . R-B; 16
Kt-K3, B-QB4; 17 Q-K4, KtxKt;
18 BxKt, BxB; 19 QxKB, P-
QKt3=.

16 Q-K4	Q-R4
17 Kt-Q4	BxKt
18 QxB	KR-Q
19 B-Kt5	

"Naturally I saw that after the
simple move 19 B-Q2 the game
would be perfectly level, for example 19 . . . Q-Kt4; 20 KR-Q,
R-Q2; 21 B-QB3, KtxB; 22 QxKt
etc., but I felt that there was more
than a draw in the position" (Tartakower).

19	R-Q2
20 P-QR3	

This and the 22nd move lead to
a troublesome weakening of the
white squares on the Q side.

20	Kt-Kt3!

Lasker immediately espies the
weak point in his opponent's
armor.

21 Q-KR4	Kt-B5
22 P-QKt4	Q-Kt3
23 KR-K	P-KR3

"Here I had the moral satisfaction of having caused the champion
to reflect on this important move
for more than half an hour, because he had fully considered all
the possible results of 24 B-K4. As
a result he later got into time-
pressure, although noted for the
rapidity of his tournament play"
(Tartakower).

24 B-K7	

Tartakower points out that 24
B-K4 would be answered by 24
. . . Kt-Q7 (not 24 . . . P-B4;
25 BxRP, PxB; 26 Qx
P, KtxB; 27 RxKt, B-B4 and wins,
or else 25 BxKt, RxB∓.

The text move is in a manner
forced, because the Kt's dominating
position makes it rather awkward
for the B to retreat along his original diagonal.

24	Q-B2

After 24 . . . P-Kt4 White
could obtain a draw by 25 QxP,
RxB; 26 QxPch, K-B; 27 Q-R6ch,
K-Kt etc., or 25 BxP(Kt5), PxB;
26 QxPch, K-B; 27 Q-R6ch, K-
K2; 28 Q-Kt5ch, K-B; 29 Q-R6ch,
K-K2; 30 Q-Kt5ch, K-B etc. (but
not 30 . . . P-B3? 31 Q-Kt7ch,
K-Q3; 32 RxBch, KxR; 33 B-R3
ch, P-B4; 34 R-Kch, K-Q3; 35 R-
Qch and wins).

| 25 | B-B5 | Kt-K4! |
| 26 | B-K3 | |

Not 26 BxKtP? Kt-Kt3! and Black wins a piece.

| 26 | . . . . | Kt-Q6 |

The maneuvers with the Kt are executed in masterly style; as will soon become apparent, it is even more strongly posted here than at B5.

| 27 | KR-Q | B-Kt6! |

Driving away the R from the Q file, for if now 28 R-Q2, Q-B6; 29 R-KB, B-Q4! 30 BxB, RxB; 31 R(B)-Q, QxRP.

| 28 | R-KB | B-Q4! |

The logical conclusion to Lasker's play on the white squares is the elimination of the hostile B, which creates a new and critical weakness in White's game.

| 29 | BxB | RxB |

"The occupation of the Q file, the superiority of the Kt to the B, and the weakness of White's Q side Ps, give Black a decided superiority. Lasker's positional play in this game is unsurpassable" (Marco).

30	Q-K4	Q-Q2
31	R-R2	R-K
32	Q-Kt2	P-QKt3
33	R-B2	R-Q
34	Q-K4	P-QKt4!

Preventing Q-QB4. Now that Black has obtained a dominating position, he threatens to crush all further resistance with . . . P-B4 and . . . P-Kt4 (Lasker).

| 35 | P-B4 | |

Hence Tartakower is driven to this move, which weakens his position on the K file, undermining in particular the position of his B.

35	. . . .	R-K
36	Q-B3	Q-K3
37	B-B2	R-Q2!
38	K-Kt2	Q-Kt6

A little excursion to convince the opponent of his helplessness.

| 39 | Q-B6 | R(K)-Q |
| 40 | Q-QB3 | |

After 40 R-B3, Q-Kt7 White is practically in *Zugzwang;* there is nothing better than 41 R-B2, Qx RP; 42 QxKtP, QxP; 43 QxQ, Kt xQ etc.

| 40 | . . . . | Q-Q4ch |
| 41 | K-Kt | Q-K5! |

Completing the maneuver begun on the 37th move—of which every Hypermodern might well be proud!

| 42 | Q-Kt3 | |

Had White played 42 Q-QB6, the point of Lasker's last move would have been revealed, namely 42 . . . KtxB! 43 R(B)xKt (43 KxKt? R-Q7ch), R-Q8ch; 44 R-B, RxRch; 45 KxR, R-Q8ch; 46 K-B2, R-Q7ch and wins.

(See diagram on next page)

| 42 | . . . . | P-Kt4! |

This fine move puts an end to White's resistance.

| 43 | Q-R2 | |

Not 43 PxP, Kt-K4; 44 B-B5, R-Q6; 45 Q-R2, Kt-B6ch.

| 43 | . . . . | PxP |
| 44 | R-K2 | Q-Kt3 |

Position after White's 42nd move

45	Q-B2	K-R2
46	Q-B3	R-KKt
47	K-R	Q-R4
48	R-Q2	PxP
49	BxP	RxB
50	Q-QB6	Kt-K4
51	Q-K4ch	K-Kt
52	R(Q2)-KB2	R-Kt4

Resigns.

GAME No. 57

St. Petersburg 1909

French Defense

White   Black

Dr. E. Lasker   E. A. Snosko-Borowski

1	P-K4	P-K3
2	P-Q4	P-Q4
3	Kt-QB3	Kt-KB3
4	B-Kt5	B-Kt5
5	PxP	QxP

Regarding this variation see Game No. 53. The continuation adopted by Lasker leads to equality.

6	Kt-B3	Kt-K5
7	B-Q2	BxKt
8	PxB	KtxB

9	QxKt	Kt-Q2
10	B-Q3	P-QB4
11	P-B4	Q-Q3
12	P-B3	P-QKt3
13	O-O	B-Kt2
14	Q-K3	O-O

The position is quite even: White has more terrain and commands K5, while Black has a finely posted B and some possibility of attack on the QBP.

15 QR-Q

Lasker criticizes this move and recommends 15 B-K4, BxB; 16 Qx B, QR-B; 17 QR-B, but it would seem that after 17 . . . R-B2; 18 Kt-Q2, Kt-B3 followed by . . . R-Q, Black has some advantage or at any rate the initiative.

15	. . . .	QR-Q

This shows poor judgment, . . . QR-B being indicated.

16	KR-K	Q-B2
17	B-B	

Lasker pursues the policy of "masterful inactivity" which netted so many useful points.

17	. . . .	P-QR3?

A positional blunder which deprives the B of a valuable square at R3 and weakens the QKtP.

18	Kt-Q2	Kt-B3
19	Kt-Kt3	R-B
20	R-Kt!	

With his characteristic flair for sensing the turning point of a game, Lasker has alertly taken advantage of Black's weak 17th move.

20	. . . .	KR-Q

In view of the troublesome pressure exercised by White against the weak QKtP, Black decides to give up a P—at first sight a promising project, as White's Q side Ps will be quite weak.

21	PxP	PxP
22	QxBP!	QxQ
23	KtxQ	RxKt

If instead 23 . . . BxP; 24 Ktx KP, PxKt; 25 KxB.

| 24 | RxB | R-QR4 |

Position after Black's 24th move

This is the position Snosko-Borowski aimed for: his Rs have ample scope and his opponent's extra P is to all intents and purposes worthless. All the more surprising is the unexpected series of charming moves by which Lasker solidifies his grip on the position.

25 R-Q!

This is not merely a piece of pretty "fireworks," as it wrests command of the Q file from Black.

| 25 | . . . . | R-QB |
| 26 | R-B7! | |

Forcing the advance of the passed P, which suddenly becomes a menace to be warded off only with the greatest difficulty.

| 26 | . . . . | R-Kt |
| 27 | P-B5! | Kt-Q4 |

After 27 . . . RxRP? 28 P-B6 White would win quickly, for example 28 . . . R(R7)-Kt7; 29 Bx P, R-Kt8; 30 RxR, RxRch; 31 B-B, R-Kt; 32 R-Kt7.

| 28 | R-Q7! | K-B |

Not 28 . . . RxRP; 29 P-QB4!

29	P-B6	R-B4
30	P-QB4	Kt-B3
31	P-B7!	

Better than 31 R-Kt7, R-B etc.

31	. . . .	R-K
32	R(Q7)-Q6	P-QR4
33	R-R6	K-K2
34	R-Kt!	

Black can no longer prevent the loss of a P after R-Kt5.

| 34 | . . . . | RxP(B2) |
| 35 | RxP | Kt-K5 |

It is still rather difficult for White to utilize his Q side Ps; his technical difficulties are far from inconsiderable.

36 R-B

Black threatened to regain his P by . . . Kt-Q7 etc.

| 36 | . . . . | R-Q |
| 37 | P-B3 | Kt-Q7? |

Better 37 . . . Kt-B4; the text hastens the end.

| 38 | B-K2 | R-Q5 |
| 39 | K-B2 | P-K4 |

The Kt is trapped! If 39 . . . KtxQBP; 40 R-R4 and . . . Kt-Kt3 is impossible because of RxR ch; or else 39 . . . K-Q3; 40 P-B 5ch! (40 K-K3, KtxPch!), K-Q4; 41 P-B6 dis ch! K-Q3; 42 K-K3, P-K4; 43 B-Q3, P-B4; 44 R-B2! (not 44 R-Q? Kt-B5ch), Kt-Kt8; 45 R(B2)-B5! Kt-Q7 (or 45 . . . Kt-R6; 46 R-B and wins); 46 Rx P winning easily.

40 RxPch	K-B3

Or 40 . . . K-Q3; 41 R-QR5, KtxQBP; 42 R-R4 and White exchanges all the pieces with a won K and P ending.

41 R-QKt5	KtxQBP
42 R-Kt4	Resigns

For if 42 . . . Kt-R4; 43 R-Kt 6ch, or 42 . . . Kt-Q3; 43 RxR (Q4).

GAME No. 58

St. Petersburg 1909

Ruy Lopez

White	Black
Dr. E. Lasker	**Dr. M. Vidmar**
1 P-K4	P-K4
2 Kt-KB3	Kt-QB3
3 B-Kt5	P-Q3
4 P-Q4	B-Q2
5 Kt-B3	PxP
6 KtxP	P-KKt3

In order to avoid the loss of time incurred in playing . . . B-K2, . . . R-K, . . . B-B, . . . P-KKt3 and . . . B-Kt2. But in the present instance the maneuver proves faulty, White being able to exploit the weakness of KB6 and KR7 in a decisive manner (Lasker).

7 B-K3	B-Kt2
8 Q-Q2	Kt-B3

After 8 . . . KKt-K2 Lasker would have played P-KR4-5 at once.

9 P-B3

In order to guard against . . . Kt-KKt5. White does not play the more customary P-KR3, as he intends to open the KR file by means of the advance of his KRP, after O-O-O.

9	O-O
10 O-O-O	P-QR3

Preparing a counter-attack which turns out to be too slow.

11 B-K2	P-QKt4
12 P-KR4	Kt-K4

This move is very finely refuted by Lasker. Schlechter suggests 12 . . . R-K and if 13 B-R6, B-R; this is however incorrect, since 13 B-R6 would lose a piece after 13 . . . KtxKt. White could very well answer 12 . . . R-K with 13 P-KKt4.

13 B-R6	Kt-B5

At first glance Black seems to obtain a promising attack with 13 . . . P-B4; 14 Kt-Kt3, P-Kt5; 15 Kt-Q5, P-B5. But after 13 . . . P-B4 the continuation would be 14 BxB!

I   14 . . . PxKt; 15 BxKt, Qx B (15 . . . PxKt; 16 QxQP); 16 QxP.

II   14 . . . KxB; 15 Kt-Kt3, P-B5 or . . . P-Kt5; 16 QxP. If instead 15 . . . Kt-B5; 16 Q-B4! (Lasker) and White has considerably the better of it, for example

16 . . . Kt-K; 17 BxKt, PxB; 18 Kt-Q2, B-K3; 19 P-K5±.

It should be noted, however, that after 13 . . . P-B4; 14 BxB, KxB; 15 Kt-Kt3, Kt-B5 White would derive little advantage from 16 B xKt, PxB; 17 KtxP, PxKt; 18 P-K5, B-K3; better is 16 BxKt, PxB; 17 QxP! PxKt; 18 P-K5, PxRP; 19 PxKtch, QxP; 20 KtxP, B-K3; 21 Kt-B3 etc.

14 BxKt   PxB

Position after Black's 14th move

15 P-R5!

Very well played! The capture of the RP would lead to a clearly lost game:

I 15 . . . KtxRP; 16 BxB, Kx B; 17 P-KKt4, Kt-B3; 18 Q-R6ch, K-Kt; 19 P-Kt5, Kt-R4; 20 Kt-Q5 (Lasker), P-KB4; 21 RxKt, PxR; 22 Kt-B6ch and wins.

II 15 . . . PxP; 16 Q-Kt5, Kt-K; 17 QxP or possibly even stronger is 16 BxB, KxB; 17 P-KKt4!

15 . . . .   P-B3

This weakens the QP irreparably, but 15 . . . B-K3 instead is impossible because of 16 BxB, Kx B; 17 PxP, RPxP; 18 Q-R6ch and mate next move, or else 15 . . . Q-K2; 16 P-KKt4, KR-K (not 16 . . . B-K3; 17 BxB, KxB; 18 PxP, BPxP; 19 Q-R6ch, K-Kt; 20 P-Kt5 and wins); 17 BxB, KxB; 18 PxP, BPxP; 19 Q-R6ch, K-R; 20 QxP or 19 . . . K-Kt; 20 P-Kt5, Kt-R4; 21 RxKt, PxR; 22 Kt-Q5 etc.

These variations go to show that White's Kt must be kept out of Q5.

16 BxB   KxB
17 PxP   BPxP
18 KKt-K2

Taking advantage of the fact that Black cannot play 18 . . . Kt-K; 19 Q-R6ch.

18 . . . .   R-B2
19 QxP   Q-Kt3
20 Q-Q4   P-B4

The end-game resulting from 20 . . . QxQ; 21 RxQ, B-K3; 22 Kt-B4 would be quite hopeless.

21 Kt-Q5!

If now 21 . . . PxQ; 22 KtxQ and Black's center Ps are decimated.

21 . . . .   Q-Kt2

Shortening the agony.

22 Q-B3

White consistently exploits his opponent's weaknesses on the black squares to the very end.

22 . . . .   QR-KB

White threatened 23 KtxKt, Rx Kt; 24 RxPch, or 23 RxPch, KxR; 24 KtxKtch etc.

23 KtxKt   RxKt
24 R-Q6   Resigns

He cannot parry the threat of 25 RxR, RxR; 26 RxPch as well as 25 RxR, RxR; 26 P-K5, R-K3; 27 Kt-B4.

A vigorously played game on Lasker's part.

GAME No. 59

St. Petersburg 1909

Scotch Game

White	Black
J. Mieses	**Dr. E. Lasker**
1 P-K4	P-K4
2 Kt-KB3	Kt-QB3
3 P-Q4	PxP
4 KtxP	B-B4

. . . Kt-B3 is also good.

| 5 B-K3 | B-Kt3 |

An innovation; the usual course is 5 . . . Q-B3; 6 P-QB3, KKt-K2 with a satisfactory game for Black.

| 6 Kt-QB3 | P-Q3 |
| 7 Kt-Q5 | |

Faulty; better 7 B-K2 and 8 O-O.

7	Kt-B3
8 KtxB	RPxKt
9 KtxKt	

The exchange is pointless. White has played the whole opening aimlessly and now has the inferior game.

| 9 . . . . | PxKt |
| 10 B-Q3 | Q-K2! |

A very good move which sets off Black's advantage, whereas if 10 . . . O-O; 11 B-KKt5, Q-K2; 12 P-B4! and White has an excellent game.

| 11 O-O | Q-K4! |

Of course not 11 . . . KtxP; 12 BxKt, QxB; 13 R-K±.

| 12 Q-B | O-O |
| 13 R-K | |

Indirectly protecting the KP.

| 13 . . . . | R-K |
| 14 P-KB3 | |

P-KB4 would weaken the KP.

| 14 . . . . | Kt-Q2! |
| 15 P-B3 | |

A weakening move; but White's game is inferior and it is not easy to hit on anything better.

15	Kt-B
16 Q-Q2	Q-KR4
17 B-KB4	P-B3!

Preventing P-K5, and at the same time preparing a retreat for the Q.

| 18 P-QR3 | |

White has only a choice of evils: the text weakens the white squares, P-QKt3 would weaken the QRP.

18	B-K3
19 B-Kt3	Kt-Q2
20 R-K3	Q-B2
21 QR-K	B-B5
22 B-QB2	

Exchanging Bs would accentuate the weakness of the white squares.

| 22 . . . . | R-R4! |

Allowing Black to double Rs on the K or QR file, according to circumstances.

| 23 Q-B | K-R |
| 24 Q-Q | R-K2 |

Although Black's position is superior, he is as yet unwilling to undertake any decisive action.

| 25 Q-Q2 | B-Kt6 |
| 26 BxB? | |

A bad positional blunder. The exchange is not forced and should therefore have been avoided.

26 . . . .   QxB
27 R-QB   Q-B2

White threatened P-QB4, which could now be answered by . . . P-QB4 and . . . Kt-Kt-B3∓.

28 R-Q   K-Kt
29 Q-QB2   R-R
30 R(K3)-K   P-QKt4
31 R-R

Intending P-QR4.

31 . . . .   Kt-B4
32 B-B2   Kt-Kt6
33 QR-Q   R(K2)-K
34 B-K3   Q-B5
35 Q-K2   R-K2
36 Q-QB2   QR-K
37 B-B2   R-K3

Black intends playing his K to the Q side, so as to be able to exploit the weakness of the white squares (after an exchange of pieces).

38 Q-Kt   P-R4

If 38 . . . K-B2; 39 P-K5 gives White chances.

39 P-R3   K-B2
40 P-Kt4?

Considerably facilitating Black's task; but Mieses evidently lacked the patience to defend himself passively.

40 . . . .   PxP
41 RPxP   P-Q4!

Lasker loses no time in exploiting his opponent's mistake.

(See diagram next column)

Position after Black's 41st move

42 PxP   RxRch
43 BxR

Forced: if 43 RxR, Kt-Q7; 44 Q-Q, RxRch; 45 BxR, Q-B8ch and wins.

43 . . . .   Q-K7!
44 PxP   QxBP
45 R-Q7ch   K-Kt
46 Q-Q   R-K7!!

White must now give up a piece to avoid mate, for if 47 QxKtch, K-R2 and White is helpless.

47 Q-Q5ch   QxQ
48 RxQ   RxBch
49 K-B2   R-K3
50 RxP   Kt-Q7

Winning the QBP, for if 51 R-QB5? Kt-K5ch.

51 P-R4   Kt-K5ch
52 K-Kt2   RxP
53 P-R5   K-B2
54 P-Kt4

White chooses to die quickly. Against 54 . . . K-K3 followed by . . . R-B4, he had no good continuation.

54 . . . .   Kt-Q3!
the simplest. If instead 54 . . . RxP; 55 R-Kt7, Kt-Q3; 56 P-R6! and White has chances.

55 R-Kt8	RxP
56 P-R6	R-QR6
57 R-QR8	K-Kt3
58 R-R7	Kt-Kt4
59 R-Kt7	P-B3
60 R-Kt6	Kt-Q5
61 K-B2	K-Kt4
62 K-K	KxP
63 K-Q2	P-KB4
64 K-B	P-B5
65 K-Kt2	P-B6!

A final elegant touch; if 66 Kx R, P-B7; 67 P-R7, P-B8=Q; 68 P-R8=Q, Q-R8 mate. White resigns.

GAME No. 60

St. Petersburg 1909

Ruy Lopez

White	Black
Dr. E. Lasker	**R. Teichmann**
1 P-K4	P-K4
2 Kt-KB3	Kt-QB3
3 B-Kt5	P-QR3
4 B-R4	Kt-B3
5 O-O	B-K2
6 Q-K2	

This move, reintroduced into master play by Yates and Thomas, was rarely played previously.

6 . . . .   P-QKt4

Not 6 . . . O-O? 7 BxKt, QPx QPxB; 8 KtxP, Q-Q5; 9 Kt-KB3, QxKP; 10 QxQ, KtxQ; 11 R-K.

| 7 B-Kt3 | P-Q3 |
| 8 P-B3 | O-O |

A better alternative is 8 . . . Kt-QR4; 9 B-B2, P-B4; 10 P-Q3 (10 P-Q4, Q-B2 and White cannot play QKt-Q2), O-O etc.

9 P-Q4   PxP

Giving up the center, which (1) leaves Black without any good squares for his pieces and (2) allows White to develop his Kt at QB3 instead of at Q2. The right move was . . . B-Kt5.

10 PxP

It is instructive to see how quickly Teichmann's game disintegrates after this unfortunate exchange.

10 . . . .   B-Kt5
11 R-Q

Tarrasch points out that White is already threatening to advance in the center, for example 12 P-K5, Kt-Q2; 13 B-Q5, or 12 . . . PxP; 13 PxP, Kt-Q2; 14 P-K6 and wins.

11 . . . .   P-Q4

Subsequently the P becomes weak, but it is difficult to suggest a better combination for Black.

| 12 P-K5 | Kt-K5 |
| 13 Kt-B3 | |

Removing Black's only well-placed piece and at the same time strengthening his own center.

13 . . . .   KtxKt
14 PxKt   P-B3?

A decisive blunder! He should have played 14 . . . Kt-R4; 15 B-B2, P-KB3 (Lasker).

15 P-KR3!   B-R4

15 . . . BxKt loses the exchange and a P after 16 QxB, while 15 . . . B-K3 would be refuted by 16 PxP, RxP; 17 B-Kt5, R-Kt3; 18 B-B2.

16 P-Kt4   B-B2

Evidently in order to provoke the further advance of the P in order to be able to play . . . B-Q3 later on. After 16 . . . B-Kt3 could continue with 17 Kt-R4, leaving Black's game in a hopeless state (17 . . . PxP; 18 KtxB, Px Kt; 19 PxP and wins, or 17 . . . B-K5? 18 QxB).

| 17 P-K6 | B-Kt3 |
| 18 Kt-R4 | |

Threatening 19 KtxB, PxKt; 20 Q-B3 among other things.

| 18 . . . . | Kt-R4 |
| 19 KtxB | PxKt |

19 . . . KtxB? would cost a piece after 20 KtxBch.

| 20 B-B2 | P-KB4 |
| 21 K-R! | |

In order to be able to obtain a devastating attack by bringing the R to the KKt file.

| 21 . . . . | B-Q3 |

"In order to bring the Q to R5 so as to prevent White's Q from carrying out the same maneuver (after PxP, PxP). But now the passed P is no longer blocked, and its advance later on decides the game" (Tarrasch). Black, however, has little choice: if instead 21 . . . Kt-B5; 22 PxP, PxP; 23 R-KKt, Kt-Q3; 24 B-R6, B-B3; 25 P-K7! or 24 . . . Kt-K; 25 Q-R5 and White must win.

| 22 PxP | Q-R5 |

After 22 . . . PxP the continuation might well have been 23 Q-R5, Q-B3; 24 R-KKt, QxKP; 25 B-R6, R-B2; 26 BxP, RxB; 27 BxP (Tarrasch), with an overwhelming

attack: 27 . . . Q-B3; 28 RxRch, KxR; 29 Q-R7ch, K-B; 30 R-KKt, Q-B2 (. . . K-K allows mate in two); 31 Q-R6ch winning the Q.

| 23 Q-B3 | PxP |
| 24 R-KKt | |

Now White has an ideal attacking position, the chief threats being 25 B-Kt5 or else 25 BxP, Q-B3; 26 Q-Kt2 etc.

| 24 . . . . | P-B5 |
| 25 R-Kt4 | Q-R3 |

Position after Black's 25th move

26 P-K7!

Crushing all further resistance. If now 26 . . . KR-K or . . . R-B2; 27 B-Kt6.

| 26 . . . . | BxP |
| 27 BxP | Q-K3 |

Black resigned without awaiting his opponent's reply, as 28 RxPch would soon lead to mate. Had he played 27 . . . Q-B3; 28 QxPch, Q-B2; 29 RxPch would have won easily.

GAME No. 61

First Match 1909

Ruy Lopez

White	Black
Dr. E. Lasker	**D. Janowski**

1	P-K4	P-K4
2	Kt-KB3	Kt-QB3
3	B-Kt5	P-QR3
4	BxKt	

Seemingly a queer continuation under the circumstances. The present match consisted of four games of which Lasker had won the first and lost the next two. Hence he had to win this, the last game, in order to draw the match! The text-move does not seem a very forcible method of bringing about this result, but its psychological value is inestimable: the ever impetuous Janowski must needs play for a win—although a draw would suffice!

4	....	QPxB
5	Kt-B3	B-QB4
6	P-Q3	Q-K2

For . . . B-KKt5 see Game No. 27.

7 B-K3

In reply to this, Marco recommends . . . B-Q3 and . . . P-B3, as previously played in a consultation game between these players. But in that event, why not play 5 . . . P-B3 directly, instead of losing time as Black does here?

7	....	BxB
8	PxB	

Now White has a strong center and attacking chances on the open file (Marco).

8	....	B-Kt5
9	Q-K2	Kt-R3

Avoiding the customary development of the Kt at B3 in order to be able to play . . . P-B3 presently.

10	O-O-O	O-O-O
11	P-KR3	B-R4
12	P-Q4	

This is White's only chance of creating complications, but it had to be considered carefully, since the center might have become weak later on.

12 . . . . PxP

Janowski sums up the position too optimistically. It would have been better to hold the center with 12 . . . P-B3, making it difficult for White to formulate any far-reaching plan. This was Black's best course from an objective point of view; but it would hardly be congenial to a player of Janowski's temperament.

13	PxP	KR-K
14	KR-K	P-B3

In order to fix White's KP, which however, is not so weak as Janowski seems to think!

14 . . . P-KB4; 15 P-K5, P-KKt4 was a far superior alternative.

15 P-KKt4 B-B2

Marco suggests . . . B-Kt3 instead, but the maneuver Kt-KR4-B5 is bound to give White the advantage in any event.

16 Q-B2!

A good move which (1) strengthens White's grip on the KB file and (2) decreases Black's pressure on the K file.

16 . . . . K-Kt

Forestalling P-Q5.

17 K-Kt	B-Kt

To what lengths did not Janow-ski go to preserve his beloved Bishops?! Surely it would have been better to have exchanged on the 11th move.

18 Kt-KR4	Kt-B2
19 Kt-B5	Q-B

The mobility of Black's B leaves something to be desired.

20 P-Kt3	Kt-Q3
21 R-Q3!	Kt-Kt4

Black does not accomplish a great deal with this maneuver, but he has a difficult game no matter what he does. If for example . . . P-KKt3; 22 Kt-Kt3 and the BP is weak, or . . . KtxKt; 22 KtPxKt and White's game is distinctly su-perior.

22 Kt-QR4	P-QKt3
23 P-B4!	

After this Black has little choice, for if now 23 . . . Kt-Q3; 24 Ktx Kt, QxKt; 25 P-B5 with a formid-able position.

23	Kt-R6ch

Now Janowski has an interesting problem on his hands: is the Kt to get out alive?!

24 K-B!	

Not 24 K-Kt2, KtxPch; 25 Px Kt, Q-Kt5ch.

24	P-Kt3

In order to get more room for his pieces, Black drives away the obstreperous Kt. But now he is troubled by the resulting weakness of the BP, on which Lasker soon trains his guns.

25 Kt-Kt3	Q-K2
26 Q-Q2!	K-Kt2

If 26 . . . P-QR4 White would double Rs, as in the game.

27 Q-B3	P-QR4

This move is too late, as Lasker demonstrates by his energetic play.

28 R-B3	R-KB
29 R(K)-KB	P-R4!?

The burden of protecting the Kt *and* the BP is too great for Black; he attempts a tactical demonstra-tion which is elegantly refuted.

30 PxP	PxP

Hoping for 31 KtxRP, QxP; 32 K-Kt2, KtxPch; 33 PxKt, RxP; 34 KtxBP, RxKt; 35 RxR, RxP and wins (Marco).

Position after Black's 30th move

31 Kt-B5!

A crushing reply.

31	Q-Kt5

. . . QxP would not do because of 32 K-Kt2 and the QP is pro-tected. White now begins a fine and deeply considered combination, by means of which he definitely maintains the advantage (Marco).

32 P-Q5!	B-R2

Or 32 . . . P-B4; 33 Kt-K7!

33 Kt-Q4!

The point! Black is forced to ex-change Qs, after which his Kt is trapped—this time with fatal results.

33 . . . .   BxP

33 . . . P-QB4; 34 Kt-B6, Qx Qch; 35 KtxQ or 33 . . . PxP; 34 KPxP, QxQch; 35 KtxQ are clearly just as hopeless.

34	KtxBP	QxQch
35	KtxQ	BxR
36	KtxRch	RxKt
37	RxB	P-Kt4
38	PxP	K-Kt3
39	RxPch	R-Q3

Now it seems as if Black can rescue his Kt after all.

40 R-B8!   Resigns

GAME No. 62

Second Match 1909
Four Knights' Game

White	Black
D. Janowski	**Dr. E. Lasker**
1 P-K4	P-K4
2 Kt-KB3	Kt-QB3
3 Kt-B3	Kt-B3
4 B-Kt5	B-Kt5
5 O-O	O-O
6 P-Q3	P-Q3

About the time this match was played, the Swedish analyst Svenonius recommended 6 . . . BxKt; 7 PxB, P-Q4—which leads to intricate and difficult play.

7 B-Kt5	BxKt
8 PxB	Kt-K2

An old-fashioned variation which has been replaced by . . . Q-K2 after Rubinstein's successful adoption of this move in several notable post-war games. Alapin has suggested the following interesting

line of play: 8 . . . P-KR3; 9 B-KR4, P-Kt4; 10 KtxKtP, KtxP! 11 Kt-B3, Kt-Kt4; 12 K-R, B-Kt5 with a good game.

9 B-QB4

The best move at White's disposal in this position is 9 Kt-R4 with 10 P-KB4 to follow.

9 . . . .   Kt-Kt3
10 Kt-R4

There is really nothing better now, else Black simply releases the pin with . . . P-KR3.

10 . . . .   Kt-B5!

This strong move (an invention of Pillsbury's) does not leave White much choice, for if 11 Q-B3, P-KR3; 12 BxQKt, PxB; 13 QxP? Kt-R4, or if 11 Kt-B5, P-Q4, or 11 P-Kt3? Kt-R6ch. On other moves Black can continue with . . . P-KR3 (Alapin).

11 BxQKt   PxB
12 Kt-B3

In order to parry the threat of . . . KtxP. As will be seen subsequently, however, the P at B5 is destined to be very troublesome for White and hence P-Kt3, leading to about an even game, was his best course. Janowski evidently considered the doubled P weak and therefore deliberately avoided P-Kt3.

12 . . . .   B-Kt5
13 P-KR3

If White intends playing Q-Q2, it would be well to do so directly, as the text-move induces a critical weakness in his game.

13 . . . .   B-R4
14 R-Kt   P-QKt3
15 Q-Q2?

This turns out badly, but White's reasons for playing it are obvious enough: he rids himself of the unpleasant pin and at the same time he prepares an attack on the resulting open file.

15	BxKt
16 PxB	Kt-R4
17 K-R2	Q-B3

The position now arrived at is rather deceptive, for Black's superiority, though considerable, is unobtrusive. White can double his Rs on the KKt file, but nothing will come of the "attack"; his B seems better placed than the Kt, but the nature of the Pawn position renders this B quite ineffective, while the Kt can readily be brought into play. White's position has reached its maximum power, while Black's game contains stores of potential energy.

| 18 R-Kt | QR-K |
| 19 P-Q4 | |

White has an imposing center, but there is absolutely nothing to be done with it; the P at B5 cripples his game (Tarrasch).

| 19 . . . . | K-R |
| 20 R-QKt5 | |

An ingenious maneuver, but quite fruitless: Lasker protects himself with the greatest ease.

| 20 . . . . | Q-R3 |

After . . . P-B4 (which would only needlessly complicate matters) White would get a good game by 21 P-K5 or P-R4-5.

| 21 QR-Kt5 | P-KB3 |
| 22 QR-Kt4 | P-Kt3 |

Tarrasch suggests . . . P-KB4 directly, with the following possible continuations: 23 R(Kt4)-Kt2, Px P; 24 PxP, RxP; 25 B-K2.

I   25 . . . Kt-Kt6? 26 B-B3.

II   25 . . . P-B6; 26 QxQ, Px Q; 27 BxP.

III   25 . . . RxB; 26 QxR, P-B6; 27 Q-K7, Q-B5ch; 28 R-Kt3 "with a better position than in the game," although Black maintains a winning advantage with 28 . . . KtxR; 29 RxKt, Q-B2 etc.

23 B-Q3

Doubtless directed against . . . P-KB4, but it would have been better to play non-committal moves, keeping the B on B4. Janowski was not the player to pursue a waiting policy!

| 23 . . . . | R-K2 |
| 24 P-B4? | |

This is distinctly bad, not only because it devaluates the B, but because it allows Lasker to improve his position by an alert tactical finesse.

| 24 . . . . | Kt-Kt2! |

Taking advantage of White's slip to post the Kt on better squares; if now 25 QxP, QxQ; 26 RxQ, Kt-K3 and . . . KtxP with a won ending.

25 P-B3?

Very poor play! 25 P-Q5 was essential to keep the Kt out of the game.

| 25 . . . . | Kt-K3! |
| 26 B-B | |

Somewhat better was 26 P-Q5, Kt-B4; 27 B-K2, P-KKt4; 28 R-KR and if 28 . . . Kt-Q2; 29 R (Kt4)-Kt, Kt-K4; 30 K-Kt2, P-KB4; 31 PxP, RxP; 32 K-B although Black should win.

26 . . . .   P-KB4!
27 R(Kt4)-Kt2

Or 27 PxP, RxP followed by
. . . R-KR4 and . . . Kt-Kt4.

27 . . . .   R-B3!
28 B-Q3   P-KKt4!

Threatening mate in two.

29 R-KR

In order to create a flight square;
29 PxP? would merely postpone
the mate for another two moves.

29 . . . .   P-Kt5!

Once more threatening . . . Kt-
Kt4 with decisive effect.

30 B-K2   Kt-Kt4!

A crushing move to which there
is no reply. White must lose a
piece.

Position after Black's 30th move

31 BPxP

Not 31 QxP? KtxPch; 32 K-
Kt3, Q-R5 mate.

31 . . . .   P-B6
32 R-Kt3   PxB
Resigns

A beautiful game on Lasker's
part—played with considerable energy and not without finesse.

Match 1910
Queen's Gambit Declined

White   Black
Dr. E. Lasker   C. Schlechter

1 P-Q4   P-Q4
2 P-QB4   P-QB3
3 Kt-KB3   Kt-B3
4 P-K3   P-KKt3

An idea which later found many
supporters. Why Schlechter chose
this fighting defense instead of an
easier, more tranquil one, would be
difficult to say. A draw would have
won the match and the championship of the world! And yet time
and again we find Schlechter refusing to play for a draw, always
choosing the riskier alternative.

5 Kt-B3   B-Kt2
6 B-Q3

Dr. Lasker, in his turn, must
play for a win if he is to retain his
title. The text prepares for a K
side attack. 6 Q-Kt3 followed by
B-Q2 and R-B is now considered
White's best line of play.

6 . . . .   O-O
7 Q-B2   Kt-R3?!

Again Schlechter adopts an aggressive but risky line of play instead of the "natural" . . . QKt-
Q2.

8 P-QR3

Of course he must prevent . . .
Kt-QKt5.

8 . . . .   PxP

Preparing the following advance
of the QKtP, which, however, results in a serious weakening of
Black's Q side. Much better is
Tarrasch's suggestion of . . . Kt-

B2-K-Q3 followed by . . . B-B4
and . . . Kt-K5.

9 BxBP	P-QKt4
10 B-Q3	P-Kt5
11 Kt-QR4	

Stronger than 11 BxKt, PxKt;
12 B-Q3, PxP; 13 BxQKtP, B-Kt2.

11	PxP
12 PxP	B-Kt2
13 QR·Kt	Q-B2

White's position is decidedly superior: his pieces are more aggressively placed, while Black has the
serious weakness of a backward P
on an open file.

14 Kt-K5

An unnecessary but harmless excursion. White should have played
14 O-O followed by B-Q2 and
KR-B, with decisive positional advantage.

14	Kt-R4
15 P-Kt4?!	

A vigorous "attacking" move
which weakens the K side. 15 Bx
Kt, BxB; 16 QxBP would, to be
sure, *not* win a P because of 16
. . . BxKt; 17 QxB, BxRP (or
even . . . QR-Kt); 18 P-Kt3, Bx
P; 19 RxKt, PxR; 20 PxB, QxP
ch∓ (Tarrasch). However, White
has two good lines of play at his
disposal: (1) 15 P-B4, defending
the Kt a second time, or (2) 15
Kt-B3!, avoiding complications and
not really losing any time since
Black's KKt must also retreat eventually. Either move would leave
White with a considerable advantage.

15	BxKt
16 PxKt	

16 PxB, Kt-Kt2; 17 P-B4, KR-
Q is too dangerous for White

16	B-Kt2
17 PxP	RPxP
18 Q-B4	B-B!
19 R-Kt	

19 BxP would win a P, but after
19 . . . B-K3; 20 QxKt (or 20
BxPch, BxB; 21 QxKt, B-Q4), Px
B etc. Black has a strong attack.

19	Q-R4ch
20 B-Q2	Q-Q4

If now 21 QxQ, PxQ; 22 R-Q
Kt5, R-Q! and White has nothing
definite.

21 QR-B	B-Kt2
22 Q-B2	Q-KR4

White was threatening 23 RxP!

23 BxP?!

After the game Lasker wrote,
"My 23rd move was refuted by
Schlechter . . . Much simpler and
better was 23 R-Kt . . . Further
23 Q-Kt3 was worth considering."

23	QxP
24 R-B	PxB!
25 Q-Kt3ch	R-B2
26 QxB	QR-KB!

Now the profound idea behind
Schlechter's attacking defense
comes to light: 27 QxKt would be
ruinous for Lasker because of 27
. . . RxP.

27 Q-Kt3

P-B4 at once would have been
stronger, as Black would lose time
saving his Kt.

27	K-R
28 P-B4	P-Kt4
29 Q-Q3?	

White could—and should—
have taken the proffered P. After

29 RxP Black's best move is 29
. . . Kt-Kt (if 29 . . . PxP; 30
PxP, Kt-Kt; 31 R-QB3! with decisive advantage). But White replies 30 R-B7 and Black's game
is untenable, for example 30 . . .
PxP; 31 PxP, BxP; 32 Q-Q5±.

29	PxP
30 PxP	Q-R5ch
31 K-K2	Q-R7ch
32 R-B2	

If 32 K-Q, Q-R4ch; 33 K-B2,
Q-KB4 and White cannot win.

| 32 . . . . | Q-R4ch |
| 33 R-B3 | |

Intending 34 R-KR, QxR; 35
R-R3ch.

| 33 . . . . | Kt-B2! |

Black rightly decides to give up
the P. If 33 . . . Q-QKt4 (the alternative . . . Kt-Kt is hardly
good); 34 R-B4±.

| 34 RxP | Kt-Kt4! |

Schlechter, who has displayed
remarkable energy, here disdains an
easy draw by . . . Kt-Q4. Marco
gives the following variations:

I 34 . . . Kt-Q4; 35 R-B5,
RxP; 36 BxR, KtxBch; 37 K-Q,
Kt-Q4 (or even 37 . . . P-K4).

II 34 . . . Kt-Q4; 35 Q-Kt6,
QxQ; 36 RxQ, KtxPch; 37 BxKt,
RxB.

35 R-B4

But not 35 R-B5, KtxPch; 36
QxKt, QxRch.

(See diagram next column)

| 35 . . . . | RxP?! |

A hallucination! With 35 . . .
R-Q Schlechter would have won
the game, the match and the cham-

Position after White's 35th move

pionship! If White replies 36 B-
K3, then 36 . . . P-K4!

Schlechter explained later that
he relied on 36 BxR, RxB; 37 R-
B8ch, B-B; 38 K-B2, Q-R5ch; 39
K-Kt2 best, Q-Kt5ch and saw too
late that White can reply 40 R-Kt
3! QxR; 41 Q-Kt6! winning. The
text-move should however still
draw.

36 BxR	RxB
37 R-B8ch	B-B
38 K-B2	

Obviously the only move.

| 38 . . . . | Q-R7ch |
| 39 K-K | Q-R8ch? |

The decisive blunder. 39 . . .
Q-R5ch would have drawn, as
shown by the following variations:

I 40 K-Q2, Q-R7ch; 41 K-K3,
RxRch; 42 KxR, Q-R6ch; 43 K-
K2, QxR; 44 QxKt.

II 40 K-B, Q-R6ch; 41 K-B2,
RxRch; 42 QxR, QxR; 43 Q-R5
ch, K-Kt; 44 QxKt.

III 40 R-Kt3? Q-R8ch; 41 K-
Q2, R-B7ch and Black wins.

40 R-B	Q-R5ch
41 K-Q2	RxR
42 QxR	QxPch
43 Q-Q3	Q-B7ch

44 K-Q   Kt-Q3

Black still has a slight attack, but White's material advantage will now decide the day. He is bound to force further simplifica-tion (as on the 51st move, when he threatens 52 R-KKt5). There followed: 45 R-B5, B-R3; 46 R-Q5, K-Kt; 47 Kt-B5, Q-Kt8ch; 48 K-B2, Q-B8ch; 49 K-Kt3, B-Kt2; 50 Kt-K6, Q-Kt7ch; 51 K-R4, K-B2; 52 KtxB, QxKt; 53 Q-QKt3, K-K; 54 Q-Kt8ch, K-B2; 55 QxP, Q-Kt5ch; 56 Q-Q4, Q-Q2ch; 57 K-Kt3, Q-Kt2ch; 58 K-R2, Q-B3; 59 Q-Q3, K-K3; 60 R-KKt5, K-Q 2; 61 R-K5, Q-Kt7ch; 62 R-K2, Q-Kt5; 63 R-Q2, Q-QR5; 64 Q-B5ch, K-B2; 65 Q-B2ch, QxQ; 66 RxQch, K-Kt3; 67 R-K2, Kt-B; 68 K-Kt3, K-B3; 69 R-B2ch, K-Kt2; 70 K-Kt4, Kt-R2; 71 K-B5 and Black resigned.

An exciting game which despite its mistakes is worthy of these two great masters and the occasion on which it was played.

GAME No. 64

Match 1910

Queen's Gambit Declined

White	Black
D. Janowski	**Dr. E. Lasker**

1 P-Q4	P-Q4
2 Kt-KB3	Kt-KB3
3 P-K3	P-B4
4 P-B4	P-K3
5 B-Q3	Kt-B3
6 O-O	PxBP
7 BxBP	

The position has transposed into the Queen's Gambit Accepted, al-though White has lost a tempo by moving his KB twice.

7 . . . .   P-QR3
8 P-QR4

This costs another tempo and gives Black a useful square at QKt5 for his pieces, but likewise after 8 Q-K2, P-QKt4; 9 B-Kt3, B-Kt2; 10 R-Q, Q-Kt3 Black would have a good position.

8	B-K2
9 Kt-B3	O-O
10 P-QKt3	PxP!
11 PxP	Kt-QKt5!
12 B-Kt2	P-QKt3
13 Q-K2	B-Kt2
14 QR-Q	KKt-Q4
15 Kt-K5	

It is clear that Black's prospects have greatly improved. He block-ades the isolated QP; his posses-sion of QKt5 assures him excellent squares for his pieces; his QB has a beautiful open diagonal, while White's corresponding B is de-graded to the status of a P and in addition leaves KB4 unpro-tected; finally White's weak Ps (Q 4 and QKt3) virtually force him to play willy-nilly for the attack, since an end-game would be dis-advantageous for him.

All these difficulties, as Tarrasch points out, stem more or less from White's 8th move.

15 . . . .   Kt-B5

Leads to interesting play.

16 Q-Kt4

Now 16 . . . KtxP would be answered by 17 P-Q5! Kt-R5; 18 PxP, P-B4 (not 18 . . . Q-B2; 19 PxPch, K-R; 20 Kt-K4); 19 Q-Kt3±. Lasker is fully alive to the danger of allowing the advance of the QP, as his next move shows.

16 . . . .   Kt(Kt5)-Q4

Threatening 17 . . . P-KR4; 18
Q-Kt3, B-R5; 19 Q-B3, KtxKt; 20
QxKt(B3), BxP and wins.

17 KtxKt   KtxKt
18 KR-K

In order to be able to get up an
attack by advancing the BP—at
present impossible because of . . .
Kt-K6.

18 R-Q3 (in order to play R-
R3) would be useless because of 18
. . . P-KR4 and White must play
19 Q-B3 with a bad game (but not
19 Q-Q, Kt-B5; 20 R-Kt3, B-R5).

18 . . . .   B-Kt5!

Lasker's method of utilizing the
hole at QKt5 is very skilful. Not
only does the text permit of the
defense of the K side by the QR
(see Black's 20th move), but it
also paves the way for the subsequent gain of the exchange.

19 R-K2   R-B
20 P-B4   R-B2!

Very good! The R not only
protects the K side but also guards
the QB; so that 21 . . . P-KR4
becomes a strong threat now, for if
22 Q-B3, Kt-B6.

21 P-B5

Leading to the loss of a P or of
the exchange; but Janowski prefers
to lose the game in his own way:
a somewhat dubious satisfaction.

21 . . . .   P-KR4!
22 QxP

This gives White attacking
chances, while after 22 Q-Kt3, Px
P he would have no counter-play
at all.

22 . . . .   Kt-B5
23 Q-Kt4   KtxRch
24 QxKt   PxP
25 Q-R5

The open file lends a superficial
appearance of danger to Black's
game, but Lasker's cold-blooded
precision soon dispels all difficulty.

25 . . . .   B-Q4

White threatened Kt-Kt6 and
mate next move.

Position after Black's 25th move

26 R-Q3

Threatening R-R3; but 26 QxP
would have given Black more difficulty:

I   26 QxP, BxB; 27 PxB, Q-B3;
28 Q-Kt4, Q-K3; 29 Q-Kt3, P-B3;
30 P-Q5, Q-B4; 31 Kt-B6, B-B4
ch; 32 K-R, Q-QB7 and wins.

II   26 QxP, BxB; 27 KtxB, Q-
B3; 28 QxQ, PxQ; 29 KtxP, R-
B7;

(a) 30 Kt-B4, KR-B; 31 B-B
(31 P-Q5, KRxKt; 32 PxR, RxB;
33 P-Q6, R-Q7), R-B6; 32 P-Q5,
RxP; 33 P-Q6, RxKt; 34 P-Q7,
B-K2 etc.

(b) 30 B-B, R-Kt; 31 Kt-Q5, B-
B6; 32 KtxPch, K-Kt2; 33 Kt-K4,

BxPch; 34 RxB, RxBch; 35 K-B2, RxP; 36 Kt-Q2, R-KR6 and wins.

26 . . . .   P-B3
27 R-R3

This is Janowski's first logical move in the whole game, as the situation clearly calls for hari-kari! If instead 27 Kt-Kt6, R-K; 28 Qx P (28 BxBch, QxB; 29 R-R3, R-K8ch is obviously ruinous, and if 28 R-R3, BxB; 29 PxB, RxP; 30 Q-R7ch, K-B2; 31 Kt-R8ch, RxKt and wins), BxB; 29 PxB, RxP; 30 R-R3, RxP etc.

27 . . . .   PxKt
28 Q-R7ch

In return for the piece Janowski obtains two Ps and four checks.

28 . . . .   K-B2
29 QxBPch   K-K
30 Q-R5ch

Or 30 QxPch, R-K2; 31 QxB? R-K8ch and mate next move.

30 . . . .   B-B2
31 QxPch   Q-K2
Resigns

Just in time to prevent mate in four after 32 QxP, Q-K8ch; 33 B-B, QxBch; 34 KxQ, B-B5 dbl ch, etc.

One of those remarkable games in which Lasker makes his oppon-ent look childish.

GAME No. 65

Match 1910

Queen's Gambit Declined

White	Black
Dr. E. Lasker	**D. Janowski**
1 P-Q4	P-Q4
2 P-QB4	P-K3
3 Kt-QB3	P-QB4
4 BPxP	KPxP
5 Kt-B3	B-K3
6 P-K4	

White can isolate the QP at will in this variation—so why ex-change off the weak P by means of the text move? More usual nowa-days—and superior to the text—is the Rubinstein Variation begin-ning with 6 P-KKt3.

6 . . . .   QPxP
7 KtxP   Kt-QB3
8 B-K3

To capture the P and attempt to retain it would be too risky, for example:

I   8 PxP, QxQch; 9 KxQ, O-O-Och; 10 K-B2, Kt-Kt5ch; 11 K-Kt, B-B4 winning two pieces for a R.

II   8 KtxP, BxKt; 9 PxB, Qx Qch; 10 KxQ, O-O-Och; 11 B-Q2, Kt-B3 and Black's position is easily worth a P.

8 . . . .   PxP
9 KtxP?

A mistake. 9 BxP was necessary and if 9 . . . KtxB; 10 QxKt (Tarrasch).

9 . . . .   Q-R4ch!
10 Kt-B3

This should have resulted in the loss of two pieces for a R. White has however no satisfactory reply:

I   10 B-Q2, Q-K4 and Black wins a piece.

II   10 Kt-Q2, KtxKt; 11 BxKt, O-O-O; 12 B-B3, B-QKt5; 13 Q-B, K-Kt; 14 BxB, QxB; 15 Q-B3, QxQ; 16 PxQ, Kt-B3 followed by . . . KR-K winning.

III   10 Q-Q2, B-QKt5; 11 Kt-

QB3, O-O-O∓.

10 . . . .   O-O-O
11 P-QR3

He cannot parry the opponent's
chief threat: 11 . . . KtxKt; 12
BxKt, B-QB4 or even 11 . . . B-
QB4.

11 . . . .   Kt-R3

Now Black begins to slip. He
could have won easily (as Tarrasch
points out) by 11 . . . B-QB4; 12
P-QKt4, BxKt; 13 PxQ (or 13
BxB, Q-KKt4; 14 Kt-K2, KtxB;
15 KtxKt, Q-K4ch), BxKtch; 14
B-Q2, RxB; 15 QxR, BxQch; 16
KxB, KtxP. 11 . . . KKt-K2 also
wins more easily than the text-
move (which gains only a P), as
will be seen from the note to
Black's 13th move.

12 P-QKt4   Q-K4
13 QKt-Kt5

QKt-K2 leads to too cramped a
position.

13 . . . .   Kt-B4

After this White must lose at
least a P, whereas after 13 . . .
P-R3 White could play 14 Q-B! P
xKt; 15 KtxKt, PxKt; 16 QxPch,
Q-B2; 17 Q-R6ch with an attack
sufficiently strong to compensate
for the sacrificed piece (Tarrasch).

14 R-B   KtxB

(See diagram next column)

A very tempting move for
White at this point is 15 KtxPch,
but after 15 . . . K-B2; 16 Kt
(Q4)-Kt5ch, K-Kt3; 17 RxKtch,
PxR; 18 QxRch, K-Kt2; 19 KtxP,
BxPch; 20 PxB, KtxP dbl ch; 21
K-Q2, RxQch; 22 KtxRch, K-Kt3;
23 BxKt, KxKt Black wins without
difficulty.

Position after Black's 14th move

15 PxKt   QxPch
16 B-K2   B-K2

Better than 16 . . . P-QR3; 17
Kt-R7ch, K-B2; 18 Kt(R7)xKt, P
xKt; 19 KtxBch, PxKt; 20 Q-B2
with good chances for White.

Tarrasch recommends 16 . . .
B-Kt6; 17 Q-Q2, QxQch; 18 Kx
Q, K-Kt; but Snosko-Borowski
cleverly refutes 16 . . . B-Kt6 with
17 KtxPch! K-B2 (forced); 18 Kt
(Q4)-Kt5ch, K-Kt3 (18 . . . K-Kt;
19 QxRch! KtxQ; 20 R-B8 mate);
19 RxKtch and wins.

17 R-B3

If 17 KtxPch, K-Kt; 18 KtxKt
ch, PxKt; 19 KtxPch, K-Kt2; 20
KtxRch, RxKt; 21 Q-B2, R-QB
and wins.

17 . . . .   B-R5ch

The attack now passes into
White's hands. To maintain the
initiative, Black should have sacrificed his Q by 17 . . . QxRch; 18
KtxQ, KtxKt∓ with a strong attack.

18 P-Kt3   Q-K5

Even now . . . QxRch would
have been preferable, though not
so strong as on the previous move.

| 19 | O-O | B-B3 |

. . . K-Kt would not do because of 20 B-B3.

20 RxB

This obvious sacrifice of the exchange allows White to snatch the attack from his opponent and conclude the game in forceful style.

20	. . . .	PxR
21	B-B3	Q-K4
22	KtxPch	K-B2
23	Kt(R7)xKt	PxKt
24	RxPch	K-Kt
25	R-Kt6ch	K-B
26	Q-Bch	K-Q2
27	KtxB	PxKt
28	R-Kt7ch	K-K
29	B-B6ch	Resigns

29 . . . K-B allows mate in two.

GAME No. 66

Moscow 1914 (Exhibition Game)

Ruy Lopez

| White | Black |
| **Dr. O. S. Bernstein** | **Dr. E. Lasker** |

1	P-K4	P-K4
2	Kt-KB3	Kt-QB3
3	B-Kt5	Kt-B3
4	O-O	P-Q3
5	P-Q4	B-Q2
6	Kt-B3	B-K2
7	R-K	PxP
8	KtxP	O-O
9	BxKt	PxB
10	B-Kt5	P-KR3

In a game between the same players at St. Petersburg 1909 (where White had played Q-Q3 instead of R-K), Lasker continued 10 . . . P-B4, but after 11 Kt-B5,

BxKt; 12 PxB, Kt-Q2; 13 BxB, QxB; 14 QR-K, Q-Q; 15 R-K2, Kt-B3; 16 KR-K, Q-Q2; 17 P-KR3, KR-K; 18 Kt-K4! the position was quite favorable for White.

| 11 | B-R4 | Kt-R2 |

The customary liberating move in this variation.

12	BxB	QxB
13	Q-Q3	KR-K
14	R-K3	Kt-B
15	Q-B4	

Thus far the game has proceeded on the usual lines, but now Bernstein begins an original and aggressive plan which is most ingeniously refuted by Lasker.

| 15 | . . . . | P-QB4 |
| 16 | Kt-Q5 | |

But here he over-reaches himself. He should have played 16 Kt-B3 or else 16 Kt-B5 and if . . . Bx Kt; 17 PxB, Q-Kt4; 18 Kt-Q5! P-QB3; 19 RxR, RxR; 20 Kt-K3±. Black's best line would be 17 . . . Q-B3, with chances for both sides

| 16 | . . . | Q-K4! |

Position after Black's 16th move

17 Kt-Kt3

The only move, as Black cannot play . . . QxKtP now.

17 . . . .   B-K3!

Threatening . . . P-QB3; White cannot go in for 18 Q-B3, BxKt and Black wins a P, or 18 P-B4, BxKt winning a piece.

18 Q-K2   QxKtP!

Well-timed: White cannot reply 19 KtxP because of . . . BxKt.

19 P-QB4

White must allow the exchange of Qs, else Black wins by . . . P-QB3 followed by . . . BxKt; while if 19 R-K, then simply . . . BxKt; 20 PxB, RxR winning another P.

19 . . . .   QxQ
20 RxQ   BxKt
21 BPxB   P-QR4!

Not only has Black a P ahead, but this move gives him command of the QKt file with an overwhelming position.

22 P-QR4   Kt-Q2
23 P-B3   KR-Kt!
24 R-K3   R-Kt5
25 Kt-B   Kt-Kt3
26 R(K3)-R3   P-B4!

Lasker carries out the whole game with a tactical verve which is delightful.

27 Kt-Q3   PxP!

A neat finish to a smartly played game.

28 KtxR   RPxKt
29 R-K3   KtxQP
30 RxP   Kt-B6
31 R-K7   P-Kt6
32 RxP   P-Kt7
33 R-KB   RxP
Resigns.

GAME No. 67

Moscow 1914
Ruy Lopez

White	Black
Dr. E. Lasker	**B. Blumenfeld**
	—. Estrin
	—. Pawlow

1 P-K4	P-K4
2 Kt-KB3	Kt-QB3
3 B-Kt5	P-QR3
4 B-R4	Kt-B3
5 O-O	B-K2
6 R-K	P-Q3
7 P-B3	

At this point White could transpose, if so inclined, into the Steinitz Defense Deferred by 7 Bx Ktch, PxB; 8 P-Q4 etc.

7 . . . .   P-QKt4
8 B-Kt3   B-Kt5

More usual is . . . O-O. The text has the desired effect of preventing White from playing P-Q4 at once, although this continuation would also be quite satisfactory for White.

9 P-Q3   O-O
10 QKt-Q2   Kt-QR4
11 B-B2   P-B4
12 P-KR3   B-K3

After . . . B-R4 the B would be out of play, but . . . B-Q2, as we shall see later, was best.

13 P-Q4   Q-B2
14 Kt-B   BPxP
15 PxP   KR-B
16 B-Q3   B-B5

This move can hardly be avoided, since the position of the B at K3 makes it impossible for the Kt to return to B3. But after the ensuing exchange, the QB file will be blocked.

17 BxB   PxB

The recapture with the Kt was probably better, but Black evidently hoped to exert some pressure on the QKtP.

18 B-Q2!   Kt-B3
19 B-B3   PxP

Again Black chooses the greater evil; it was preferable to allow the possibility of P-Q5 rather than free White's pieces for a K side attack.

20 KtxP   Kt-K4
21 Kt-B5   QR-Kt
22 Kt(B)-K3   B-B

If instead 22 . . . Kt-Q6; 23 KtxBch, QxKt; 24 Kt-B5, Q-Q; 25 R-K3, KtxKtP? 26 Q-Q4 followed by R-Kt3 with a winning attack.

23 P-B4!   Kt(K4)-Q2

And not 23 . . . Kt-Q6; 24 Bx Kt, KtxR; 25 Q-Kt4, P-Kt3; 26 RxKt winning easily; or 24 . . . PxB; 25 Q-Kt4ch, K-R; 26 Kt-Q5, Q-B4ch; 27 R-K3! and wins.

24 Kt-Q5!   KtxKt

After 24 . . . Q-Q White would obtain a powerful bind on the position with 25 Q-Q4.

Position after Black's 24th move

25 Kt-R6ch!

Winning a P, as the Kt is of course immune from capture.

25 . . .   K-R
26 KtxPch   K-Kt
27 Kt-R6ch   K-R

But of course not 27 . . . Px Kt; 28 QxKt mate!

28 PxKt   Kt-B3
29 Kt-Kt4!   KtxKt

If the Kt retreats, then P-B5 followed by R-K6 etc.

30 QxKt   Q-B2
31 R-K6   B-K2
32 P-B5   B-B3
33 BxB   PxB
34 Q-Q4   Q-KKt2
35 QR-K   Resigns

At least another P must fall.

GAME No. 68

St. Petersburg 1914
Scotch Game

White   Black
J. H. Blackburne Dr. E. Lasker

1 P-K4   P-K4
2 Kt-KB3   Kt-QB3
3 P-Q4   PxP
4 KtxP   B-B4

An old defense seldom played of late, . . . Kt-B3 being more usual.

5 B-K3   Q-B3
6 P-QB3   KKt-K2
7 Kt-B2   P-QKt3

An interesting move. After the exchange of Bs, which is inevitable, Black will have the open QKt file at his disposal. Another good line is 7 . . . BxB; 8 KtxB, Q-K4.

8 Kt-Q2   Q-Kt3

Hindering the development of White's KB.

9 BxB

If 9 B-KB4, P-Q4! (not 9 . . . P-Q3; 10 P-QKt4).

9 . . . .   PxB
10 Kt-K3   QR-Kt

Provoking a weakness on the Q side.

11 P-QKt3   O-O
12 B-B4

Else Black could play 12 . . . P-B4 with a good game.

12 . . . .   P-Q3
13 P-B4?!

A sacrifice or an oversight? The natural continuation was 13 O-O, K-R; 14 P-B4, P-B4 and Black stands well.

13 . . . .   Q-B3!
14 O-O

He cannot defend the P, for if 14 Kt-Q5, KtxKt; 15 BxKt (15 PxKt, R-Kch; 16 B-K2, B-Kt5), Kt-K2; 16 Q-B3, KtxB; 17 PxKt, R-Kch; 18 K-B2, Q-Kt3 threatening . . . B-Kt5 as well as . . . Q-B7.

14 . . . .   QxQBP
15 R-B3

White now threatens to threaten everything; one doesn't know just what!—but these are the situations which are the most dangerous (Marco).

15 . . . .   Q-Q5!

Gaining a valuable tempo for defensive purposes, as he threatens . . . B-Kt5.

16 K-R   B-K3

Black strives for . . . P-B4.

17 QR-B   BxB

18 RxB   Q-Kt7!
19 R-QB2   Q-B3
20 Kt-Kt4   Q-Kt3

Blackburne must have been praying for 20 . . . Q-R5? 21 R-R3.

21 R-Kt3   P-B4!

Lasker's handling of the technical part of the game is very fine: White's BP is now weak.

22 Kt-K5   Q-K3
23 KtxKt   KtxKt
24 P-K5

Hoping to disrupt Black's Pawn position, say 24 . . . PxP; 25 Px P, QxP; 26 R(Kt3)-QB3.

24 . . . .   Kt-Kt5!

Far better than 24 . . . Kt-Q5; 25 R-B4, PxP; 26 RxP, PxP; 27 R-Q3 etc. (Marco).

25 R-B4   PxP

Whereas if now 26 PxP, QxP; 27 R(Kt3)-QB3, Kt-Q4 wins the exchange.

26 Q-R!

An ingenious resource.

26 . . . .   Q-Q2!

A more ingenious reply: White's Kt is attacked and the mate at Kt2 is defended.

27 Kt-B3

If 27 QxP, QR-K; 28 Q-R, R-K7!∓.

27 . . . .   PxP
28 Kt-K5   Q-K2
29 RxKBP   QR-K
30 Kt-B4

Kt-B3 would avoid the exchange of Qs, but White is two Ps down with a hopeless game in any case.

30 . . . .   Q-K8ch
31 R-B   QxQ
32 RxQ   KtxP!

33	P-R3	P-B5
34	R-Q3	Kt-Kt5
35	R-Q7	P-B6!

Preparing a mating net: just in time, Black's Q side Ps being so weak.

36	PxP	RxP
37	RxRP	Kt-Q6!

Threatening mate in six by 38 . . . R-K8ch; 39 K-Kt2, R-B7ch; 40 K-Kt3, R-Kt8ch; 41 K-R4, R-B5ch; 42 K-R5, P-Kt3ch; 43 K-R6, R-R5 mate.

Position after Black's 37th move

38	R-R	Kt-K8!

Now the threat is 39 . . . R-B8ch; 40 K-R2, R-K7ch; 41 K-Kt3, R-Kt7ch; 42 K-R4, Kt-B6ch and mate next move.

39	Kt-Q2	RxPch
40	K-Kt	R-Kt6ch
41	K-R2	R-Q6!

Forcing further exchanges.

42	RxKt	RxKtch

A piquant position!

43	RxR	RxR
44	R-Q7	R-K6
45	RxP	RxP
46	RxP	P-R3

There followed: 47 R-B6, K-R2; 48 K-Kt2, P-R4; 49 R-R6, P-Kt3; 50 R-R4, K-R3; 51 R-QB4, R-Kt4; 52 K-Kt3, K-Kt4; 53 R-B3, P-R5ch; 54 K-R3, K-R4; 55 R-B4, R-Kt6ch; 56 K-R2, P-Kt4; 57 R-R4, R-Kt7ch; 58 K-R, P-R6; 59 R-QB4, P-Kt5; 60 K-Kt, P-Kt6; 61 R-B5ch, K-Kt3; 62 R-B, K-B4; 63 R-R, R-Q7; 64 R-K, K-B5; 65 R-R, K-K6; 66 R-R3ch, R-Q6; 67 R-R, K-K7; White resigns.

A certain melancholy historical interest attaches to this game: both players must have been looking back to their first meeting more than a quarter of a century previous; and it may well be that Blackburne deliberately selected one of the favorite openings of his younger days by way of affirming his loyalty to a style of chess that has disappeared, perhaps forever, from master play.

GAME No. 69

St. Petersburg 1914

Ruy Lopez

White	Black
Dr. E. Lasker	**A. Rubinstein**
1 P-K4	P-K4
2 Kt-KB3	Kt-QB3
3 B-Kt5	P-QR3
4 B-R4	Kt-B3
5 O-O	KtxP
6 P-Q4	P-QKt4
7 B-Kt3	P-Q4
8 PxP	B-K3
9 P-B3	B-QB4

The relative merits of this and 9 . . . B-K2 are still a subject for controversy.

10 QKt-Q2	O-O

| 11 B-B2 | KtxKt |

Not good. 11 . . . P-B4; 12 PxP e. p., KtxP(B3) or 12 Kt-Kt3, B-Kt3; 13 KKt-Q4, KtxKt; 14 Px Kt, P-B5; 15 P-B3, Kt-Kt6! gives Black a playable game.

| 12 QxKt | P-B3 |
| 13 PxP | RxP |

Better 13 . . . QxP; 14 Kt-Kt5, P-Kt3.

| 14 Kt-Q4 | KtxKt |

Remaining with a backward QBP. The alternative . . . Kt-K2 was safer.

| 15 PxKt | B-Kt3 |

To keep an eye on the QP; but the B would have been more useful at Q3.

16 P-QR4!

White has come out of the opening with an advantage because of Black's backward BP. Lasker's immediate object is now to prevent . . . P-B4; but P-QKt4 at once could have been answered by . . . P-QR4.

| 16 . . . . | R-Kt |

Not 16 . . . P-B4? 17 QPxP, BxP; 18 BxPch, KxB; 19 Q-B2ch etc.

17 PxP	PxP
18 Q-B3	Q-Q3
19 B-K3	B-KB4
20 KR-B	BxB
21 RxB	R-K
22 QR-QB	KR-K3

Preventing Q-B6, which would be answered by 23 . . . QxQ; 24 RxQ, RxR; 25 RxR, BxP.

| 23 P-R3 | R-K5 |

Again preventing Q-B6, since the Q must guard the QP.

24 Q-Q2

Not 24 Q-Q3, BxP∓.

| 24 . . . . | QR-K3 |

Black now intends . . . Q-Q2, after which his defense will be impregnable.

| 25 R-B6! | Q-Q2? |

Consistent, but bad. After 25 . . . QxR; 26 RxQ, RxR; 27 Q-Kt4, R-Q3; 28 QxP, P-R3 White would be a P ahead, but a win would be almost impossible.

26 RxR	QxR
27 Q-Q3	Q-K
28 Q-B3	K-B2
29 Q-Q3	K-Kt
30 Q-B3	Q-K3
31 R-R	Q-K
32 K-B!	P-R3
33 Q-Q3	K-B2
34 R-B	K-Kt
35 Q-Kt3	

Black must now choose between two evils: 1) he can play . . .P-B3 and thereby subject his BP to attack or 2) he can relinquish the K file (as in the text), permitting White to drive away the R from K5, thus releasing the pressure on White's QP.

| 35 . . . . | Q-B2 |

Submitting to both of the evils mentioned in the previous note. 35 . . . Q-Q2 was better.

36 R-Q

Not 36 QxKtP? RxB and wins.

| 36 . . . . | P-B3 |

If now 36 . . . Q-Q2 (to avoid the weakening text-move); 37 P-B3, R-K3; 38 B-B4 and B-K5, with appreciable advantage for White.

| 37 P-B3 | Q-B3 |

38 Q-Q3

If 38 B-B2, RxP! 39 BxR, BxB would have proved embarrassing for White because of the weakness of his black squares.

38	R-K2
39 B-B2	Q-Q3
40 Q-B2	K-B2
41 R-B	R-K3
42 Q-B5ch	R-B3

If 42 . . . K-Kt; 43 R-R maintains the pressure.

43 Q-K5!   R-K3

The exchange of Qs is by no means desirable for Black, but 43 . . . Q-Q2; 44 B-R4 would be no better, say 44 . . . B-B2; 45 Q-R5ch, R-Kt3; 46 R-K, B-Q3; 47 P-B4! and wins; while after 44 . . . R-B4; 45 Q-K3 the threat of P-KKt4 forces further weaknesses in Black's game.

44 QxQ	RxQ
45 K-K2	K-K2
46 K-Q3	R-Kt3

Preventing B-Kt3-K5.

47 P-KKt3	R-B3
48 P-B4	K-Q2
49 R-K	R-B
50 R-QR	P-R4

This is weakening, but no suitable defensive plan for Black is available. If for example 50 . . . R-K; 51 B-K3, R-K5; 52 R-R6, K-B2; 53 R-R8 or 50 . . . P-Kt4; 51 B-K3, B-B2; 52 R-KB. In both cases White maintains his superiority.

51 B-K3	P-Kt3
52 R-KB	K-Q3
53 P-KKt4	PxP
54 PxP	

(See diagram next column)

Position after White's 54th move

54 . . . .   P-B4

Leading to a lost R and P ending, but if 54 . . . K-K3 (recommended in the Tournament Book); 55 R-K! and Black's difficulties are far from over:

I 55 . . . B-B2; 56 P-B5ch, K-B2 (56 . . . K-B3; 57 P-Kt5ch followed by 58 P-B6; of course if 57 . . . KxP? 58 R-Bch wins a R); 57 B-Kt5, B-Q (or 57 . . . B-Q3; 58 R-K6); 58 PxPch, KxP (the alternative 58 . . . K-Kt2; 59 BxB, RxB; 60 R-K6, R-QB; 61 P-QKt4! would not suffice to hold the game); 59 BxB, RxB; 60 R-K6ch, K-Kt4; 61 RxP, KxP; 62 R-Kt6 with a winning position.

II 55 . . . K-Q2; 56 R-KR, B-B2; 57 R-R7ch, K-B (57 . . . K-Q; 58 P-B5, PxP; 59 B-Kt5ch transposes into the main variation); 58 P-B5! PxP; 59 B-R6, R-B3; 60 B-Kt7! R-B2; 61 P-Kt5, P-B5; 62 P-Kt6, R-B4; 63 B-R6, P-B6; 64 P-Kt7, P-B7; 65 P-Kt8=Qch, K-Kt2; 66 RxBch, KxR; 67 Q-R7 ch and wins. An elegant variation! After the lapse on the 25th move, Black had no clear drawing line.

55 PxPch   BxP

56 BxBch	KxB
57 P-B5	PxP
58 PxP	R-B3
59 R-B4!	P-Kt5

Or 59 . . . P-Q5; 60 K-K4, K-B5; 61 K-K5 and wins.

60 P-Kt3

Now Black must either allow White's K to enter or White's P to advance.

60	R-B2
61 P-B6	K-Q3
62 K-Q4	K-K3
63 R-B2!	K-Q3

After 63 . . . RxP; 64 RxRch, KxR; 65 KxP, K-K2; 66 K-B4, K-Q2; 67 KxP, the ending is won for White.

64 R-QR2	R-B2
65 R-R6ch	K-Q2
66 R-Kt6	Resigns

A splendid game on Lasker's part. His conduct of the ending has the same iron consistency which characterizes the R and P ending won by Rubinstein from Lasker at St. Petersburg 1909!

GAME No. 70

St. Petersburg 1914
Queen's Gambit Declined

| White | Black |
| **D. Janowski** | **Dr. E. Lasker** |

1 P-Q4	P-Q4
2 Kt-KB3	P-QB4
3 P-B4	P-K3
4 P-K3	

White has no reason for avoiding the Schlechter-Rubinstein Variation (4 BPxP, KPxP; 5 Kt-B3, Kt-QB3; 6 P-KKt3) which is assuredly stronger than the continua-tion actually adopted.

4	Kt-QB3
5 B-Q3	Kt-B3
6 O-O	B-Q3
7 P-QKt3	O-O
8 B-Kt2	P-QKt3
9 QKt-Q2	B-Kt2
10 Kt-K5	Q-K2
11 P-QR3	

In order to forestall . . . BPxP followed by . . . B-R6.

11 . . . .   QR-Q!!

Concerning this subtle move Tarrasch pedantically remarks: "It will soon be obvious that the KR should have been played here." But Hans Kmoch writes more understandingly: "Lasker's last move is a typical avoidance of the obvious. What Tarrasch says is quite correct—objectively. We may be certain that ten out of any other ten masters would have played . . . KR-Q and . . . QR-B without a thought. We may be equally certain that the move played by the other ten masters would have been weaker than the one adopted by Lasker, which reveals for the first time in this game his will to win and the extraordinary power of his personality. Whoever wishes to get to the heart of Lasker's greatness must devote more study to such simple moves than to the most brilliant combinations . . . For it is this quality that separates Lasker from all other players, his genius for taking his opponent out of the accustomed routine and putting him on his own resources . . . How many dangers Lasker voluntarily takes upon himself, merely to avoid a drawish position!—for this is the secret of 11 . . . QR-Q.

After 11 . . . KR-Q White would hardly play 12 Q-B2 (because of the self-evident 12 . . . QR-B), choosing instead 12 Q-K2. The position would then be almost symmetrical, and Black's winning chances reduced to a minimum."

12 Q-B2

Threatening to win the KRP after the necessary preliminary exchanges in the center.

12 . . . .   QPxP
13 QKtxP

With this move Janowski posts the QKt to advantage. Yet 13 KtP xP was perhaps better, for 1) it would keep Black's pieces out of Q4, thus reducing their mobility, and 2) the Pawn formation in the center would be fluid, giving White's QB a great deal of latent power.

13 . . . .   PxP
14 PxP   R-B

Dr. Tarrasch comments that if Black had both Rs developed now, he would have a beautiful game. "Quite right," adds Kmoch, "but if Lasker had played 11 . . . KR-Q (as recommended by Tarrasch), then the present position would never have arisen! Just as some players sacrifice Ps to obtain an at-tack, Lasker frequently sacrifices tempi and terrain in order to main-tain the tension."

15 Q-K2   B-Kt
16 P-B4   Kt-Q4
17 QR-K

A demonstration without any real sting. Tarrasch rightly sug-gests 17 P-B5, PxP; 18 BxP, QR-K and White's position is full of promise after 19 QR-K, the im-

mediate threat being 20 BxPch, Kx B (20 . . . K-R; 21 Q-R5, Kt-B3; 22 RxKt); 21 Q-R5ch, K-Kt; 22 KtxP! and wins.

17 . . . .   P-B4!

This makes a bad impression on first sight, but as compensation for the backward KP, Lasker succeeds in preventing P-B5, whereupon White's QB is very badly placed (Lasker's QB, on the contrary, has an open diagonal and plays a lead-ing part in the subsequent maneuv-ers right down to the last move).

18 Q-Q2   KtxKt
19 KtxKt

In order to keep the K file open so as to be able to attack the back-ward P—more promising in ap-pearance than it actually turns out to be.

QPxKt has been recommended as more likely to lead to a draw, but even then Black has a per-ceptible advantage in the superior diagonals of his Bs, his command of the open files, the strong position of his Kt, and the possibility of an attack along the KKt file with . . . P-KKt4.

19 . . . .   P-QR3

Doubtless intending . . . P-QKt4 and . . . B-R2; but White's next move leads Lasker's thoughts in a different direction.

20 B-Kt   B-Q3!

Compelling White to retreat his only well-posted piece, as 21 P-QKt4 would be followed by 21 . . . KtxKtP; 22 PxKt, BxQKtP ∓.

21 Kt-B4   P-QKt4
22 Kt-R5

After 22 KtxB, QxKt Black would sooner or later force the entrance of his Kt at QB5, followed by . . . B-Q4 and the occupation of the QB and Q files.

22 . . . .   B-R
23 P-QKt4

Threatening Kt-Kt3-B5 and at the same time setting a deep trap which Black avoids, namely: 23 . . . KtxKtP; 24 PxKt, BxQKtP (seemingly winning the Kt) ; 25 Rx P! BxQ (there is nothing better) ; 26 RxQ, BxKt; 27 B-R2ch, K-R; 28 P-Q5, B-B6; 29 BxB, RxB; 30 R-Q±. White's passed P is very dangerous (Kmoch).

23 . . . .   Kt-Kt3!

Lasker wishes to bring the QB to Q4 in order to protect the weak KP, at the same time preparing . . . Kt-B5.

24 Kt-Kt3   B-Q4
25 Kt-B5   Kt-B5
26 Q-B3

Threatening KtxRP as well as KtxKP followed by P-Q5—according to Tarrasch. This comment is erroneous, since 27 KtxKP, BxKt; 28 P-Q5 is answered by 28 . . . KtxB; 29 QxKt, Q-R2ch followed by . . . B-Q2 with a piece ahead.

26 . . . .   R-KB3!

A powerful move, after which Black's attacking chances begin to materialize. He need not fear 27 KtxRP because of the reply . . . BxKKtP!

27 B-B

The uselessness of this B (hemmed in by the Ps at QKt4, Q4 and B4) shows how weak White's 17th move was—and correspondingly illustrates the strength of 17. . . . P-B4! (Kmoch).

27 . . . .   P-QR4!
28 R-B2   PxP
29 PxP   R-R

Now all of Lasker's pieces are admirably posted.

30 B-R2

In order to rid himself of the terrible Kt. If only he could rid himself of his QB!

30 . . . .   Q-KB2
31 BxKt   BxB
32 B-Kt2

Hoping either to exchange Rs on the QR file or to unmask the B's diagonal. White carries out both of these aims—but the result is not wholly pleasing.

32 . . . .   R-Kt3

Beginning the final phase.

33 R-R

Better would have been B-B; but the continuation now adopted by Lasker was not easy to foresee.

33 . . . .   RxRch
34 BxR   Q-B2!

The first move of an extraordinarily complicated and daring maneuver which shows Lasker at the height of his tactical skill.

35 Q-K3   R-Kt5!

In order to force P-Kt3, which Janowski could still have avoided if his B were on the right diagonal.

36 P-Kt3

Forced: if 36 KtxP? Q-K2.

(See diagram on next page)

36 . . . .   P-Kt4!!

Despite its apparent boldness, the move is quite sound and absolutely decisive! In order to appre-

Position after White's 36th move

ciate the move fully, one must bear in mind that Lasker, before venturing on it, had to calculate its consequences and foresee that he would ultimately obtain a definite advantage.

37 P-Q5

37 PxP would be ruinous because of 37 . . . BxP. The text is White's best chance.

37	BxQP
38 Q-Q4	PxP
39 Q-R8ch	K-B2
40 QxPch	K-K
41 Q-R8ch	B-B
42 B-K5	Q-B2
43 RxP	RxR

Lasker's combination has been carefully planned to the last detail: if now 44 PxR, Q-Kt3ch; 45 K-B2, Q-Kt7ch; 46 K-K3 (threatening B-Q6 as well as Q-R5ch followed by Q-Kt5ch. If instead 46 K-K, B-B6 and mate follows), B-B6! 47 Kt-Q3 (if 47 KtxP, Q-K7ch; 48 K-Q4, Q-Q7 mate; or 47 B-Q6, Q-K7ch; 48 K-Q4, Q-Kt7ch winning the Q, or 47 K-Q3, B-Q8! and wins), Q-K7ch; 48 K-Q4, B-K5! and Black must win: 49 Q-R3 (obviously the Kt cannot move),

BxP! (if now 50 KtxB; Q-B5ch; 51 K-K3, Q-Kt6ch winning the Q); 50 Q-R8ch (there is nothing better), B-B; 51 Q-R3, BxKt; 52 QxB, B-B4ch; 53 K-B3, B-Kt5ch! 54 K-Q4, Q-B7ch; 55 Q-K3, B-B4ch and White's Q is lost. An impressive example of the power of the Bs on the open board.

44 BxR

Now White's prospects seem excellent; he has regained his P, the game is considerably simplified, and he threatens B-Q6.

44 . . . .   Q-KKt2!

To this simple move there is no adequate reply! Either White must exchange Qs (which gives him a lost ending because of his weak QKtP and the opponent's powerful Bs and passed P) or else he falls into a mating net. Janowski chooses the latter alternative as being more interesting.

45 Q-R5ch

45 B-K5 would be worthless because of the fatal reply 45 . . . Q-Kt5 and if then 46 B-Q6? Q-Q8 ch; 47 K-B2, Q-Q7ch; 48 K-B, B-B5ch; 49 K-Kt, Q-K8ch; 50 K-Kt2, Q-B8 mate.

45	K-Q
46 B-Kt5ch	K-B2
47 B-B4ch	B-Q3

White is forced to exchange: the rest is easy.

| 48 BxBch | KxB |
| 49 Q-R4 | |

If 49 Q-Q, Q-Kt7 wins; or 49 Q-K2, Q-Q5ch etc.

| 49 . . . . | Q-R8ch |
| 50 K-B2 | Q-Kt7ch |

51 K-K

51 K-K3 would likewise lose after 51 . . . Q-B8ch; 52 K-Q3, B-B5ch or 52 K-Q4? Q-Q7ch; 53 Kt-Q3, P-K4 mate.

| 51 . . . . | Q-B8ch |
| 52 K-K2 | B-B5ch |

White resigns, for if 53 Kt-Q3, Q-B7ch; or 53 K-B2, Q-Q7ch; 54 K-Kt, Q-K8ch and mate next move; or finally 53 K-B3, Q-B8ch.

This game, so masterfully conducted by Lasker through all its difficult phases, is perhaps the finest of his whole career.

GAME No. 71

St. Petersburg 1914
Albin Counter Gambit

White	Black
Dr. E. Lasker	**Dr. A. Alekhine**
1 P-Q4	P-Q4
2 P-QB4	P-K4
3 QPxP	P-Q5
4 Kt-KB3	Kt-QB3
5 P-QR3	B-Kt5
6 QKt-Q2	

6 B-B4 would not hold the P: 6 . . . KKt-K2; 7 QKt-Q2, Kt-Kt3; 8 B-Kt3, Q-K2 etc. Lasker, however, is not interested in retaining the gambit P, as he wishes to wrest the attack from his youthful opponent.

| 6 . . . . | Q-K2 |
| 7 P-R3 | BxKt |

After this move White's advantage becomes clear. 7 . . . B-R4; 8 P-KKt4, B-Kt3; 9 B-Kt2 (whereby some weak points are created in White's game) would have been more in the spirit of the opening.

| 8 KtxB | O-O-O |
| 9 Q-Q3 | |

Again the opportunity of remaining a P ahead presented itself with 9 B-Kt5, but after 9 . . . P-B3; 10 PxP, PxP; 11 B-B4, B-R3; 12 BxB, KtxB; 13 Q-Q3, Kt-K4; 14 KtxKt, PxKt; 15 Q-K4, Kt-B2; 16 P-KKt3, Kt-Q3; 17 Q-Q3, P-B4; 18 B-Kt2, P-K5 Black has a strong attack.

9 . . . .   P-KR3

Not 9 . . . KtxP; 10 Q-B5ch, Kt-Q2; 11 KtxP.

| 10 P-KKt3 | P-KKt3 |
| 11 B-Kt2 | B-Kt2 |

After 11 . . . KtxP; 12 KtxKt, QxKt; 13 O-O White can develop his QB without loss of time.

12 O-O	KtxP
13 KtxKt	BxKt
14 P-QKt4	P-KB4

Black is still unable to develop his Kt, for if 14 . . . Kt-B3; 15 P-B4, B-Q3; 16 P-QB5.

15 P-B5   Q-K3

. . . Kt-B3? is still impossible.

16 P-B6!   Kt-K2

Alekhine prefers to complicate matters still further, since the acceptance of the sacrifice would give him a difficult game: 16 . . . PxP; 17 B-Kt2, Kt-K2; 18 QR-B.

I 18 . . . R-Q3; 19 Q-R6ch, K-Q; 20 QxRP, P-Kt4; 21 P-Kt5 ±.

II 18 . . . Kt-Q4; 19 Q-R6 ch, K-Q2; 20 P-Kt5, PxP; 21 QxP ch, K-K2; 22 R-B5 and wins.

| 17 PxPch | K-Kt |
| 18 B-Kt2 | |

Not a good square for the B;

it would be far more preferable to develop it at Q2, a post which is useful for both attack and defense.

An even stronger continuation, however, is 18 P-Kt5 and if in reply 18 . . . R-Q3; 19 P-QR4 wins quickly, for example 19 . . . KR-Q; 20 P-R5, Kt-Q4; 21 B-R3, R(Q3)-Q2; 22 B-B5 and Black cannot defend himself against P-Kt6. Thus if 22. . . P-Kt4; 23 P-Kt6, BPxP; 24 PxP, KtxP; 25 Q-R6, K-B2; 26 QxP and wins.

18 . . . .   R-Q3

If 18 . . . P-B5 White can force an advantageous ending by 19 PxP, BxP; 20 Q-K4, QxQ (20 . . . Q-Q3? 21 KR-Q±); 21 Bx Q etc.

19 QR-B   KR-Q
20 R-B2   P-B5

After B-Q2 it would not have been so easy to play this move.

21 PxP   BxP
22 R-Q

If instead 22 Q-K4, B-K4; 23 P-B4, B-B3; 24 QxQ, RxQ and White has too many weaknesses to expect to win. Nor would 22 B-B, B-K4; 23 BxP, Kt-Q4; 24 B-Q2, Kt-B6 be a satisfactory continuation for White.

22 . . . .   Kt-B4

Not 22 . . . Kt-Q4; 23 BxP!

23 B-QB?

Here 23 Q-K4 would have prevented the ensuing complications, as Black would be forced to exchange Qs:

I   23 . . . B-K4; 24 R-B5.

II   23 . . . Q-Kt6; 24 B-QB, BxB (or 24 . . . R-K3; 25 Q-Q3); 25 KRxB, R(Q3)-Q2;   26 Q-

B4, Q-B2; 27 P-Kt5 and White should win.

23 . . . .   Kt-K6!
24 R-B5!   Q-B3

If 24 . . . KtxR; 25 BxB, Kt-Kt7; 26 BxR!

Tarrasch is of the opinion that after 24 . . . KtxB; 25 KxKt the game would be about even; if now 25 . . . BxB; 26 KRxB, R(Q)-Q2 ;27 Q-KB3, R-B2 and White has only a slight advantage. The move actually made, however, still keeps the draw in hand.

25 Q-K4

The alternative 25 R-K would force Black to play 25 . . . KtxB; 26 KxKt, BxB; 27 KRxB with a draw as the probable result.

25 . . . .   KtxR!
26 BxB

Position after White's 26th move

26 . . . .   Kt-B6?

Tarrasch considers Black's 25th move the decisive blunder, but in point of fact Alekhine's last move deserves that dubious honor. Black could still have held the game with 26 . . . KtxP!

I   27 BxR, RxB! 28 Q-K8ch, R-Q; 29 Q-K5, QxQ; 30 RxQ, P-Q6! 31 PxP, KtxP; 32 R-K4 (to

stop. . . Kt-B5), P-Kt4; 33 R-K6,
Kt-B5; 34 RxP, KtxB; 35 KxKt,
R-Q6=.

II   27 BxR, RxB! 28 Q-K5, P-
Q6! 29 QxQ, RxQ; 30 PxP (or
30 R-Q5, R-Q3! 31 RxR? PxR; 32
KxKt, P-Q7), KtxP; 31 R-Q5, R-
Q3; 32 RxR, PxR and Black can
hardly lose.

III   27 KxKt? P-Q6!! (27 . . .
P-Kt4? R-B5); 28 K-Kt, QxB! 29
QxQ, P-Q7; 30 R-B (or 30 Qx
QP), PxR = Qch; 31 QxQ, R-
Q8ch and wins.

IV   27 Q-B3, P-Q6! 28 BxR,
RxB; 29 PxP (or 29 QxQ, transposing into Variation II), KtxP
and Black should draw without
difficulty.

27 BxR!!	QxB

But not 27 . . . KtxQ; 28 Bx
Pch, KxP; 30 BxKtch, K-R3; 31
P-Kt5 mate.

28 Q-K5	Q-Kt3
29 Q-K7	Q-Q3
30 R-K5	P-Q6
31 PxP	QxQP
32 R-K3	Q-Q8ch
33 K-R2	Kt-Kt4
34 R-K6	KtxP
35 R-KB6	Resigns

He has no defense against 36 R-
B8. A game worthy of the champion and the champion-to-be!

GAME No. 72

St. Petersburg 1914

Queen's Gambit Declined

White	Black
Dr. E. Lasker	**Dr. S. Tarrasch**
1 P-Q4	P-Q4
2 Kt-KB3	P-QB4
3 P-B4	P-K3

Transposing into the defense
which Tarrasch advocated so stub-
bornly for a good forty years in
the controversy which he somewhat
magniloquently termed *Tarrasch
contra mundum.*

4 BPxP	KPxP
5 P-KKt3	Kt-QB3
6 B-Kt2	Kt-B3
7 O-O	B-K2
8 PxP	BxP
9 QKt-Q2	

An innovation of some theoretical importance. White plans to
blockade the isolated QP by playing one of his Kts to Q4. Black
has nothing better than to allow
his opponent to carry out his plan.

9	P-Q5?

Distinctly bad. Tarrasch crosses
his adversary's plan, to be sure, but
the game soon takes an unfavorable
turn for Black because of this
move.

10 Kt-Kt3	B-Kt3
11 Q-Q3!	

Now Black must defend himself
against the threat of R-Q.

11	B-K3
12 R-Q	BxKt
13 QxB	

Still threatening to win the QP
(14 P-K3 etc.). Hence Black's
reply.

13	Q-K2
14 B-Q2!	

Far stronger than the more
plausible B-B4, as White's next
move shows.

14	O-O
15 P-QR4!!	

"An exceptionally fine move: the
P is to be advanced in order to

undermine the position of Black's Q side pieces" (Tarrasch).

15 . . . .   Kt-K5

There is no wholly satisfactory move available; if for example 15 . . . B-B4; 16 P-R5, P-QR3 (recommended by Tarrasch); 17 QR-B, B-R2; 18 Kt-R4, whereupon 18 . . . QxP would be bad because of 19 QxP; or if 18 . . . QR-B; 19 Q-Q3±.

Black must of course avoid 15 . . . QxP? 16 R-K, Q-R3; 17 B-KB and the Q is trapped.

16 B-K   QR-Q

Losing valuable time: the R should have been brought to the QB file directly. If instead 16 . ⊥ . Kt-B4; 17 Q-Kt5.

17 P-R5   B-B4
18 P-R6!   PxP

Black is confronted with a choice of evils. After the text Black's pieces are very awkwardly placed on the QB file. An examination of the consequences of 18 . . . P-QKt3 shows that Lasker's 15th move was a deeply considered demonstration against the QP, namely 18 . . . P-QKt3; 19 Q-R4, R-B; 20 QR-Kt and White wins the QP after the advance of his QKtP.

19 QR-B

Now all of Black's pieces "hang" badly, the chief threat being Kt-R4 winning a piece.

19 . . . .   R-B

The loss of time incurred in this R's moves is now evident. If instead 19 . . . Kt-Kt; 20 Kt-R4, B-Kt3; 21 B-Kt4 or 20 . . . B-Q3; 21 RxP±.

(See diagram next column)

Position after Black's 19th move

20 Kt-R4   B-Kt3

Costs the exchange, but there is no wholly satisfactory alternative:

I   20 . . . B-Q3? 21 Kt-B5, Q-K4; 22 BxKt etc.

II   20 . . . Kt-B3; 21 B-R3, R-B2 (forced); 22 Kt-B5, Q-K4; 23 B-Q2 etc.

III   20 . . . Kt-Kt; 21 Q-KB3 (21 Q-B2, P-Q6!), Kt-KB3; 22 Kt-B5, Q-K4; 23 B-Q2±.

IV   20 . . . Kt-Q; 21 Kt-B5, Q-K4; 22 BxKt, QxB; 23 Kt-Q6 and wins.

21 Kt-B5   Q-K4
22 BxKt   QxB
23 Kt-Q6   QxP
24 KtxR   RxKt

Black has a strong passed P, but his game must fall to pieces as soon as his remaining R is exchanged.

25 Q-Q5   Q-K3

Not 25 . . . Kt-K2? 26 RxRch, KtxR; 27 Q-R8, Q-K; 28 R-B, Kt-Q3; 29 QxQch ,KtxQ; 30 R-B8, K-B; 31 B-Kt4ch.

26 Q-B3

Lasker decides to defer the exchange of Qs, as he has a strong position with the present set-up of forces. But 26 QxQ, PxQ; 27 R-B4, Kt-K2 (forced); 28 RxRch, KtxR; 29 R-B was also good enough to win: 29 . . . Kt-K2; 30 B-Kt4 followed by B-B5 etc.

26 . . . .   P-R3
27 B-Q2!

Threatening 28 R-K, Q-Q2; 29 R-B4 and Black has no good de-fense against KR-QB. If 29 . . . Kt-K2; 30 RxKt; or 29 . . . Kt-R4; 30 R-K7, QxR; 31 RxRch winning a piece; or 29 . . . Kt-Kt; 30 R-K7 etc.

27 . . . .   Kt-K4
28 RxRch   QxR
29 Q-K4   Kt-Q2

The Kt would be safer at Kt3, but out of play (Tarrasch).

30 R-QB   Q-B

This costs a P, but . . . Q-Q could be met by Q-Q5 or Q-Kt7.

31 BxP   Kt-B4

31 . . . PxB; 32 Q-Kt4ch would be even more hopeless for Black.

32 Q-Kt4   P-B4
33 Q-Kt6   Q-B2

Or 33 . . . P-R4 (White threatened to win outright by 34 P-QKt4, Kt-Q2; 35 R-B8); 34 R-K, Kt-K5; 35 P-B3, P-Q6 dis ch; 36 K-Kt2, Kt-B3 (36 . . . Kt-Q3; 37 R-K6, B-B4; 38 B-B4); 37 B-Kt5 etc.

34 QxQch   KxQ
35 B-Kt5

The ending is easily won for White with a little care.

35 . . . .   Kt-Q6
36 R-Kt   K-K3
37 P-Kt3

This and the next move prevent

Black's K from getting into play, after which the QP might become dangerous.

37 . . . .   K-Q4
38 P-B3   P-R4
39 P-R4   Kt-B4
40 P-R5   P-Q6
41 K-B   P-R5?

Cutting short what promised to be a very interesting end-game. Absorbed in his own plans, Black overlooks his opponent's threat.

42 PxP   KtxP
43 B-B6!   K-K3

Sorrowful homecoming. The B is of course immune from capture.

44 BxP   K-B2
45 B-K5   Kt-B4
46 R-Q   Resigns

For B-Q4 will win the QP. Tarrasch unstintedly praises Las-ker's fine play in this game.

GAME No. 73

St. Petersburg 1914

Ruy Lopez

White	Black
Dr. A. Alekhine	**Dr. E. Lasker**

1 P-K4   P-K4
2 Kt-KB3   Kt-QB3
3 B-Kt5   P-QR3
4 BxKt   QPxB
5 Kt-B3   P-B3

Regarding this move see Games Nos. 27 and 32.

6 P-Q4   PxP
7 QxP   QxQ
8 KtxQ   B-Q3
9 B-K3   Kt-K2
10 O-O-O

With the White pieces against Capablanca the following day,

Lasker castled K side. The text is at least equally good.

10 . . . .   O-O

Black, however, should castle Q side, in order to defend the Ps on that wing. Being a point and a half behind Capablanca and desperately in need of a win at this stage, Lasker purposely takes chances.

11 Kt-Kt3

To gain control of QB5. If now 11 . . . P-QKt3? 12 BxP.

11	Kt-Kt3
12 B-B5	B-B5ch
13 K-Kt	R-K.

In order to be able to answer P-Kt3 with . . . B-K4, threatening . . . BxKt as well as . . . B-Kt5.

14 KR-K	P-Kt3
15 B-K3	B-K4
16 B-Q4	Kt-R5
17 R-Kt	B-K3

An excellent alternative is 17 . . . P(KKt4! and if then 18 BxB, PxB; 19 Kt-Q2, B-Kt5; 20 P-B3, B-K3; 21 P-KKt3, Kt-Kt3; 22 QR-KB, R-KB∓.

| 18 P-B4! | B-Q3 |
| 19 B-B2 | |

Of course not 19 BxKtP, BxP.

| 19 . . . . | Kt-Kt3 |
| 20 P-B5! | |

Relatively best. 20 P-KKt3 would leave the KP subject to attack, while 20 BxP loses a P after 20 . . . BxP; 21 B-Q4, BxP.

| 20 . . . | BxKt |
| 21 RPxB | |

Superior to 21 PxKt, B-K3; 22 PxPch, K-R; 23 BxP, BxP; 24 R-R.

| 21 . . . . | Kt-B |

22 BxP	BxP
23 R-R	PxB
24 RxB	P-QKt4
25 R-K	Kt-Q2
26 Kt-Q	P-QR4

Tarrasch expresses surprise at the fact that Lasker does not concentrate on the backward KP, but instead starts a belated attack on White's K. But Lasker judges the position more profoundly. In order to remain in the running for first prize, he must win this game. A stereotyped, attack on the KP would lead to nothing, since White can defend the P as many times as it is attacked. Lasker therefore decides to allow the advance of the KP, in order to create complications which may turn out in his favor.

| 27 R-R3 | P-Kt5 |
| 28 Kt-B2 | Kt-B4 |

More promising than 28 . . . Kt-K4; 29 Kt-Q3.

29 R(R3)-K3	P-R5
30 PxP	KtxRP
31 P-K5	PxP
32 RxP	KR-Kt

Now Black has attacking chances. Thus 33 R-K4? would lose because of 33 . . . Kt-B6ch; 34 PxKt, PxP dis ch; 35 K-B, R-R8 mate.

| 33 Kt-K4 | P-Kt6 |

If 33 . . . Kt-B6ch; 34 KtxKt, PxKt; 35 P-QKt3±.

34 R-K2

34 P-B3 would strengthen Black's attack, while if 34 PxP, Rx P; 35 R-K2, QR-Kt and Black wins a P.

| 34 . . . . | Kt-Kt3 |

34 . . . KtxP; 35 KxKt, R-R7
ch; 36 K-B3, P-Kt7; 37 Kt-Q2 is
not good for Black (Tarrasch).

35 PxP	Kt-Q4
36 P-KKt4	P-R3
37 P-Kt5	PxP
38 KtxP	Kt-B3

38 . . . RxP? allows mate in
two.

39 R-K7

White's attempt at attack is
faulty policy. R(K5)-K3 or R-Q
B5 or R-QB2 would have been
sufficient to draw.

| 39 . . . . | RxP |
| 40 R-Kt2 | |

To prevent . . . R-Kt6.

| 40 . . . . | Kt-Q4 |
| 41 R-Q7? | |

A blunder which loses the exchange; it must be admitted that
the winning move is extremely fine
and difficult to foresee. White
should have played 41 R-K, after
which he could hardly lose.

Position after White's 41st move

41 . . . .   R-Q6!!

Forcing the win of the exchange!
The immediate threat is 42 . . .
Kt-B6ch. If White avoids this by

42 R-Kt7, then 42 . . . R-Q8ch;
43 K-B2, Kt-K6ch winning a R!
42 K-B would save both Rs but
lead to mate: 42 . . . R-R8ch; 43
K-B2, Kt-Kt5 mate.

42 RxKt	RxR
43 Kt-K6	K-B2
44 RxPch	K-B3
45 R-B7	R-Q3

Black must not lose this P, without which the game cannot be won.

46 Kt-B5   KxP

As Tarrasch points out, Black's
chief problem in the ensuing end-
game is practically solved by the
exchange of Rs, for Black's K will
then become an attacking piece.

47 R-B7ch	K-K4
48 K-B2	R-KR3
49 Kt-Q3ch	K-Q3
50 R-B5	R-QKt
51 K-B3	K-B2
52 R-B7ch	K-Kt3
53 R-Q7	

This is of course the most favorable square for the R, as its mobility is greatest at this point. But
Black can easily drive it away by
playing a R to Q4.

| 53 . . . . | R-R6 |
| 54 R-Q4 | R(Kt)-KR |

Threatening . . . R(R)-R5 followed by . . . R-R4-Q4.

55 R-Kt4ch	K-B2
56 K-B2	R(R)-R5
57 R-Kt3	R-R7ch

Tarrasch points out a far speed-
ier win here by 57 . . . P-B4; 58
R-B3, K-Q3; 59 R-R3, P-B5; 60
R-R6ch, K-Q4; 61 Kt-Kt4ch, K-
Q5 and Black should win quickly.
"But we must bear in mind," he
continues, "that the advance of the

QBP determines first prize! . . .
And the advance would still be
possible if the other methods turned
out to be insufficient."

58 K-B3	R(R5)-R6
59 R-Kt4	R-R4
60 R-Kt4	R(R7)-R6

Threatening . . . R-Q4.

61 K-B2	R-Q4
62 Kt-B4	R-B4ch
63 K-Kt	R-R8ch
64 K-R2	R-R4ch
65 K-Kt3	R-Kt4ch
66 K-B3	K-Kt3
67 Kt-Q3	R-R6

Lasker bides his time and slowly
moves towards his goal. The text
threatens . . . R-Q4.

68 K-B2	R-Q4
69 R-Kt4ch	K-B2
70 R-Kt3	R-R7ch
71 K-B3	K-Q3
72 R-R3	R-Kt7
73 R-R	R-Kt6
74 R-Q	K-B2
75 R-Q2	K-Kt3
76 R-Q	K-Kt4

Now 77 R-Q2 would lose
quickly: 77 . . . R-B4ch; 78 K-
Kt3 (or 78 K-Q4, R-B5ch; 79 K-
K5, R-K6ch; 80 K-B5, R-Q5), R-
B5; 80 R-Q, P-B4; 81 R-Q2, R-
R6; 82 R-Q, R-K6; 83 R-Q2, R
(B5)-K5 and the exchange of Rs
cannot be prevented (Tarrasch).

| 77 K-B2 | K-B5 |
| 78 P-Kt3ch | K-Kt4 |

Black has now forced a serious
weakness in White's game.

79 R-Q2	R-R6
80 R-Q	R-R7ch
81 K-B3	R-Q
82 R-KKt	R-R6

| 83 R-Q | R(Q)-KR |

Threatening 84 . . . R-R8; 85
R-Q2, R(R)-R7; 86 Kt-B2, R-B8.

84 R-KKt	R(R)-R4
85 K-B2	R-Q4
86 R-Q	R-Kt4
87 R-Q2?	

A slip probably due to fatigue.
Correct was 87 R-KB, after which
Black would double Rs on the
seventh rank and attack the QKtP.
This would paralyze White's R,
but the win would still be quite
difficult.

87	R(R6)-Kt6
88 Kt-B	R-Kt7
89 Kt-K2	K-Kt3!

White resigns, since he cannot
avoid the exchange of Rs, which
will leave Black with an easy win.
This game, by reason of its inherent difficulty as well as the
nerve-racking circumstances under
which it was played, belongs in the
same class with Game No. 63.

GAME No. 74

St. Petersburg 1914
Ruy Lopez

White	Black
Dr. E. Lasker	**J. R. Capablanca**

1 P-K4	P-K4
2 Kt-KB3	Kt-QB3
3 B-Kt5	P-QR3
4 BxKt	QPxB
5 P-Q4	PxP
6 QxP	QxQ
7 KtxQ	B-Q3
8 Kt-QB3	Kt-K2
9 O-O	

Unusual, but good: the K is to
support the advance of the K side

Ps.

9 . . . .   O-O

Also unusual, but this time less good. As pointed out in the notes to Game No. 73, Black should castle Q side in order to guard his weak Ps. If instead 9 . . . P-KB 4; 10 R-K, PxP; 11 KtxP±.

10 P-B4

Having the majority of Ps on the K side, Lasker immediately sets out to utilize this advantage.

10 . . . .   R-K

After White's last move 10 . . . B-QB4 suggests itself, but the continuation 11 B-K3, R-Q; 12 QR-Q, B-KKt5; 13 R-Q3, R-Q2; 14 P-KR3, QR-Q; 15 PxB, BxKt; 16 BxB, RxB; 17 KR-Q would be in White's favor, although the resulting position would be exceedingly difficult to win. Superior to the text was 10 . . . P-KB4; 11 P-K5, B-B4; 12 B-K3, BxKt! (White was threatening KtxKBP, while if 12 . . . B-Kt3; 13 QKt-K2±); 13 Bx B, P-QKt3; 14 QR-Q, P-B4; 15 B-K3, B-K3 and in view of the Bs of opposite color and Black's initiative on the Q side, the position is about even.

11 Kt-Kt3

Black was threatening 11 . . . B-QB4; 12 B-K3, Kt-Q4∓.

11 . . . .   P-B3

Preventing P-K5 but weakening his K3. Preferable was 11 . . . B-K3 and if 12 P-K5, B-QKt5 with good chances, for example 13 Kt-K4, B-KB4 or 13 Kt-Q4, B-QB4; 14 B-K3, BxKt; 15 BxB, P-QKt3=.

12 P-B5!

A surprising and courageous move which gives White a definite advantage. The move creates a hole for Black's pieces at K4, but it helps White in three ways: 1) it fixes Black's KBP, enabling White to undertake a K side attack with P-KKt4-5; 2) it confines Black's QB; and 3) it will later enable White to plant a Kt at K6. The fact that Lasker was able to carry out every one of these objectives, shows that Capablanca did not properly grasp the essentials of the position.

12 . . . .   P-QKt3

A wiser continuation was 12 . . . B-Q2 and if 13 B-B4, BxB; 14 RxB, QR-Q; 15 R-Q, B-B and White will find it difficult to press home his advantage.

13 B-B4   B-Kt2

"Capablanca decided upon this move only after prolonged deliberation. The alternative was . . . BxB; 14 RxB, P-B4. In that case White would be unable to establish a Kt on K6, but would exchange Rs on the Q file and virtually be a P ahead, e g. 15 R-Q, B-Kt2; 16 R-B2, QR-Q; 17 RxR, RxR; 18 R-Q2, RxR; 19 KtxR. Many complications might yet arise, but with best play, White can retain a slight advantage" (Lasker).

14 BxB

Good: now Black has a new weakness at Q3.

14 . . .   PxB

15 Kt-Q4   QR-Q?

After this he will never be able to drive White's Kt from K6. The alternative was 15 . . . R-R2; 16 QR-Q, B-B but after 17 P-KKt4 followed by Kt(Q4)-K2 White's game remains much superior.

16 Kt-K6   R-Q2
17 QR-Q   Kt-B

If instead 17 . . . P-Q4; 18 R-B2-Q2 would practically stalemate all of Black's pieces.

18 R-B2   P-QKt4

In order to obtain some more room. But the move eventually leads to the opening of the QR file, which can only result in White's favor because of his superior mobility. Black's best chance was to give up the exchange.

19 KR-Q2

To prevent Black from moving his Kt.

19 . . . .   R(Q2)-K2
20 P-QKt4

Stops . . . P-QB4 or . . . P-Kt5.

20 . . . .   K-B2
21 P-QR3   B-R
22 K-B2

Preparing to advance on the K side.

22 . . . .   R-R2
23 P-Kt4   P-R3
24 R-Q3   P-QR4

The opening of the file, as previously pointed out, only helps White. Giving up the exchange was still Black's best course.

25 P-KR4   PxP
26 PxP   R(R2)-K2
27 K-B3   R-Kt
28 K-B4   P-KKt3
29 R-Kt3   P-Kt4ch
30 K-B3!   Kt-Kt3

A desperate attempt to obtain some counter-play. If 31 RxP Black intends 31 . . . Kt-B5; 32

R-Q, Kt-K4ch; 33 K moves, PxP with a good game.

31 PxP   RPxP

After 31 . . . BPxP; 32 R-R3 the RP is lost.

32 R-R3!

Lasker is faithful to his strategical plan: it is more important to command the KR file than to win the QP.

32 . . . .   R-Q2
33 K-Kt3!

In order to threaten 34 P-K5! B PxP (34 . . . QPxP? 35 RxRch, KtxR; 36 R-R7ch, K-K; 37 Kt-K4 and mate in two); 35 Kt-K4 with a winning position. With this in view, Lasker removes the K from the diagonal.

33 . . . .   K-K
34 QR-KR

If 34 P-K5, P-Q4! (the only move); 35 PxP, K-B2 and Black still has some play left. The text wins very simply, since Black has no good moves.

34 . . . .   B-Kt2

Black is helpless: if 34 . . . R-QR2; 35 R-R8 wins a R; if 34 . . . Kt-B5; 35 R-R8 wins the B; and if 34 . . . P-Q4; 35 PxP, Ktx P; 36 Kt-K4 followed by R-R8 wins.

(See diagram on next page)

35 P-K5!

A pretty finishing touch.

35 . . . .   QPxP

Alternatives were:

I 35 . . . P-Q4; 36 Kt-B5, R-K2; 37 R-R8, RxR; 38 RxRch, K-B2; 39 R-R7ch, K-K; 40 RxRch, KxR; 41 PxPch, KxP; 42 KtxB.

Position after Black's 34th move

II 35 . . . BPxP; 36 Kt-K4, Kt-Q4; 37 R-R8, RxR; 38 RxRch, K-K2; 39 Kt(K6)xP, Kt-B3 (forced); 40 KtxKt, KxKt; 41 R-R6ch! K-K2 (41 . . . KxKt? 42 R-Kt6 mate); 42 P-B6ch, K-Q; 43 P-B7 winning easily.

36 Kt-K4	Kt-Q4
37 Kt(K6)-B5	

Winning the exchange, for if 37 . . . R-K2; 38 KtxB, RxKt; 39 Kt-Q6ch etc.

37	B-B
38 KtxR	BxKt
39 R-R7	R-B
40 R-R	K-Q
41 R-R8ch	B-B
42 Kt-B5	Resigns

He cannot meet the threats of R-Q7ch, Kt-K6ch and Kt-Kt7ch.

This fine game uniquely epi-tomizes Lasker's genius.

GAME No. 75

St. Petersburg 1914
Petroff Defense

White	Black
Dr. E. Lasker	**F. J. Marshall**
1 P-K4	P-K4
2 Kt-KB3	Kt-KB3
3 KtxP	P-Q3
4 Kt-KB3	KtxP
5 Q-K2	

Lasker's choice of the opening variation was conditioned by the circumstances under which this game was played. It took place in the last round, with Lasker half a point ahead of Capablanca. Hence the text-move, which assures him a draw, and possibly — against Marshall's attempt to complicate matters—winning chances.

5	Q-K2
6 P-Q3	Kt-KB3
7 B-Kt5	B-K3

This is Black's only move if he wishes both to avoid the exchange of Qs and the doubling of his Ps.

8 Kt-B3	QKt-Q2

Black evidently dislikes 8 . . . Kt-B3; 9 P-Q4, P-Q4; 10 BxKt, P xB; but after the text he also gets into difficulties.

9 O-O-O	P-KR3

A forcible attempt to free his position, for after 9 . . . O-O-O; 10 P-Q4, P-Q4; 11 Kt-K5 White would have the better game.

10 B-R4	P-KKt4

The natural complement to the previous move, but this violent demonstration only accentuates the inferiority of Black's game.

11 B-Kt3	Kt-R4

Or 11 . . . O-O-O; 12 P-Q4, P-Q4; 13 P-KR4, P-Kt5; 14 Kt-K5±.

12 P-Q4	KtxB

In order to be able to play . . . P-Q4, but this move is by no means good, as Lasker convincingly demonstrates. Somewhat better (though insufficient to equalize) was . . . O-O-O.

13 RPxKt	P-Kt5

Putting the Kt more or less out of play, but after White's reply the threat of P-Q5 becomes even more acute.

14 Kt-KR4	P-Q4?

The decisive mistake. Tarrasch rightly recommends . . . Kt-Kt3.

15 Q-Kt5!

Winning at least a P by force.

15 . . . .   O-O-O

Black has no satisfactory alternative, for if 15 . . . Q-Kt5; 16 Kt xP, QxQ; 17 KtxPch etc; or 15 . . . B-Kt2; 16 QxKtP, O-O and Black does not have adequate compensation for his material inferiority. The text-move sets an amusing trap: 16 KtxP, BxKt; 17 Qx B, Q-Kt4ch winning a piece.

16 Q-R5	P-R3

Again Black has nothing better, 16 . . . K-Kt being answered by 17 Kt-Kt5.

17 BxP!	PxB
18 QxRPch	K-Kt
19 Kt-Kt5	Kt-Kt3
20 R-Q3	

Intending R-Kt3 followed by P-R4-5.

(See diagram next column)

20 . . . .   Q-Kt4ch?

Marshall misses the best defense, which consisted in 20 . . . Kt-B5;

Position after White's 20th move

21 R-K (in order to interpose this R after . . . Q-Kt4ch. It would be a mistake to play 21 R-Kt3, Q-Kt4ch; 22 K-Kt, Kt-Q7ch), R-Q3; 22 KtxR, QxKt; 23 R-Kt3ch, Kt-Kt3; 24 P-R4, B-B; 25 R-K8, Q-Q2; 26 Q-Kt5! QxQ; 27 RxQ and White finally comes out a P ahead, for example . . . K-Kt2; 28 P-R 5, B-Q2; 29 RxB etc. (Tarrasch) and White wins the ending without much difficulty.

21 K-Kt	B-Q3
22 R-Kt3	KR-K

Black is helpless against the advance of the RP.

23 P-R4	B-KB4

Hoping for . . . R-K7, but Lasker's next move puts an end to this plan.

24 Kt-R7	B-Q2
25 P-R5	Q-Q7
26 PxKt	R-K8ch
27 K-R2	

By way of emphasizing the futility of Black's struggles.

27	P-QB3
28 Kt-Kt5	PxKt
29 Q-R7ch	Resigns

. . . K-B leads to mate in two by 30 Q-R8ch, B-Kt; 31 Q-R6 mate.

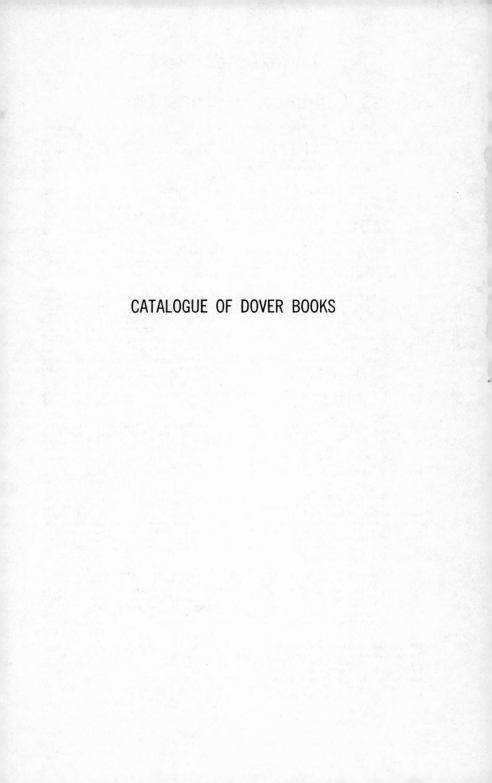
CATALOGUE OF DOVER BOOKS

Chess, Checkers, Games, Go

THE ADVENTURE OF CHESS, Edward Lasker. A lively history of chess, from its ancient beginnings in the Indian 4-handed game of Chaturanga, through to the great players of our day, as told by one of America's finest masters. He introduces such unusual sidelights and amusing oddities as Maelzel's chess-playing automaton that beat Napoleon 3 times. Major discussion of chess-playing machines and personal memories of Nimzovich, Capablanca, etc. 5-page chess primer. 11 illustrations, 53 diagrams. 296pp. 5⅜ x 8. S510 Paperbound **$1.45**

A TREASURY OF CHESS LORE, edited by Fred Reinfeld. A delightful collection of anecdotes, short stories, aphorisms by and about the masters, poems, accounts of games and tournaments, photography. Hundreds of humorous, pithy, satirical, wise, and historical episodes, comments, and word portraits. A fascinating "must" for chess players; revealing and perhaps seductive to those who wonder what their friends see in the game. 48 photographs (14 full page plates) 12 diagrams. xi + 306pp. 5⅜ x 8. T458 Paperbound **$1.75**

HOW DO YOU PLAY CHESS? by Fred Reinfeld. A prominent expert covers every basic rule of chess for the beginner in 86 questions and answers: moves, powers of pieces, rationale behind moves, how to play forcefully, history of chess, and much more. Bibliography of chess publications. 11 board diagrams. 48 pages. **FREE**

THE PLEASURES OF CHESS, Assiac. Internationally known British writer, influential chess columnist, writes wittily about wide variety of chess subjects: Anderssen's "Immortal Game;" only game in which both opponents resigned at once; psychological tactics of Reshevsky, Lasker; varieties played by masters for relaxation, such as "losing chess;" sacrificial orgies; etc. These anecdotes, witty observations will give you fresh appreciation of game. 43 problems. 150 diagrams. 139pp. 5⅜ x 8. T597 Paperbound **$1.25**

WIN AT CHESS, F. Reinfeld. 300 practical chess situations from actual tournament play to sharpen your chess eye and test your skill. Traps, sacrifices, mates, winning combinations, subtle exchanges, show you how to WIN AT CHESS. Short notes and tables of solutions and alternative moves help you evaluate your progress. Learn to think ahead playing the "crucial moments" of historic games. 300 diagrams. Notes and solutions. Formerly titled CHESS QUIZ. vi + 120pp. 5⅜ x 8. T438 Paperbound **$1.00**

THE ART OF CHESS, James Mason. An unabridged reprinting of the latest revised edition of the most famous general study of chess ever written. Also included, a complete supplement by Fred Reinfeld, "How Do You Play Chess?", invaluable to beginners for its lively question and answer method. Mason, an early 20th century master, teaches the beginning and intermediate player more than 90 openings, middle game, end game, how to see more moves ahead, to plan purposefully, attack, sacrifice, defend, exchange, and govern general strategy. Supplement. 448 diagrams. 1947 Reinfeld-Bernstein text. Bibliography. xvi + 340pp. 5⅜ x 8. T463 Paperbound **$1.85**

THE PRINCIPLES OF CHESS, James Mason. This "great chess classic" (N. Y. Times) is a general study covering all aspects of the game: basic forces, resistance, obstruction, opposition, relative values, mating, typical end game situations, combinations, much more. The last section discusses openings, with 50 games illustrating modern master play of Rubinstein, Spielmann, Lasker, Capablanca, etc., selected and annotated by Fred Reinfeld. Will improve the game of any intermediate-skilled player, but is so forceful and lucid that an absolute beginner might use it to become an accomplished player. 1946 Reinfeld edition. 166 diagrams. 378pp. 5⅜ x 8. T646 Paperbound **$1.85**

LASKER'S MANUAL OF CHESS, Dr. Emanuel Lasker. Probably the greatest chess player of modern times, Dr. Emanuel Lasker held the world championship 28 years, independent of passing schools or fashions. This unmatched study of the game, chiefly for intermediate to skilled players, analyzes basic methods, combinations, position play, the aesthetics of chess, dozens of different openings, etc., with constant reference to great modern games. Contains a brilliant exposition of Steinitz's important theories. Introduction by Fred Reinfeld. Tables of Lasker's tournament record. 3 indices. 308 diagrams. 1 photograph. xxx + 349pp. 5⅜ x 8. T640 Paperbound **$2.00**

THE ART OF CHESS COMBINATION, E. Znosko-Borovsky. Proves that combinations, perhaps the most aesthetically satisfying, successful technique in chess, can be an integral part of your game, instead of a haphazard occurrence. Games of Capablanca, Rubinstein, Nimzovich, Bird, etc. grouped according to common features, perceptively analyzed to show that every combination begins in certain simple ideas. Will help you to plan many moves ahead. Technical terms almost completely avoided. "In the teaching of chess he may claim to have no superior," P. W. Sergeant. Introduction. Exercises. Solutions. Index. 223pp. 5⅜ x 8. T583 Paperbound **$1.45**

CATALOGUE OF DOVER BOOKS

MODERN IDEAS IN CHESS, Richard Reti. An enduring classic, because of its unrivalled explanation of the way master chess had developed in the past hundred years. Reti, who was an outstanding theoretician and player, explains each advance in chess by concentrating on the games of the single master most closely associated with it: Morphy, Anderssen, Steinitz, Lasker, Alekhine, other world champions. Play the games in this volume, study Reti's perceptive observations, and have a living picture of the road chess has travelled. Introduction. 34 diagrams. 192pp. 5⅜ x 8.   T638 Paperbound **$1.25**

THE BOOK OF THE NEW YORK INTERNATIONAL CHESS TOURNAMENT, 1924, annotated by A. Alekhine and edited by H. Helms. Long a rare collector's item, this is the book of one of the most brilliant tournaments of all time, during which Capablanca, Lasker, Alekhine, Reti, and others immeasurably enriched chess theory in a thrilling contest. All 110 games played, with Alekhine's unusually penetrating notes. 15 photographs. xi + 271pp. 5⅜ x 8.
T752 Paperbound **$1.85**

KERES' BEST GAMES OF CHESS, selected, annotated by F. Reinfeld. 90 best games, 1931-1948, by one of boldest, most exciting players of modern chess. Games against Alekhine, Bogolyubov, Capablanca, Euwe, Fine, Reshevsky, other masters, show his treatments of openings such as Giuoco Piano, Alekhine Defense, Queen's Gambit Declined; attacks, sacrifices, alternative methods. Preface by Keres gives personal glimpses, evaluations of rivals. 110 diagrams. 272pp. 5⅜ x 8.   T593 Paperbound **$1.35**

HYPERMODERN CHESS as developed in the games of its greatest exponent, ARON NIMZOVICH, edited by Fred Reinfeld. An intensely original player and analyst, Nimzovich's extraordinary approaches startled and often angered the chess world. This volume, designed for the average player, shows in his victories over Alekhine, Lasker, Marshall, Rubinstein, Spielmann, and others, how his iconoclastic methods infused new life into the game. Use Nimzovich to invigorate your play and startle opponents. Introduction. Indices of players and openings. 180 diagrams. viii + 220pp. 5⅜ x 8.   T448 Paperbound **$1.35**

THE DEVELOPMENT OF A CHESS GENIUS: 100 INSTRUCTIVE GAMES OF ALEKHINE, F. Reinfeld. 100 games of the chess giant's formative years, 1905-1914, from age 13 to maturity, each annotated and commented upon by Fred Reinfeld. Included are matches against Bogolyubov, Capablanca, Tarrasch, and many others. You see the growth of an inexperienced genius into one of the greatest players of all time. Many of these games have never appeared before in book form. "One of America's most significant contributions to the chess world," Chess Life. New introduction. Index of players, openings. 204 illustrations. xv +227pp. 5¾ x 8.
T551 Paperbound **$1.35**

RESHEVSKY'S BEST GAMES OF CHESS, Samuel Reshevsky. One time 4-year-old chess genius, 5-time winner U. S. Chess Championship, selects, annotates 110 of his best games, illustrating theories, favorite methods of play against Capablanca, Alekhine, Bogolyubov, Kashdan, Vidmar, Botvinnik, others. Clear, non-technical style. Personal impressions of opponents, autobiographical material, tournament match record. Formerly "Reshevsky on Chess." 309 diagrams, 2 photos. 288pp. 5⅜ x 8.   T606 Paperbound **$1.25**

ONE HUNDRED SELECTED GAMES, Mikhail Botvinnik. Author's own choice of his best games before becoming World Champion in 1948, beginning with first big tournament, the USSR Championship, 1927. Shows his great power of analysis as he annotates these games, giving strategy, technique against Alekhine, Capablanca, Euwe, Keres, Reshevsky, Smyslov, Vidmar, many others. Discusses his career, methods of play, system of training. 6 studies of endgame positions. 221 diagrams. 272pp. 5⅜ x 8.   T620 Paperbound **$1.50**

RUBINSTEIN'S CHESS MASTERPIECES, selected, annotated by Hans Kmoch. Thoroughgoing mastery of opening, middle game; faultless technique in endgame, particularly rook and pawn endings; ability to switch from careful positional play to daring combinations; all distinguish the play of Rubinstein. 100 best games, against Janowski, Nimzowitch, Tarrasch, Vidmar, Capablanca, other greats, carefully annotated, will improve your game rapidly. Biographical introduction, B. F. Winkelman. 103 diagrams. 192pp. 5⅜ x 8.
T617 Paperbound **$1.25**

TARRASCH'S BEST GAMES OF CHESS, selected & annotated by Fred Reinfeld. First definitive collection of games by Siegbert Tarrasch, winner of 7 international tournaments, and the leading theorist of classical chess. 183 games cover fifty years of play against Mason, Mieses, Paulsen, Teichmann, Pillsbury, Janwoski, others. Reinfeld includes Tarrasch's own analyses of many of these games. A careful study and replaying of the games will give you a sound understanding of classical methods, and many hours of enjoyment. Introduction. Indexes. 183 diagrams. xxiv + 386pp. 5⅜ x 8.   T644 Paperbound **$2.00**

MARSHALL'S BEST GAMES OF CHESS, F. J. Marshall. Grandmaster, U. S. Champion for 27 years, tells story of career; presents magnificent collection of 140 of best games, annotated by himself. Games against Alekhine, Capablanca, Emanuel Lasker, Janowski, Rubinstein, Pillsbury, etc. Special section analyzes openings such as King's Gambit, Ruy Lopez, Alekhine's Defense, Giuoco Piano, others. A study of Marshall's brilliant offensives, slashing attacks, extraordinary sacrifices, will rapidly improve your game. Formerly "My Fifty Years of Chess." Introduction. 19 diagrams. 13 photos. 250pp. 5⅜ x 8.   T604 Paperbound **$1.45**

CATALOGUE OF DOVER BOOKS

THE HASTINGS CHESS TOURNAMENT, 1895, edited by Horace F. Cheshire. This is the complete tournament book of the famous Hastings 1895 tournament. One of the most exciting tournaments ever to take place, it evoked the finest play from such players as Dr. Lasker, Steinitz, Tarrasch, Harry Pillsbury, Mason, Tchigorin, Schlecter, and others. It was not only extremely exciting as an event, it also created first-rate chess. This book contains fully annotated all 230 games, full information about the playing events, biographies of the players, and much other material that makes it a chess classic. 22 photos, 174 diagrams. x + 370pp. 5⅜ x 8½.   T288 Paperbound **$2.00**

THE BOOK OF THE NOTTINGHAM INTERNATIONAL CHESS TOURNAMENT, 1936, Annotated by Dr. Alexander Alekhine. The Nottingham 1936 tournament is regarded by many chess enthusiasts as the greatest tournament of recent years. It brought together all the living former world champions, the current chess champion, and the future world champion: Dr. Lasker, Capablanca, Alekhine, Euwe, Botvinnik, and Reshevsky, Fine, Flohr, Tartakover, Vidmar, and Bogoljubov. The play was brilliant throughout. This volume contains all 105 of the games played, provided with the remarkable annotations of Alekhine. 1 illustration, 121 diagrams. xx + 291pp. 5⅜ x 8½.   T189 Paperbound **$1.85**

CHESS FOR FUN AND CHESS FOR BLOOD, Edward Lasker. A genial, informative book by one of century's leading masters. Incisive comments on chess as a form of art and recreation, on how a master prepares for and plays a tournament. Best of all is author's move-by-move analysis of his game with Dr. Emanuel Lasker in 1924 World Tournament, a charming and thorough recreation of one of the great games in history: the author's mental processes; how his calculations were upset; how both players blundered; the surprising outcome. Who could not profit from this study-in-depth? For the enthusiast who likes to read about chess as well as play it. Corrected (1942) edition. Preface contains 8 letters to author about the fun of chess. 95 illustrations by Maximilian Mopp. 224pp. 5⅜ x 8½.   T146 Paperbound **$1.25**

HOW NOT TO PLAY CHESS, Eugene A. Znosko-Borovsky. Sticking to a few well-chosen examples and explaining every step along the way, an outstanding chess expositor shows how to avoid playing a hit-or-miss game and instead develop general plans of action based on positional analysis: weak and strong squares, the notion of the controlled square, how to seize control of open lines, weak points in the pawn structure, and so on. Definition and illustration of typical chess mistakes plus 20 problems (from master games) added by Fred Reinfeld for the 1949 edition and a number of good-to-memorize tips make this a lucid book that can teach in a few hours what might otherwise take years to learn. 119pp. 5⅜ x 8. T920 Paperbound **$1.00**

THE SOVIET SCHOOL OF CHESS, A. Kotov and M. Yudovich. 128 master games, most unavailable elsewhere, by 51 outstanding players, including Botvinnik, Keres, Smyslov, Tal, against players like Capablanca, Euwe, Reshevsky. All carefully annotated, analyzed. Valuable biographical information about each player, early history of Russian chess, careers and contributions of Chigorin and Alekhine, development of Soviet school from 1920 to present with full over-all study of main features of its games, history of Russian chess literature. The most comprehensive work on Russian chess ever printed, the richest single sourcebook for up-to-date Russian theory and strategy. New introduction. Appendix of Russian Grandmasters, Masters, Master Composers. Two indexes (Players, Games). 30 photographs. 182 diagrams. vi + 390pp. 5⅜ x 8.   T26 Paperbound **$2.00**

THE ART OF THE CHECKMATE, Georges Renaud and Victor Kahn. Two former national chess champions of France examine 127 games, identify 23 kinds of mate, and show the rationale for each. These include Legal's pseudo sacrifice, the double check, the smothered mate, Greco's mate, Morphy's mate, the mate of two bishops, two knights, many, many more. Analysis of ideas, not memorization problems. Review quizzes with answers help readers gauge progress. 80 quiz examples and solutions. 299 diagrams. vi + 208pp. T106 Paperbound **$1.35**

HOW TO SOLVE CHESS PROBLEMS, K. S. Howard. Full of practical suggestions for the fan or the beginner—who knows only the moves of the chessmen. Contains preliminary section and 58 two-move, 46 three-move, and 8 four-move problems composed by 27 outstanding American problem creators in the last 30 years. Explanation of all terms and exhaustive index. "Just what is wanted for the student," Brian Harley. 112 problems, solutions. vi +171pp. 5⅜ x 8. T748 Paperbound **$1.00**

CHESS STRATEGY, Edward Lasker. Keres, Fine, and other great players have acknowledged their debt to this book, which has taught just about the whole modern school how to play forcefully and intelligently. Covers fundamentals, general strategic principles, middle and end game, objects of attack, etc. Includes 48 dramatic games from master tournaments, all fully analyzed. "Best textbook I know in English," J. R. Capablanca. New introduction by author. Table of openings. Index. 167 illustrations. vii + 282pp. 5⅜ x 8.

                                                                                   T528 Paperbound **$1.50**

REINFELD ON THE END GAME IN CHESS, F. Reinfeld. Formerly titled PRACTICAL END-GAME PLAY, this book contains clear, simple analyses of 62 end games by such masters as Alekhine, Tarrasch, Marshall, Morphy, Capablanca, and many others. Primary emphasis is on the general principles of transition from middle play to end play. This book is unusual in analyzing weak or incorrect moves to show how error occurs and how to avoid it. Covers king and pawn, minor piece, queen endings, weak squares, centralization, tempo moves, and many other vital factors. 62 diagrams. vi + 177pp. 5⅜ x 8.   T417 Paperbound **$1.25**

CATALOGUE OF DOVER BOOKS

THE AMERICAN TWO-MOVE CHESS PROBLEM, Kenneth S. Howard. One of this country's foremost contemporary problem composers selects an interesting, diversified collection of the best two-movers by 58 top American composers. Involving complete blocks, mutates, line openings and closings, other unusual moves, these problems will help almost any player improve his strategic approach. Probably has no equal for all around artistic excellence, surprising keymoves, interesting strategy. Includes 30-page history of development of American two-mover from Loyd, its founder, to the present. Index of composers. vii + 99pp. 5⅜ x 8½.
T997 Paperbound **$1.00**

WIN AT CHECKERS, M. Hopper. (Formerly CHECKERS). The former World's Unrestricted Checker Champion discusses the principles cf the game, expert's shots and traps, problems for the beginner, standard openings, locating your best move, the end game, opening "blitzkrieg" moves, ways to draw when you are behind your opponent, etc. More than 100 detailed questions and answers anticipate your problems. Appendix. 75 problems with solutions and diagrams. Index. 79 figures. xi + 107pp. 5⅜ x 8.
T363 Paperbound **$1.00**

GAMES ANCIENT AND ORIENTAL, AND HOW TO PLAY THEM, E. Falkener. A connoisseur's selection of exciting and different games: Oriental varieties of chess, with unusual pieces and moves (including Japanese shogi); the original pachisi; go; reconstructions of lost Roman and Egyptian games; and many more. Full rules and sample games. Now play at home the games that have entertained millions, not on a fad basis, but for millennia. 345 illustrations and figures. iv + 366pp. 5⅜ x 8.
T739 Paperbound **$2.00**

GO AND GO-MOKU, Edward Lasker. A fascinating Oriental game, Go, is winning new devotees in America daily. Rules that you can learn in a few minutes—a wealth of combinations that makes it more profound than chess! This is an easily followed step-by-step explanation of this 2000-year-old game, beginning with fundamentals. New chapter on advanced strategy in this edition! Also contains rules for Go-Moku, a very easy sister game. 72 diagrams. xix + 215pp. 5⅜ x 8.
T613 Paperbound **$1.50**

HOW TO FORCE CHECKMATE, F. Reinfeld. Formerly titled CHALLENGE TO CHESSPLAYERS, this is an invaluable collection of 300 lightning strokes selected from actual masters' play, which will demonstrate how to smash your opponent's game with strong decisive moves. No board needed — clear, practical diagrams and easy-to-understand solutions. Learn to plan up to three moves ahead and play a superior end game. 300 diagrams. 111pp. 5⅜ x 8.
T439 Paperbound **$1.25**

CHESSBOARD MAGIC! A COLLECTION OF 160 BRILLIANT ENDINGS, I. Chernev. Contains 160 endgame compositions, all illustrating not only ingenuity of composition, but inherent beauty of solution. In one, five Knights are needed to force mate; in another White forces stalemate though Black finishes eight passed pawns ahead; 150 more, all remarkable, all will sharpen your imagination and increase your skill. "Inexhaustible source of entertainment, an endless feast of delight," Reuben Fine, Grandmaster. Introduction. 160 diagrams. Index of composers. vii + 172pp. 5⅜ x 8.
T607 Paperbound **$1.00**

LEARN CHESS FROM THE MASTERS, F. Reinfeld. Formerly titled CHESS BY YOURSELF, this book contains 10 games which you play against such masters as Marshall, Bronstein, Najdorf, and others, and an easy system for grading each move you make against a variety of other possible moves. Detailed annotations reveal the principles of the game through actual play. 91 diagrams. viii + 144pp. 5⅜ x 8.
T362 Paperbound **$1.00**

MORPHY'S GAMES OF CHESS, edited by Philip W. Sergeant. You can put boldness into your game by following the brilliant, forceful moves of the man who has been called the greatest chess player of all time. Here are 300 of Morphy's best games carefully annotated to reveal Morphy's principles. 54 classics against masters like Anderssen, Harrwitz, Bird, Paulsen, and others. 52 games at odds; 54 blindfold games; plus over 100 others. Unabridged reissue of the latest revised edition. Bibliography. New introduction by Fred Reinfeld. Annotations and introduction by Sergeant. Index. 235 diagrams. x + 352pp. 5⅜ x 8. T386 Paperbound **$1.85**

CHESS PRAXIS, Aron Nimzovich. Nimzovich was the stormy petrel of chess in the first decades of this century, and his system, known as hypermodern chess, revolutionized all play since his time. Casting aside the classical chess theory of Steinitz and Tarrasch, he created his own analysis of chess, considering dynamic patterns as they emerge during play. This is the fullest exposition of his ideas, and it is easily one of the dozen greatest books ever written on chess. Nimzovich illustrates each of his principles with at least two games, and shows how he applied his concepts successfully in games against such masters as Alekhine, Tarrasch, Reti, Rubinstein, Capablanca, Spielmann and others. Indispensable to every serious chess player. Translated by J. DuMont. 135 diagrams, 1 photo. xi + 364pp. 5½ x 8⅝.
T296 Paperbound **$2.00**

CHESS AND CHECKERS: THE WAY TO MASTERSHIP, Edward Lasker. Complete, lucid instructions for the beginner—and valuable suggestions for the advanced player! For both games the great master and teacher presents fundamentals, elementary tactics, and steps toward becoming a superior player. He concentrates on general principles rather than a mass of rules, comprehension rather than brute memory. Historical introduction. 118 diagrams. xiv + 167pp. 5⅜ x 8.
T657 Paperbound **$1.15**

Nature

AN INTRODUCTION TO BIRD LIFE FOR BIRD WATCHERS, Aretas A. Saunders. Fine, readable introduction to birdwatching. Includes a great deal of basic information on about 160 different varieties of wild birds—elementary facts not easily found elsewhere. Complete guide to identification procedures, methods of observation, important habits of birds, finding nests, food, etc. "Could make bird watchers of readers who never suspected they were vulnerable to that particular virus," CHICAGO SUNDAY TRIBUNE. Unabridged, corrected edition. Bibliography. Index. 22 line drawings by D. D'Ostilio. Formerly "The Lives of Wild Birds." 256pp. 5⅜ x 8½. **T1139 Paperbound $1.00**

LIFE HISTORIES OF NORTH AMERICAN BIRDS, Arthur Cleveland Bent. Bent's historic, all-encompassing series on North American birds, originally produced under the auspices of the Smithsonian Institution, now being republished in its entirety by Dover Publications. The twenty-volume collection forms the most comprehensive, most complete, most-used source of information in existence. Each study describes in detail the characteristics, range, distribution, habits, migratory patterns, courtship procedures, plumage, eggs, voice, enemies, etc. of the different species and subspecies of the birds that inhabit our continent, utilizing reports of hundreds of contemporary observers as well as the writings of the great naturalists of the past. Invaluable to the ornithologist, conservationist, amateur naturalist, and birdwatcher. All books in the series contain numerous photographs to provide handy guides for identification and study.

LIFE HISTORIES OF NORTH AMERICAN BIRDS OF PREY. Including hawks, eagles, falcons, buzzards, condors, owls, etc. Index. Bibliographies of 923 items. 197 full-page plates containing close to 400 photographs. Total of 907pp. 5⅜ x 8½.　　Vol. I: T931 Paperbound **$2.50**
Vol. II: T932 Paperbound **$2.50**
The set Paperbound **$5.00**

LIFE HISTORIES OF NORTH AMERICAN SHORE BIRDS. Including 81 varieties of such birds as sandpipers, woodcocks, snipes, phalaropes, oyster catchers, and many others. Index for each volume. Bibliographies of 449 entries. 121 full-page plates including over 200 photographs. Total of 860 pp. 5⅜ x 8½.　　Vol. I: T933 Paperbound **$2.35**
Vol. II: T934 Paperbound **$2.35**
The set Paperbound **$4.70**

LIFE HISTORIES OF NORTH AMERICAN WILD FOWL. Including 73 varieties of ducks, geese, mergansers, swans, etc. Index for each volume. Bibliographies of 268 items. 106 full-page plates containing close to 200 photographs. Total of 685pp. 5⅜ x 8½.
Vol. I: T285 Paperbound **$2.50**
Vol. II: T286 Paperbound **$2.50**
The set Paperbound **$5.00**

LIFE HISTORIES OF NORTH AMERICAN GULLS AND TERNS. 50 different varieties of gulls and terns. Index. Bibliography. 93 plates including 149 photographs. xii + 337pp. 5⅜ x 8½.
T1029 Paperbound $2.75

LIFE HISTORIES OF NORTH AMERICAN GALLINACEOUS BIRDS. Including partridge, quail, grouse, pheasant, pigeons, doves, and others. Index. Bibliography. 93 full-page plates including 170 photographs. xiii + 490pp. 5⅜ x 8½. **T1028 Paperbound $2.75**

THE MALAY ARCHIPELAGO, Alfred Russel Wallace. The record of the explorations (8 years, 14,000 miles) of the Malay Archipelago by a great scientific observer. A contemporary of Darwin, Wallace independently arrived at the concept of evolution by natural selection, applied the new theories of evolution to later scientific discoveries, and made significant contributions to biology, zoology, and botany. This work is still one of the classics of natural history and travel. It contains the author's reports of the different native peoples of the islands, descriptions of the island groupings, his accounts of the animals, birds, and insects that flourished in this area. The reader is carried through strange lands, alien cultures, and new theories, and will share in an exciting, unrivalled travel experience. Unabridged reprint of the 1922 edition, with 62 drawings and maps. 3 appendices, one on cranial measurements. xvii + 515pp. 5⅜ x 8. **T187 Paperbound $2.00**

THE TRAVELS OF WILLIAM BARTRAM, edited by **Mark Van Doren.** This famous source-book of American anthropology, natural history, geography is the record kept by Bartram in the 1770's, on travels through the wilderness of Florida, Georgia, the Carolinas. Containing accurate and beautiful descriptions of Indians, settlers, fauna, flora, it is one of the finest pieces of Americana ever written. Introduction by Mark Van Doren. 13 original illustrations. Index. 448pp. 5⅜ x 8. **T13 Paperbound $2.00**

COMMON SPIDERS OF THE UNITED STATES, J. H. Emerton. Only non-technical, but thorough, reliable guide to spiders for the layman. Over 200 spiders from all parts of the country, arranged by scientific classification, are identified by shape and color, number of eyes, habitat and range, habits, etc. Full text, 501 line drawings and photographs, and valuable introduction explain webs, poisons, threads, capturing and preserving spiders, etc. Index. New synoptic key by S. W. Frost. xxiv + 225pp. 5⅜ x 8. **T223 Paperbound $1.45**

CATALOGUE OF DOVER BOOKS

LIFE HISTORIES OF NORTH AMERICAN MARSH BIRDS. A wealth of data on 54 different kinds of marsh bird (flamingo, ibis, bittern, heron, egret, crane, crake, rail, coot, etc.). Index. Bibliography. 98 full-page plates containing 179 black-and-white photographs. xiv + 392pp. 5⅜ x 8½.
T1082 Paperbound **$2.75**

LIFE HISTORIES OF NORTH AMERICAN DIVING BIRDS. Thirty-six different diving birds including grebe, loon, auk, murre, puffin, and the like. Index. Bibliography. 55 full-page plates (92 photographs). xiv + 239pp. 5⅜ x 8½.
T1091 Paperbound **$2.75**

LIFE HISTORIES OF NORTH AMERICAN WOOD WARBLERS. Covers about 58 types. Index. Bibliography. 83 full-page plates containing 125 black-and-white photographs. xi + 734pp. of text. 5⅜ x 8½.
Vol. I: T1153 Paperbound **$2.50**
Vol. II: T1154 Paperbound **$2.50**
The set Paperbound **$5.00**

LIFE HISTORIES OF NORTH AMERICAN FLYCATCHERS, LARKS, SWALLOWS, AND THEIR ALLIES. Complete information on about 78 different varieties. Index. Bibliography. 70 full-page plates (117 photographs). xi + 555pp. of text. 5⅜ x 8½.
T1090 Paperbound **$2.75**

AMERICAN WILDLIFE, AND PLANTS: A GUIDE TO WILDLIFE FOOD HABITS, A. C. Martin, H. S. Zim, A. L. Nelson. Result of 75 years of research by U. S. Fish and Wildlife Service into food and feeding habits of more than 1,000 species of birds and mammals, their distribution in America, migratory habits, and the most important plant-animal relationships. Treats over 300 common species of birds, fur and game animals, small mammals, hoofed browsers, fish, amphibians, reptiles by group, giving data on their food, ranges, habits and economies. Also focuses on the different genera of plants that furnish food for our wildlife, animals that use them, and their value. Only thorough study of its kind in existence. "Of immense value to sportsmen, naturalists, bird students, foresters, landscape architects, botanists," NATURE. "Undoubtedly an essential handbook," SCIENTIFIC MONTHLY. Unabridged republication of 1951 edition. Over 600 illustrations, maps, etc. Classified bibliography. Index. x + 500pp. 5⅜ x 8.
T793 Paperbound **$2.25**

HOW TO KNOW THE WILD FLOWERS, Mrs. Wm. Starr Dana. A Guide to the names, haunts, and habits of wild flowers. Well-known classic of nature lore. Informative and delightful. Plants classified by color and season of their typical flowers for easy identification. Thorough coverage of more than 1,000 important flowering, berry-bearing and foliage plants of Eastern and Central United States and Canada. Complete botanical information about each important plant. Also history, uses, folklore, habitat, etc. Nomenclature modernized by C. J. Hylander. 174 full-page illustrations by Marion Satterlee. xii + 481pp. 5⅜ x 8½.
T332 Paperbound **$1.85**

HOW PLANTS GET THEIR NAMES, L. H. Bailey. Introduction to botanical nomenclature for the horticulturist and garden-lover. Discussions of Carl Linnaeus, "father of botany," and analysis of his definitions of genus and species, a brief history of the science before Linnaean systematization, a chapter on plant identification, a mine of information on the rules of nomenclature and Latin stems and word-endings used in botanical nomenclature, with pronunciation guides. An important section contains a full list of generic terms of horticultural literature and common Latin words and their English botanical applications and meanings. "Written with knowledge and authority, charm and eloquence and poetic imagination on the varied aspects of the author's specialty," New York Times. 11 illustrations. vi + 181pp. 5⅜ x 8½.
T796 Paperbound **$1.25**

THE CACTACEAE: DESCRIPTIONS AND ILLUSTRATIONS OF PLANTS OF THE CACTUS FAMILY, N. L. Britton and J. N. Rose. Definitive study of plants of the Cactus Family. The authors devoted more than 15 years of research to this monumental task and produced an exhaustive, rigorously scientific account never likely to be superseded. 3 major classifications, or tribes, are recognized, under which they arrange and describe in full detail 124 genera and 1,235 species of cactus from all over the world. Complete data on each species: leaves, flowers, seeds, fruit, distribution, growth, spines, stem structure, economic uses, etc. In addition, 125 keys facilitate identification of genera and species. For teachers and students of botany and forestry, naturalists, conservationists, and nature lovers, this is an indispensable work. Unabridged republication of second (1937) edition. First edition originally published under the auspices of the Carnegie Institution, Washington, D.C. 4 vols. bound as 2. 1279 illustrations, photographs, sketches, etc. 137 plates. Total of xxvii + 1039pp. 8 x 10¼.
T771 Clothbound, 2-volume set **$20.00**

GUIDE TO SOUTHERN TREES, Elwood S. and J. George Harrar. A handy, comprehensive 700-page manual with numerous illustrations and information on more than 350 different kinds of trees, covering the entire area south of the Mason-Dixon line from the Atlantic Ocean to the Florida Keys and western Texas. Descriptions range from the common pine, cypress, walnut, beech, and elm to such rare species as Franklinia, etc. A mine of information on leaves, flowers, twigs, bark, fruit, distribution etc. of each kind of tree. Eminently readable, written in non-technical language, it is an indispensable handbook for all lovers of the outdoors. Revised edition. Index. 81-item bibliography. Glossary. 200 full-page illustrations. ix + 709pp. 4⅝ x 6⅜.
T945 Paperbound **$2.25**

CATALOGUE OF DOVER BOOKS

WESTERN FOREST TREES, James B. Berry. For years a standard guide to the trees of the Western United States. Covers over 70 different subspecies, ranging from the Pacific shores to western South Dakota, New Mexico, etc. Much information on range and distribution, growth habits, appearance, leaves, bark, fruit, twigs, etc. for each tree discussed, plus material on wood of the trees and its uses. Basic division (Trees with needle-like leaves, scale-like leaves, and compound, lobed or divided, and simple broadleaf trees), along with almost 100 illustrations (mostly full-size) of buds, leaves, etc., aids in easy identification of just about any tree of the area. Many subsidiary keys. Revised edition. Introduction. 12 photos. 85 illustrations by Mary E. Eaton. Index. xii + 212pp. 5⅜ x 8.
T1138 Paperbound **$1.35**

MANUAL OF THE TREES OF NORTH AMERICA (EXCLUSIVE OF MEXICO), Charles Sprague Sargent. The magnum opus of the greatest American dendrologist. Based on 44 years of original research, this monumental work is still the most comprehensive and reliable sourcebook on the subject. Includes 185 genera and 717 species of trees (and many shrubs) found in the U.S., Canada, and Alaska. 783 illustrative drawings by C. E. Faxon and Mary W. Gill. An all-encompassing lifetime reference book for students, teachers of botany and forestry, naturalists, conservationists, and all nature lovers. Includes an 11-page analytical key to genera to help the beginner locate any tree by its leaf characteristics. Within the text over 100 further keys aid in easy identification. Synopsis of families. Glossary. Index. 783 illustrations, 1 map. Total of 1 + 891pp. 5⅜ x 8.
T277 Vol. I Paperbound **$2.25**
T278 Vol. II Paperbound **$2.25**
The set **$4.50**

TREES OF THE EASTERN AND CENTRAL UNITED STATES AND CANADA, W. M. Harlow, Professor of Wood Technology, College of Forestry, State University of N. Y., Syracuse, N. Y. This middle-level text is a serious work covering more than 140 native trees and important escapes, with information on general appearance, growth habit, leaf forms, flowers, fruit, bark, and other features. Commercial use, distribution, habitat, and woodlore are also given. Keys within the text enable you to locate various species with ease. With this book you can identify at sight almost any tree you are likely to encounter; you will know which trees have edible fruit, which are suitable for house planting, and much other useful and interesting information. More than 600 photographs and figures. xiii + 288pp. 4⅝ x 6½.
T395 Paperbound **$1.35**

FRUIT KEY AND TWIG KEY TO TREES AND SHRUBS (FRUIT KEY TO NORTHEASTERN TREES, TWIG TREE TO DECIDUOUS WOODY PLANTS OF EASTERN NORTH AMERICA), W. M. Harlow. The only guides with photographs of every twig and fruit described—especially valuable to the novice. The fruit key (both deciduous trees and evergreens) has an introduction explaining seeding, organs involved, fruit types and habits. The twig key introduction treats growth and morphology. In the keys proper, identification is easy and almost automatic. This exceptional work, widely used in university courses, is especially useful for identification in winter, or from the fruit or seed only. Over 350 photos, up to 3 times natural size. Bibliography, glossary, index of common and scientific names, in each key. xvii + 125pp. 5⅝ x 8⅜.
T511 Paperbound **$1.25**

HOW TO KNOW THE FERNS, F. T. Parsons. Ferns, among our most lovely native plants, are all too little known. This modern classic of nature lore will enable the layman to identify any American fern he is likely to come across. After an introduction on the structure and life of ferns, the 57 most important ferns are fully pictured and described (arranged upon a simple identification key). Index of Latin and English names. 61 illustrations and 42 full-page plates. xiv + 215pp. 5⅜ x 8.
T740 Paperbound **$1.35**

OUR SMALL NATIVE ANIMALS: THEIR HABITS AND CARE, R. Snedigar, Curator of Reptiles, Chicago Zoological Park. An unusual nature handbook containing all the vital facts of habitat, distribution, foods, and special habits in brief life histories of 114 different species of squirrels, chipmunks, rodents, larger mammals, birds, amphibians, lizards and snakes. Liberally sprinkled with first-hand anecdotes. A wealth of information on capturing and caring for these animals: proper pens and cages, correct diet, curing diseases, special equipment required, etc. Addressed to the teacher interested in classroom demonstrations, the camp director, and to anyone who ever wanted a small animal for a pet. Revised edition, New preface. Index. 62 halftones. 14 line drawings. xviii + 296pp. 5⅜ x 8⅛.
T1022 Paperbound **$1.75**

INSECT LIFE AND INSECT NATURAL HISTORY, S. W. Frost. Unusual for emphasizing habits, social life, and ecological relations of insects, rather than more academic aspects of classification and morphology. Prof. Frost's enthusiasm and knowledge are everywhere evident as he discusses insect associations, and specialized habits like leaf-mining, leaf-rolling, and case-making, the gall insects, the boring insects, aquatic insects, etc. He examines all sorts of matters not usually covered in general works, such as: insects as human food; insect music and musicians; insect response to electric and radio waves; use of insects in art and literature. The admirably executed purpose of this book, which covers the middle ground between elementary treatment and scholarly monographs, is to excite the reader to observe for himself. Over 700 illustrations. Extensive bibliography. x + 524pp. 5⅜ x 8.
T517 Paperbound **$2.25**

Language Books and Records

GERMAN: HOW TO SPEAK AND WRITE IT. AN INFORMAL CONVERSATIONAL METHOD FOR SELF STUDY, Joseph Rosenberg. Eminently useful for self study because of concentration on elementary stages of learning. Also provides teachers with remarkable variety of aids: 28 full- and double-page sketches with pertinent items numbered and identified in German and English; German proverbs, jokes; grammar, idiom studies; extensive practice exercises. The most interesting introduction to German available, full of amusing illustrations, photographs of cities and landmarks in German-speaking cities, cultural information subtly woven into conversational material. Includes summary of grammar, guide to letter writing, study guide to German literature by Dr. Richard Friedenthal. Index. 400 illustrations. 384pp. 5⅜ x 8½.
T271 Paperbound **$2.00**

FRENCH: HOW TO SPEAK AND WRITE IT. AN INFORMAL CONVERSATIONAL METHOD FOR SELF STUDY, Joseph Lemaitre. Even the absolute beginner can acquire a solid foundation for further study from this delightful elementary course. Photographs, sketches and drawings, sparkling colloquial conversations on a wide variety of topics (including French culture and custom), French sayings and quips, are some of aids used to demonstrate rather than merely describe the language. Thorough yet surprisingly entertaining approach, excellent for teaching and for self study. Comprehensive analysis of pronunciation, practice exercises and appendices of verb tables, additional vocabulary, other useful material. Index. Appendix. 400 illustrations. 416pp. 5⅜ x 8½.
T268 Paperbound **$2.00**

DICTIONARY OF SPOKEN SPANISH, Spanish-English, English-Spanish. Compiled from spoken Spanish, emphasizing idiom and colloquial usage in both Castilian and Latin-American. More than 16,000 entries containing over 25,000 idioms—the largest list of idiomatic constructions ever published. Complete sentences given, indexed under single words—language in immediately useable form, for travellers, businessmen, students, etc. 25 page introduction provides rapid survey of sounds, grammar, syntax, with full consideration of irregular verbs. Especially apt in modern treatment of phrases and structure. 17 page glossary gives translations of geographical names, money values, numbers, national holidays, important street signs, useful expressions of high frequency, plus unique 7 page glossary of Spanish and Spanish-American foods and dishes. Originally published as War Department Technical Manual TM 30-900. iv + 513pp. 5⅜ x 8.
T495 Paperbound **$1.75**

SPEAK MY LANGUAGE: SPANISH FOR YOUNG BEGINNERS, M. Ahlman, Z. Gilbert. Records provide one of the best, and most entertaining, methods of introducing a foreign language to children. Within the framework of a train trip from Portugal to Spain, an English-speaking child is introduced to Spanish by a native companion. (Adapted from a successful radio program of the N. Y. State Educational Department.) Though a continuous story, there are a dozen specific categories of expressions, including greetings, numbers, time, weather, food, clothes, family members, etc. Drill is combined with poetry and contextual use. Authentic background music is heard. An accompanying book enables a reader to follow the records, and includes a vocabulary of over 350 recorded expressions. Two 10″ 33⅓ records, total of 40 minutes. Book. 40 illustrations. 69pp. 5¼ x 10½.
T890 The set **$4.95**

AN ENGLISH-FRENCH-GERMAN-SPANISH WORD FREQUENCY DICTIONARY, H. S. Eaton. An indispensable language study aid, this is a semantic frequency list of the 6000 most frequently used words in 4 languages—24,000 words in all. The lists, based on concepts rather than words alone, and containing all modern, exact, and idiomatic vocabulary, are arranged side by side to form a unique 4-language dictionary. A simple key indicates the importance of the individual words within each language. Over 200 pages of separate indexes for each language enable you to locate individual words at a glance. Will help language teachers and students, authors of textbooks, grammars, and language tests to compare concepts in the various languages and to concentrate on basic vocabulary, avoiding uncommon and obsolete words. 2 Appendixes. xxi + 441pp. 6½ x 9¼.
T738 Paperbound **$2.45**

NEW RUSSIAN-ENGLISH AND ENGLISH-RUSSIAN DICTIONARY, M. A. O'Brien. Over 70,000 entries in the new orthography! Many idiomatic uses and colloquialisms which form the basis of actual speech. Irregular verbs, perfective and imperfective aspects, regular and irregular sound changes, and other features. One of the few dictionaries where accent changes within the conjugation of verbs and the declension of nouns are fully indicated. "One of the best," Prof. E. J. Simmons, Cornell. First names, geographical terms, bibliography, etc. 738pp. 4½ x 6¼.
T208 Paperbound **$2.00**

96 MOST USEFUL PHRASES FOR TOURISTS AND STUDENTS in English, French, Spanish, German, Italian. A handy folder you'll want to carry with you. How to say "Excuse me," "How much is it?", "Write it down, please," etc., in four foreign languages. Copies limited, no more than 1 to a customer.
FREE

CATALOGUE OF DOVER BOOKS

Say It language phrase books

These handy phrase books (128 to 196 pages each) make grammatical drills unnecessary for an elementary knowledge of a spoken foreign language. Covering most matters of travel and everyday life each volume contains:

Over 1000 phrases and sentences in immediately useful forms — foreign language plus English.

Modern usage designed for Americans. Specific phrases like, "Give me small change," and "Please call a taxi."

Simplified phonetic transcription you will be able to read at sight.

The only completely indexed phrase books on the market.

Covers scores of important situations: — Greetings, restaurants, sightseeing, useful expressions, etc.

These books are prepared by native linguists who are professors at Columbia, N.Y.U., Fordham and other great universities. Use them independently or with any other book or record course. They provide a supplementary living element that most other courses lack. Individual volumes in:

Russian 75¢	Italian 75¢	Spanish 75¢	German 75¢
Hebrew 75¢	Danish 75¢	Japanese 75¢	Swedish 75¢
Dutch 75¢	Esperanto 75¢	Modern Greek 75¢	Portuguese 75¢
Norwegian 75¢	Polish 75¢	French 75¢	Yiddish 75¢
Turkish 75¢			

English for Italian-speaking people 75¢

English for German-speaking people 75¢
English for Spanish-speaking people 75¢

Large clear type. 128-196 pages each. 3½ x 5¼. Sturdy paper binding.

Listen and Learn language records

LISTEN & LEARN is the only language record course designed especially to meet your travel and everyday needs. It is available in separate sets for FRENCH, SPANISH, GERMAN, JAPANESE, RUSSIAN, MODERN GREEK, PORTUGUESE, ITALIAN and HEBREW, and each set contains three 33⅓ rpm long-playing records—1½ hours of recorded speech by eminent native speakers who are professors at Columbia, New York University, Queens College.

Check the following special features found only in LISTEN & LEARN:

- **Dual-language recording. 812 selected phrases and sentences**, over 3200 words, spoken first in English, then in their foreign language equivalents. A suitable pause follows each foreign phrase, allowing you time to repeat the expression. You learn by unconscious assimilation.

- **128 to 206-page manual** contains everything on the records, plus a simple phonetic pronunciation guide.

- **Indexed for convenience. The only set on the market** that is completely indexed. No more puzzling over where to find the phrase you need. Just look in the rear of the manual.

- **Practical.** No time wasted on material you can find in any grammar. LISTEN & LEARN covers central core material with phrase approach. Ideal for the person with limited learning time.

- **Living, modern expressions,** not found in other courses. Hygienic products, modern equipment, shopping—expressions used every day, like "nylon" and "air-conditioned."

- **Limited objective.** Everything you learn, no matter where you stop, is immediately useful. You have to finish other courses, wade through grammar and vocabulary drill, before they help you.

- **High-fidelity recording.** LISTEN & LEARN records equal in clarity and surface-silence any record on the market costing up to $6.

"Excellent . . . the spoken records . . . impress me as being among the very best on the market," **Prof. Mario Pei,** Dept. of Romance Languages, Columbia University. "Inexpensive and well-done . . . it would make an ideal present," CHICAGO SUNDAY TRIBUNE. "More genuinely helpful than anything of its kind which I have previously encountered," **Sidney Clark,** well-known author of "ALL THE BEST" travel books.

UNCONDITIONAL GUARANTEE. Try LISTEN & LEARN, then return it within 10 days for full refund if you are not satisfied.

Each set contains three twelve-inch 33⅓ records, manual, and album.

SPANISH	the set $5.95	GERMAN		the set $5.95
FRENCH	the set $5.95	ITALIAN		the set $5.95
RUSSIAN	the set $5.95	JAPANESE		the set $5.95
PORTUGUESE	the set $5.95	MODERN GREEK		the set $5.95
MODERN HEBREW	the set $5.95			

Trubner Colloquial Manuals

These unusual books are members of the famous Trubner series of colloquial manuals. They have been written to provide adults with a sound colloquial knowledge of a foreign language, and are suited for either class use or self-study. Each book is a complete course in itself, with progressive, easy to follow lessons. Phonetics, grammar, and syntax are covered, while hundreds of phrases and idioms, reading texts, exercises, and vocabulary are included. These books are unusual in being neither skimpy nor overdetailed in grammatical matters, and in presenting up-to-date, colloquial, and practical phrase material. Bilingual presentation is stressed, to make thorough self-study easier for the reader.

COLLOQUIAL HINDUSTANI, A. H. Harley, formerly Nizam's Reader in Urdu, U. of London. 30 pages on phonetics and scripts (devanagari & Arabic-Persian) are followed by 29 lessons, including material on English and Arabic-Persian influences. Key to all exercises. Vocabulary. 5 x 7½. 147pp.
Clothbound $1.75

COLLOQUIAL PERSIAN, L. P. Elwell-Sutton. Best introduction to modern Persian, with 90 page grammatical section followed by conversations, 35-page vocabulary. 139pp.
Clothbound $1.75

COLLOQUIAL ARABIC, DeLacy O'Leary. Foremost Islamic scholar covers language of Egypt, Syria, Palestine, & Northern Arabia. Extremely clear coverage of complex Arabic verbs & noun plurals; also cultural aspects of language. Vocabulary. xviii + 192pp. 5 x 7½.
Clothbound $2.50

COLLOQUIAL GERMAN, P. F. Doring. Intensive thorough coverage of grammar in easily-followed form. Excellent for brush-up, with hundreds of colloquial phrases. 34 pages of bilingual texts. 224pp. 5 x 7½.
Clothbound $1.75

COLLOQUIAL SPANISH, W. R. Patterson. Castilian grammar and colloquial language, loaded with bilingual phrases and colloquialisms. Excellent for review or self-study. 164pp. 5 x 7½.
Clothbound $1.75

COLLOQUIAL FRENCH, W. R. Patterson. 16th revision of this extremely popular manual. Grammar explained with model clarity, and hundreds of useful expressions and phrases; exercises, reading texts, etc. Appendixes of new and useful words and phrases. 223pp. 5 x 7½.
Clothbound $1.75

COLLOQUIAL CZECH, J. Schwarz, former headmaster of Lingua Institute, Prague. Full easily followed coverage of grammar, hundreds of immediately useable phrases, texts. Perhaps the best Czech grammar in print. "An absolutely successful textbook," JOURNAL OF CZECHO-SLOVAK FORCES IN GREAT BRITAIN. 252pp. 5 x 7½.
Clothbound $3.00

COLLOQUIAL RUMANIAN, G. Nandris, Professor of University of London. Extremely thorough coverage of phonetics, grammar, syntax; also included 70-page reader, and 70-page vocabulary. Probably the best grammar for this increasingly important language. 340pp. 5 x 7½.
Clothbound $2.50

COLLOQUIAL ITALIAN, A. L. Hayward. Excellent self-study course in grammar, vocabulary, idioms, and reading. Easy progressive lessons will give a good working knowledge of Italian in the shortest possible time. 5 x 7½.
Clothbound $1.75

COLLOQUIAL TURKISH, Yusuf Mardin. Very clear, thorough introduction to leading cultural and economic language of Near East. Begins with pronunciation and statement of vowel harmony, then 36 lessons present grammar, graded vocabulary, useful phrases, dialogues, reading, exercises. Key to exercises at rear. Turkish-English vocabulary. All in Roman alphabet. x + 288pp. 4¾ x 7¼.
Clothbound $4.00

DUTCH-ENGLISH AND ENGLISH-DUTCH DICTIONARY, F. G. Renier. For travel, literary, scientific or business Dutch, you will find this the most convenient, practical and comprehensive dictionary on the market. More than 60,000 entries, shades of meaning, colloquialisms, idioms, compounds and technical terms. Dutch and English strong and irregular verbs. This is the only dictionary in its size and price range that indicates the gender of nouns. New orthography. xvii + 571pp. 5½ x 6¼.
T224 Clothbound $2.75

LEARN DUTCH, F. G. Renier. This book is the most satisfactory and most easily used grammar of modern Dutch. The student is gradually led from simple lessons in pronunciation, through translation from and into Dutch, and finally to a mastery of spoken and written Dutch. Grammatical principles are clearly explained while a useful, practical vocabulary is introduced in easy exercises and readings. It is used and recommended by the Fulbright Committee in the Netherlands. Phonetic appendices. Over 1200 exercises; Dutch-English, English-Dutch vocabularies. 181pp. 4¼ x 7¼.
T441 Clothbound $2.25

Philosophy, Religion

GUIDE TO PHILOSOPHY, C. E. M. Joad. A modern classic which examines many crucial problems which man has pondered through the ages: Does free will exist? Is there plan in the universe? How do we know and validate our knowledge? Such opposed solutions as subjective idealism and realism, chance and teleology, vitalism and logical positivism, are evaluated and the contributions of the great philosophers from the Greeks to moderns like Russell, Whitehead, and others, are considered in the context of each problem. "The finest introduction," BOSTON TRANSCRIPT. Index. Classified bibliography. 592pp. 5⅜ x 8.
T297 Paperbound **$2.00**

HISTORY OF ANCIENT PHILOSOPHY, W. Windelband. One of the clearest, most accurate comprehensive surveys of Greek and Roman philosophy. Discusses ancient philosophy in general, intellectual life in Greece in the 7th and 6th centuries B.C., Thales, Anaximander, Anaximenes, Heraclitus, the Eleatics, Empedocles, Anaxagoras, Leucippus, the Pythagoreans, the Sophists, Socrates, Democritus (20 pages), Plato (50 pages), Aristotle (70 pages), the Peripatetics, Stoics, Epicureans, Sceptics, Neo-platonists, Christian Apologists, etc. 2nd German edition translated by H. E. Cushman. xv + 393pp. 5⅜ x 8.
T357 Paperbound **$1.85**

ILLUSTRATIONS OF THE HISTORY OF MEDIEVAL THOUGHT AND LEARNING, R. L. Poole. Basic analysis of the thought and lives of the leading philosophers and ecclesiastics from the 8th to the 14th century—Abailard, Ockham, Wycliffe, Marsiglio of Padua, and many other great thinkers who carried the torch of Western culture and learning through the "Dark Ages": political, religious, and metaphysical views. Long a standard work for scholars and one of the best introductions to medieval thought for beginners. Index. 10 Appendices. xiii + 327pp. 5⅜ x 8.
T674 Paperbound **$1.85**

PHILOSOPHY AND CIVILIZATION IN THE MIDDLE AGES, M. de Wulf. This semi-popular survey covers aspects of medieval intellectual life such as religion, philosophy, science, the arts, etc. It also covers feudalism vs. Catholicism, rise of the universities, mendicant orders, monastic centers, and similar topics. Unabridged. Bibliography. Index. viii + 320pp. 5⅜ x 8.
T284 Paperbound **$1.85**

AN INTRODUCTION TO SCHOLASTIC PHILOSOPHY, Prof. M. de Wulf. Formerly entitled SCHOLASTICISM OLD AND NEW, this volume examines the central scholastic tradition from St. Anselm, Albertus Magnus, Thomas Aquinas, up to Suarez in the 17th century. The relation of scholasticism to ancient and medieval philosophy and science in general is clear and easily followed. The second part of the book considers the modern revival of scholasticism, the Louvain position, relations with Kantianism and Positivism. Unabridged. xvi + 271pp. 5⅜ x 8.
T296 Clothbound **$3.50**
T283 Paperbound **$1.75**

A HISTORY OF MODERN PHILOSOPHY, H. Höffding. An exceptionally clear and detailed coverage of western philosophy from the Renaissance to the end of the 19th century. Major and minor men such as Pomponazzi, Bodin, Boehme, Telesius, Bruno, Copernicus, da Vinci, Kepler, Galileo, Bacon, Descartes, Hobbes, Spinoza, Leibniz, Wolff, Locke, Newton, Berkeley, Hume, Erasmus, Montesquieu, Voltaire, Diderot, Rousseau, Lessing, Kant, Herder, Fichte, Schelling, Hegel, Schopenhauer, Comte, Mill, Darwin, Spencer, Hartmann, Lange, and many others, are discussed in terms of theory of knowledge, logic, cosmology, and psychology. Index. 2 volumes, total of 1159pp. 5⅜ x 8.
T117 Vol. 1, Paperbound **$2.25**
T118 Vol. 2, Paperbound **$2.25**

ARISTOTLE, A. E. Taylor. A brilliant, searching non-technical account of Aristotle and his thought written by a foremost Platonist. It covers the life and works of Aristotle; classification of the sciences; logic; first philosophy; matter and form; causes; motion and eternity; God; physics; metaphysics; and similar topics. Bibliography. New Index compiled for this edition. 128pp. 5⅜ x 8.
T280 Paperbound **$1.00**

THE SYSTEM OF THOMAS AQUINAS, M. de Wulf. Leading Neo-Thomist, one of founders of University of Louvain, gives concise exposition to central doctrines of Aquinas, as a means toward determining his value to modern philosophy, religion. Formerly "Medieval Philosophy Illustrated from the System of Thomas Aquinas." Trans. by E. Messenger. Introduction. 151pp. 5⅜ x 8.
T568 Paperbound **$1.25**

LEIBNIZ, H. W. Carr. Most stimulating middle-level coverage of basic philosophical thought of Leibniz. Easily understood discussion, analysis of major works: "Theodicy," "Principles of Nature and Grace," "Monadology"; Leibniz's influence; intellectual growth; correspondence; disputes with Bayle, Malebranche, Newton; importance of his thought today, with reinterpretation in modern terminology. "Power and mastery," London Times. Bibliography. Index. 226pp. 5⅜ x 8.
T624 Paperbound **$1.35**

CATALOGUE OF DOVER BOOKS

THE ANALYSIS OF MATTER, Bertrand Russell. A classic which has retained its importance in understanding the relation between modern physical theory and human perception. Logical analysis of physics, prerelativity physics, causality, scientific inference, Weyl's theory, tensors, invariants and physical interpretations, periodicity, and much more is treated with Russell's usual brilliance. "Masterly piece of clear thinking and clear writing," NATION AND ATHENAE-UM. "Most thorough treatment of the subject," THE NATION. Introduction. Index. 8 figures. viii + 408pp. 5⅜ x 8. S231 Paperbound **$1.95**

CONCEPTUAL THINKING (A LOGICAL INQUIRY), S. Körner. Discusses origin, use of general concepts on which language is based, and the light they shed on basic philosophical questions. Rigorously examines how different concepts are related; how they are linked to experience; problems in the field of contact between exact logical, mathematical, and scientific concepts, and the inexactness of everyday experience (studied at length). This work elaborates many new approaches to the traditional problems of philosophy—epistemology, value theories, metaphysics, aesthetics, morality. "Rare originality . . . brings a new rigour into philosophical argument," Philosophical Quarterly. New corrected second edition. Index. vii + 301pp. 5⅜ x 8 T516 Paperbound **$1.75**

INTRODUCTION TO SYMBOLIC LOGIC, S. Langer. No special knowledge of math required — probably the clearest book ever written on symbolic logic, suitable for the layman, general scientist, and philosopher. You start with simple symbols and advance to a knowledge of the Boole-Schroeder and Russell-Whitehead systems. Forms, logical structure, classes, the calculus of propositions, logic of the syllogism, etc., are all covered. "One of the clearest and simplest introductions," MATHEMATICS GAZETTE. Second enlarged, revised edition. 368pp. 5⅜ x 8. S164 Paperbound **$1.75**

LANGUAGE, TRUTH AND LOGIC, A. J. Ayer. A clear, careful analysis of the basic ideas of Logical Positivism. Building on the work of Schlick, Russell, Carnap, and the Viennese School, Mr. Ayer develops a detailed exposition of the nature of philosophy, science, and metaphysics; the Self and the World; logic and common sense, and other philosophic concepts. An aid to clarity of thought as well as the first full-length development of Logical Positivism in English. Introduction by Bertrand Russell. Index. 160pp. 5⅜ x 8. T10 Paperbound **$1.25**

ESSAYS IN EXPERIMENTAL LOGIC, J. Dewey. Based upon the theory that knowledge implies a judgment which in turn implies an inquiry, these papers consider the inquiry stage in terms of: the relationship of thought and subject matter, antecedents of thought, data and meanings. 3 papers examine Bertrand Russell's thought, while 2 others discuss pragmatism and a final essay presents a new theory of the logic of values. Index. viii + 444pp. 5⅜ x 8. T73 Paperbound **$1.95**

TRAGIC SENSE OF LIFE, M. de Unamuno. The acknowledged masterpiece of one of Spain's most influential thinkers. Between the despair at the inevitable death of man and all his works and the desire for something better, Unamuno finds that "saving incertitude" that alone can console us. This dynamic appraisal of man's faith in God and in himself has been called "a masterpiece" by the ENCYCLOPAEDIA BRITANNICA. xxx + 332pp. 5⅜ x 8. T257 Paperbound **$2.00**

HISTORY OF DOGMA, A. Harnack. Adolph Harnack, who died in 1930, was perhaps the greatest Church historian of all time. In this epoch-making history, which has never been surpassed in comprehensiveness and wealth of learning, he traces the development of the authoritative Christian doctrinal system from its first crystallization in the 4th century down through the Reformation, including also a brief survey of the later developments through the Infallibility decree of 1870. He reveals the enormous influence of Greek thought on the early Fathers, and discusses such topics as the Apologists, the great councils, Manichaeism, the historical position of Augustine, the medieval opposition to indulgences, the rise of Protestantism, the relations of Luther's doctrines with modern tendencies of thought, and much more. "Monumental work; still the most valuable history of dogma . . . luminous analysis of the problems . . . abounds in suggestion and stimulus and can be neglected by no one who desires to understand the history of thought in this most important field," Dutcher's Guide to Historical Literature. Translated by Neil Buchanan. Index. Unabridged reprint in 4 volumes. Vol I: Beginnings to the Gnostics and Marcion. Vol II & III: 2nd century to the 4th century Fathers. Vol IV & V: 4th century Councils to the Carlovingian Renaissance. Vol VI & VII: Period of Clugny (c. 1000) to the Reformation, and after. Total of cii + 2407pp. 5⅜ x 8.

T904 Vol I Paperbound **$2.50**
T905 Vol II & III Paperbound **$2.50**
T906 Vol IV & V Paperbound **$2.50**
T907 Vol VI & VII Paperbound **$2.50**
The set **$10.00**

THE GUIDE FOR THE PERPLEXED, Maimonides. One of the great philosophical works of all time and a necessity for everyone interested in the philosophy of the Middle Ages in the Jewish, Christian, and Moslem traditions. Maimonides develops a common meeting-point for the Old Testament and the Aristotelian thought which pervaded the medieval world. His ideas and methods predate such scholastics as Aquinas and Scotus and throw light on the entire problem of philosophy or science vs. religion. 2nd revised edition. Complete unabridged Friedländer translation. 55 page introduction to Maimonides's life, period, etc., with an important summary of the GUIDE. Index. lix + 414pp. 5⅜ x 8. T351 Paperbound **$2.00**

New Books

101 PATCHWORK PATTERNS, Ruby Short McKim. With no more ability than the fundamentals of ordinary sewing, you will learn to make over 100 beautiful quilts: flowers, rainbows, Irish chains, fish and bird designs, leaf designs, unusual geometric patterns, many others. Cutting designs carefully diagrammed and described, suggestions for materials, yardage estimates, step-by-step instructions, plus entertaining stories of origins of quilt names, other folklore. Revised 1962. 101 full-sized patterns. 140 illustrations. Index. 128pp. 7⅞ x 10¾.
T773 Paperbound **$1.85**

ESSENTIAL GRAMMAR SERIES
By concentrating on the essential core of material that constitutes the semantically most important forms and areas of a language and by stressing explanation (often bringing parallel English forms into the discussion) rather than rote memory, this new series of grammar books is among the handiest language aids ever devised. Designed by linguists and teachers for adults with limited learning objectives and learning time, these books omit nothing important, yet they teach more usable language material and do it more quickly and permanently than any other self-study material. Clear and rigidly economical, they concentrate upon immediately usable language material, logically organized so that related material is always presented together. Any reader of typical capability can use them to refresh his grasp of language, to supplement self-study language records or conventional grammars used in schools, or to begin language study on his own. Now available:

ESSENTIAL GERMAN GRAMMAR, Dr. Guy Stern & E. F. Bleiler. Index. Glossary of terms. 128pp. 5⅜ x 8.
T422 Paperbound **$1.00**

ESSENTIAL FRENCH GRAMMAR, Dr. Seymour Resnick. Index. Cognate list. Glossary. 159pp. 5⅜ x 8.
T419 Paperbound **$1.00**

ESSENTIAL ITALIAN GRAMMAR, Dr. Olga Ragusa. Index. Glossary. 111pp. 5⅜ x 8.
T779 Paperbound **$1.00**

ESSENTIAL SPANISH GRAMMAR, Dr. Seymour Resnick. Index. 50-page cognate list. Glossary. 138pp. 5⅜ x 8.
T780 Paperbound **$1.00**

PHILOSOPHIES OF MUSIC HISTORY: A Study of General Histories of Music, 1600-1960, Warren D. Allen. Unquestionably one of the most significant documents yet to appear in musicology, this thorough survey covers the entire field of historical research in music. An influential masterpiece of scholarship, it includes early music histories; theories on the ethos of music; lexicons, dictionaries and encyclopedias of music; musical historiography through the centuries; philosophies of music history; scores of related topics. Copiously documented. New preface brings work up to 1960. Index. 317-item bibliography. 9 illustrations; 3 full-page plates. 5⅜ x 8½. xxxiv + 382pp.
T282 Paperbound **$2.00**

MR. DOOLEY ON IVRYTHING AND IVRYBODY, Finley Peter Dunne. The largest collection in print of hilarious utterances by the irrepressible Irishman of Archey Street, one of the most vital characters in American fiction. Gathered from the half dozen books that appeared during the height of Mr. Dooley's popularity, these 102 pieces are all unaltered and uncut, and they are all remarkably fresh and pertinent even today. Selected and edited by Robert Hutchinson. 5⅜ x 8½. xii + 244p.
T626 Paperbound **$1.00**

TREATISE ON PHYSIOLOGICAL OPTICS, Hermann von Helmholtz. Despite new investigations, this important work will probably remain preeminent. Contains everything known about physiological optics up to 1925, covering scores of topics under the general headings of dioptrics of the eye, sensations of vision, and perecptions of vision. Von Helmholtz's voluminous data are all included, as are extensive supplementary matter incorporated into the third German edition, new material prepared for 1925 English edition, and copious textual annotations by J. P. C. Southall. The most exhaustive treatise ever prepared on the subject, it has behind it a list of contributors that will never again be duplicated. Translated and edited by J. P. C. Southall. Bibliography. Indexes. 312 illustrations. 3 volumes bound as 2. Total of 1749pp. 5⅜ x 8.
S15-16 Two volume set, Clothbound **$15.00**

THE ARTISTIC ANATOMY OF TREES, Rex Vicat Cole. Even the novice with but an elementary knowledge of drawing and none of the structure of trees can learn to draw, paint trees from this systematic, lucid instruction book. Copiously illustrated with the author's own sketches, diagrams, and 50 paintings from the early Renaissance to today, it covers composition; structure of twigs, boughs, buds, branch systems; outline forms of major species; how leaf is set on twig; flowers and fruit and their arrangement; etc. 500 illustrations. Bibliography. Indexes. 347pp. 5⅜ x 8.
T1016 Clothbound **$4.50**

CATALOGUE OF DOVER BOOKS

GEOMETRY OF FOUR DIMENSIONS, H. P. Manning. Unique in English as a clear, concise introduction to this fascinating subject. Treatment is primarily synthetic and Euclidean, although hyperplanes and hyperspheres at infinity are considered by non-Euclidean forms. Historical introduction and foundations of 4-dimensional geometry; perpendicularity; simple angles; angles of planes; higher order; symmetry; order, motion; hyperpyramids, hypercones, hyperspheres; figures with parallel elements; volume, hypervolume in space; regular polyhedroids. Glossary of terms. 74 illustrations. ix + 348pp. 5⅜ x 8. **S182 Paperbound $2.00**

PAPER FOLDING FOR BEGINNERS, W. D. Murray and F. J. Rigney. A delightful introduction to the varied and entertaining Japanese art of origami (paper folding), with a full, crystal-clear text that anticipates every difficulty; over 275 clearly labeled diagrams of all important stages in creation. You get results at each stage, since complex figures are logically developed from simpler ones. 43 different pieces are explained: sailboats, frogs, roosters, etc. 6 photographic plates. 279 diagrams. 95pp. 5⅝ x 8⅜. **T713 Paperbound $1.00**

SATELLITES AND SCIENTIFIC RESEARCH, D. King-Hele. An up-to-the-minute non-technical account of the man-made satellites and the discoveries they have yielded up to September of 1961. Brings together information hitherto published only in hard-to-get scientific journals. Includes the life history of a typical satellite, methods of tracking, new information on the shape of the earth, zones of radiation, etc. Over 60 diagrams and 6 photographs. Mathematical appendix. Bibliography of over 100 items. Index. xii + 180pp. 5⅜ x 8½. **T703 Paperbound $2.00**

LOUIS PASTEUR, S. J. Holmes. A brief, very clear, and warmly understanding biography of the great French scientist by a former Professor of Zoology in the University of California. Traces his home life, the fortunate effects of his education, his early researches and first theses, and his constant struggle with superstition and institutionalism in his work on microorganisms, fermentation, anthrax, rabies, etc. New preface by the author. 159pp. 5⅜ x 8. **T197 Paperbound $1.00**

THE ENJOYMENT OF CHESS PROBLEMS, K. S. Howard. A classic treatise on this minor art by an internationally recognized authority that gives a basic knowledge of terms and themes for the everyday chess player as well as the problem fan: 7 chapters on the two-mover; 7 more on 3- and 4-move problems; a chapter on selfmates; and much more. "The most important one-volume contribution originating solely in the U.S.A.," Alain White. 200 diagrams. Index. Solutions. viii + 212pp. 5⅜ x 8. **T742 Paperbound $1.25**

SAM LOYD AND HIS CHESS PROBLEMS, Alain C. White. Loyd was (for all practical purposes) the father of the American chess problem and his protégé and successor presents here the diamonds of his production, chess problems embodying a whimsy and bizarre fancy entirely unique. More than 725 in all, ranging from two-move to extremely elaborate five-movers, including Loyd's contributions to chess oddities—problems in which pieces are arranged to form initials, figures, other by-paths of chess problem found nowhere else. Classified according to major concept, with full text analyzing problems, containing selections from Loyd's own writings. A classic to challenge your ingenuity, increase your skill. Corrected republication of 1913 edition. Over 750 diagrams and illustrations. 744 problems with solutions. 471pp. 5⅜ x 8½. **T928 Paperbound $2.25**

FABLES IN SLANG & MORE FABLES IN SLANG, George Ade. 2 complete books of major American humorist in pungent colloquial tradition of Twain, Billings. 1st reprinting in over 30 years includes "The Two Mandolin Players and the Willing Performer," "The Base Ball Fan Who Took the Only Known Cure," "The Slim Girl Who Tried to Keep a Date that was Never Made," 42 other tales of eccentric, perverse, but always funny characters. "Touch of genius," H. L. Mencken. New introduction by E. F. Bleiler. 86 illus. 208pp. 5⅜ x 8. **T533 Paperbound $1.00**

Prices subject to change without notice.

Dover publishes books on art, music, philosophy, literature, languages, history, social sciences, psychology, handcrafts, orientalia, puzzles and entertainments, chess, pets and gardens, books explaining science, intermediate and higher mathematics, mathematical physics, engineering, biological sciences, earth sciences; classics of science, etc. Write to:

Dept. catrr.
Dover Publications, Inc.
180 Varick Street, N. Y. 14, N. Y.